Criminal Justice in Native A

D0404388

Criminal Justice in Native America

Edited by
Marianne O. Nielsen and Robert A. Silverman

The University of Arizona Press   Tucson

To my late mother, Anna Margrete Nielsen,
who never did quite understand my work but did understand
that "de Indianner" needed assistance in achieving justice
in both Canada and the USA.
M. O. N.

To Elaine, love of my life.
R. A. S.

To Native American scholars and students.
M. O. N. and R. A. S.

The University of Arizona Press
© 2009 The Arizona Board of Regents
All rights reserved

www.uapress.arizona.edu

Library of Congress Cataloging-in-Publication Data

Criminal justice in Native America / edited by Marianne
O. Nielsen and Robert A. Silverman.
    p.   cm.
  Includes bibliographical references and index.
  ISBN 978-0-8165-2653-6 (pbk. : alk. paper)
  1. Indians of North America—Social conditions.
2. Crime—United States.   3. Criminal justice,
Administration of—United States.   I. Nielsen,
Marianne O.   II. Silverman, Robert A., 1943–
E98.C87C75   2009
305.897—dc22   2008037222

Publication of this book is made possible in part by the proceeds of a permanent
endowment created with the assistance of a Challenge Grant from the National
Endowment for the Humanities, a federal agency.

Manufactured in the United States of America on acid-free, archival-quality paper
and processed chlorine free.

14 13 12 11   6 5 4 3

Contents

Preface

This book was designed to meet the growing interest about the involvement of Native Americans in the criminal justice system. It therefore should be of use to students of criminal justice, criminology, Native studies (Native American or American Indian studies), law, sociology, and anthropology. It also provides resource materials for practitioners in the various criminal justice fields and in private agencies providing services to Native American peoples.

The work is a collection of original chapters by scholars who have done extensive research and/or teaching in the field. About half of the authors are of Native American ancestry and come from a wide range of disciplines and institutions.

The overall approach of the book is that because of the tragic consequences of colonialism, Native American communities and organizations need more control over their own destinies and need more resources to do so; they need to be able to determine for themselves how to best provide services to their Native American members and clients. They may choose to follow traditional practices or values, or they may choose modified Western models of justice services—either way, it is their choice. The issues are put into this overall context in the first and last chapters.

Despite some short mentions of other countries, this is a book about Native Americans in the United States. Scholars and practitioners in other countries that have suffered colonialism may find a great deal that is familiar but also much that is different.

Because this is an introductory survey book, we thought it desirable to expose the student to as wide a range of voices as possible, although the general level of writing should be comfortable for an introductory student. References are provided at the end of each chapter for readers who wish to learn more about a topic. These should be a rich source of materials for students who wish to pursue some of the topics.

Empirical research on Native Americans is relatively scarce in the crime and criminal justice literature, but we are fortunate that our authors are experts in the areas they describe and have themselves done a significant amount of the most recent cutting-edge research in these areas.

Research into some issues has been more thorough in other countries, such as Canada. In fact, it is reasonable to say that Native American issues of crime and justice have been neglected in U.S. research. Despite all our efforts, we feel that this book could have included a great deal more material. We have only brief sentences on Native Hawaiians and Alaska Natives, for example. We have very little information on restorative justice programs other than Navajo Nation peacemaking. Issues for Native Americans living in urban areas probably deserved their own chapter, but we were limited by space considerations. Yet we do discuss issues that have received little coverage elsewhere, such as female victims of sexual abuse and cultural stresses facing Native American police officers. We hope the end result is a book that provides a range of topics sufficient for the book to be useful to the reader.

Unfortunately, in our society "law and order" is a growth industry, and stereotypes of Native American involvement in the criminal justice system abound. Criminal justice system members make decisions based on this kind of inadequate or inaccurate information—decisions about new laws; new facilities; the life or death of service programs; the allotment of funding and resources for policing, courts, and corrections; even the freedom and fate of individuals. The distribution of knowledge is an important step in alleviating this situation. More educational courses are an important part of the process, but there is also a great deal of research out there waiting to be done. We encourage graduate students, especially Native American graduate students, to give serious consideration to pursuing this area of study.

This book is organized so that the reader is taken through the criminal justice system starting with an overview of the social and historical context of Native American involvement. The section on law points out that Native American peoples had well-functioning "legal" systems long before the non-Native American system was imposed on them. This section also gives an overview of some of the major pieces of non-Native

American legislation that define the criminal justice powers of tribal governments today. The section on Native American crime rates gives an overview of trends in crime statistics and highlights several categories of crime that are of particular importance to Native American communities, including juvenile crime and family violence. Please note that this book does not pretend to explain why some Native American individuals commit crime. There has been almost no rigorous empirical research in this area.

The sections on policing, courts, and corrections describe some of the most important issues, including the stressors on Native American police forces, the overrepresentation of Native American offenders in jails, and the need for Native American spirituality programs in correctional institutions. The final chapter draws together the issues that run through many of the chapters and returns the book to its opening theme of self-determination and resource needs.

We welcome your comments and suggestions about this book. The path we walk is shared.

Acknowledgments

This book project would not have been possible without the enthusiastic willingness of its contributors, who provided not only their excellent work but encouragement, collegiality, and humor when things got stressful. This project is truly a shared endeavor of which we should all be proud.

We would also like to thank Sarah Deer, who wanted to be part of this project, but life intervened; Lorraine Malcoe for her assistance; Bill Archambeault, who wrote a chapter when health issues suggested he shouldn't have; Jon'a Meyer, Barbara Perry, Eileen Luna-Firebaugh, and Larry Gould, who worked hard at conferences to raise the project's profile; and Heather Hice-McCray, who assisted with online research. We would also like to thank our colleagues and students who asked repeatedly and convincingly for an updated book on Native American criminal justice issues. Lastly, we would like to thank our anonymous reviewers and Patti Hartmann, senior editor at the University of Arizona Press, who supported the project from the moment she heard about it and trusted us to deliver.

Queen's University in Kingston, Ontario, and the University of Northern Arizona in Flagstaff provide us with environments that foster the work that we do. At Queen's, Bob is grateful for support from Hazel Metcalfe and the other ladies with whom he shares a quaint cottage that has become their office, for letting him concentrate on his work, for social interaction, and for helping him with computers, copy machines, and other useful devices. At NAU, Marianne is grateful for the unquestioning assistance provided by Denise Ayers-Mondragon, the Criminology and Criminal Justice Department's former administrative assistant; Ann Lewis, the current administrative assistant; and her colleagues, whose good-natured teasing about her book-imposed isolation kept her feeling connected.

Criminal Justice in Native America

Introduction to the Context of Native American Criminal Justice Involvement

Marianne O. Nielsen

NATIVE AMERICAN involvement in the American criminal justice system is a complex story with its roots deep in colonialism. This issue cannot be understood without recognizing its interrelatedness with other issues facing Native Americans today. Political power and its lack, land and its loss, economic development and its success or lack of success, individual esteem or individual despair—these and other issues must be considered in exploring Native American criminal justice involvement. It is important to note that in such an exploration, we are discussing much more than Native Americans in the role of offender or victim; Native Americans are also part of the criminal justice system as program developers and service providers—important roles that often get ignored by scholars.

Native Americans are the original inhabitants of what we now think of as North America. Native Americans are categorized by a variety of names, depending mainly on their legal status. Native Americans are most commonly called Indians, Native Americans, or American Indians, and include Inuit, Aleuts, and Native Hawaiians. The Inuit are Indigenous peoples who live in the circumpolar parts of the United States and Canada. Aleuts are inhabitants of the western Alaska peninsula and the Aleutian Island chain. Alaskan Inuit, Aleuts, and Indians together are sometimes referred to as "Alaska Natives." Native Hawaiians are descendents of the Polynesians who migrated to Hawaii centuries ago (Utter 2001, 34–35). In general in this book, we will use the term *Native Americans* because it is an inclusive term that applies to all of these peoples, although other terms may be used by authors depending on the context of their discussion and their concerns about respectful naming.

William Archambeault describes the naming and current status of the Native American population as follows:[1]

> When Columbus made his first report back to Spain, he called the indigenous peoples of the Americas *una gente in Dios* or *people of (in) God*. This is the origin of the Spanish word *Indios*, from which the English word *Indian* is derived. According to the July 1, 2005, report of the U.S. Census Bureau, an estimated 4 million people, or 1.5 percent of the total U.S. population, list themselves as being Indian or Alaskan Native, with approximately two-thirds living in urban and suburban areas outside of reservations. Most are stable wage earners seeking similar goals and dreams as their other neighbors. Many, however, are concentrated in "Indian ghettos" in certain larger cities, such as Minneapolis/St. Paul, Los Angeles, Albuquerque, and New York, while most Alaskan Natives live in small villages. Census numbers, however, do not reflect either the transitory or the homeless Indigenous populations. While little research exists on the Transitory Group,[2] some fall into another category on which there is extensive research: homeless Indigenous peoples. (Westerfelt and Yellow Bird 1999, 145–62)

The "self-labeling" definition of *Indian* as used by the U.S. Census Bureau is not the same as the meaning applied by the Bureau of Indian Affairs (BIA). Currently the BIA recognizes approximately 551 Indian tribes or Alaskan Native Communities,[3] whose population totals account for only a portion of the total number reported by the Census Bureau. The BIA definition is limited to people enrolled in tribes on land legally defined as *Indian country*, land that is held in trust by the U.S. government and managed by BIA and tribal authorities (see the chapter by Cardani for more on this). Except for the provision of the Jay Treaty, Indigenous people from the other countries or from the United States that do not meet this definition are not considered to be Indians by the BIA or the U.S. government, regardless of what they call themselves.

Qualifying as a "card-carrying" BIA-certified Indian is important both to the tribal community and to the individual. For example, only BIA Indians are entitled to protections and services from the federal government. These include, but are not limited to, access to

Indian Health Care Services, housing, food supports, education, and certain First Amendment rights. Also, communities are entitled to protection of natural resources or ancestral artifacts covered by laws such as the 1990 *Native America Graves Protection and Repatriation Act* or other protective laws.

People not meeting BIA requirements do not enjoy these services or protections. Who are these others? They include members of "state-only" recognized tribes, that is, members of tribes recognized by state governments only, usually in Public Law 280 states (see the chapter by Cardani); communities who consider themselves Indian and who retain elements of a tribal language or culture; people whose ancestors avoided or refused to cooperate with Dawes or other commissions; people whose ancestors were adopted by whites; and people who feel they are Indian. Also included are people who have grown up on tribal reservations and who, for insufficient blood quantum or other reason, are not enrolled tribal members.

It is important to realize that the legal categories imposed on Native Americans by the government and the different rights and obligations that accompany each category serve, more often than not, to divide the interests of Native Americans and sometimes prevent them from working together.

In terms of group identity, many Native American groups have names that are not their own; that is, the name they have now may be based on an inaccurate description, like the word *Indian* itself. The Inuit, for example, were called "Eskimo," meaning "eaters of raw meat," a name given to them by neighboring Abenaki (Algonquin) tribes who thought raw meat was an unsavory dinner item. *Inuit* means "people." Similarly, the Navajo call themselves *Diné*, which also means "people." In fact, the names that many Native American groups have for themselves simply mean "people." Morse (1989, 1) defines Native Americans as "all people who trace their ancestors in these lands to time immemorial." This definition encompasses all Native Americans, including those of partial Native American ancestry. While this is an excellent general definition to use, in specific situations the most appropriate and respectful response to this confusion of names is to find out what the Native people in question call themselves, and to use that name.

It is important to note that there is no single entity called "the Native culture" or "the Native community." Native American cultures are *not* homogeneous, nor are they static. They are dynamic and adaptive. There are differences between nations based on historical developments, economic pursuits, geography, languages, spiritual views, and so on. There are also differences among the individuals within communities. Not all Native Americans believe in or practice traditional Native culture. They vary in how acculturated they are (Garrett and Pichette 2000), with Zion (1983) classifying the population in broad categories of "traditionalists," "transitionals," and "moderns," so that Native American individuals and communities can be described as varying from being very traditional-culture-oriented to being completely assimilated into the dominant non-Native society, with the transitionals (communities and individuals who are integrated into both societies) in between. In this book it is necessary to generalize in order to familiarize students with historical contexts and current trends in justice. This is being done as respectfully as possible, realizing that there are wide variations between and within communities. Wherever feasible, the authors have included the issues and accomplishments of distinct communities and nations.

Expanding on Snipp (1989, 2–3), Native Americans as a whole are essential to the study of law, crime, and criminal justice for a number of reasons. First, Native Americans have a special historical and political status as the first peoples of this continent, making important contributions to our social, political, and legal history. Second, the history and current living conditions of Native Americans contradict this country's ideals of equality of opportunity and justice. Third, there is a body of law that applies only to Native Americans, as Cardani in this volume describes later. Native Americans are the only minority group mentioned specifically in the Constitution, and the only group to have special branches of government set up to regulate and administer them and their resources. Currently, the federal Bureau of Indian Affairs plays this role. Many states also have state-level commissions or departments.

Fourth, myths and stereotypes about Native Americans continue to influence society and criminal justice system personnel. Native Americans have been inaccurately portrayed in books, newspapers, comics, magazines, films, and other media, in some cases since contact (Mihesuah 1996). Perry's chapter in this volume provides an excellent example of how stereotypes contribute to hate crimes against Native Americans. Fifth, as mentioned earlier, Native Americans are a growing part of the population, and are no longer isolated in reservations or rural villages. This urbanization in particular has had an impact on criminal justice system involvement.

Sixth, Native American cultures and lifestyles were historically different from Euro-based North American cultures. Native American societies are still in the process of adapting to the cataclysmic changes brought by colonization. As part of this adaptation, Native Americans are developing innovative criminal justice (and other) services and programs from which the dominant society could learn a great deal. See the chapters in this volume by Hamby, Luna-Firebaugh, Meyer, and Archambeault for descriptions of such services.

Last, Native Americans are overrepresented in the criminal justice system. To illustrate, if Native American people make up 17 percent of the population of a state, as they do in Alaska, it should be expected that they will also make up 17 percent of the prison population. As it is, however, Native Americans actually make up 35 percent of Alaska's prison population (Alaska Justice Forum 1999). This defines Native Americans as an "overrepresented" population in the criminal justice system of each state. See Silverman in this volume for a description of Native American crime rates in various offense categories. As well, in some states, Native American offenders not only are overrepresented in terms of their numbers in prison but receive longer sentences and stay in prison longer than any other group (Bachman, Alvarez, and Perkins 1996). The reasons for this overrepresentation can be explained by three possible factors: differential commitment of offenses (i.e., Native Americans may commit more offenses); differential patterns of crime (i.e., Native Americans may commit crimes that are more easily detected, such as public intoxication or assault); and Native Americans may receive differential treatment by the criminal justice system (i.e., they may be overpoliced or may be treated more harshly than non-Native suspects and offenders) (LaPrairie 1990).

It should be noted that Native American issues and offenders get comparatively little attention by scholars or policy makers, because they are overshadowed by the large numbers of African American and Hispanic offenders in the system. It is also important to note that Native American overrepresentation is not just an "American problem."

This same trend of overrepresentation is found in every country where an indigenous population has been overrun by an invading group. In addition to the United States, it is found, for example, among the Aboriginal peoples of Canada, the Aborigines of Australia, the Maoris of New Zealand, and the indigenous peoples of Papua New Guinea, Scandinavia, Japan, Russia, and many African countries. With few exceptions, it seems that the processes of invasion and colonization produce conditions that increase the involvement of the original inhabitants in the criminal justice system of the dominant (colonizing) society.

To understand how justice system overrepresentation came about in this country, and the nature of the strategies to overcome it, it is necessary to understand the impact of colonization on Native American individuals and communities.

The Impact of Colonization

Before European contact, the Native Americans of North America had their own cultures, economic systems, societal structures, laws, and methods of enforcing good behavior. Their understanding of "justice" was distinctly different from that of the European colonists. Justice was not a separate institution in Native American communities; it was part of day-to-day living. When someone's behavior disrupted the community or the community's relationship with the wider world, action was taken to encourage that person to conform, to restore harmony, and to heal all involved, including the community. These remedial actions were usually some form of what we now call restorative justice, that is, counseling by elders or community leaders, reparations, and healing ceremonies, though if the problem was disruptive enough, actions could include banishment or putting to death (see, for example, Dumont 1993; Traisman 1981). Many of these holistic and restorative justice values and practices are in sharp contrast to the adversarial and punishment orientation of the Euro-based criminal justice system. Traditional justice values may still influence the expectations that some Native Americans have of the dominant justice process (Dumont 1993).

The arrival of English, Spanish, French, Dutch, Swedish and Russian Europeans severely damaged Native American societies over a relatively brief time.[4] Some of this destruction resulted from deliberate government policy; some of it was unintentional (Blaut 1993). The changes brought by the Europeans affected every aspect of Native American life and society—population demographics, technology, economic systems, ecology, culture, law, and politics. Indian nations were affected by these agents at different times, because of the differential rate of European settlement.

After contact, Native Americans and Europeans lived together more or less cooperatively, with Native Americans being the dominant group. The Native American nations provided Europeans with food, shelter, trade, knowledge of the land and its resources, and military aid. This eventually changed as the result of increasing expansion of the European population and its hunger for land. Military campaigns and massacres by colonists, along with disease epidemics against which Native Americans had no immunity, and the resulting social disorganization, took a heavy toll. It is estimated that the Native population in North America fell from somewhere between two million and seven million inhabitants pre-contact, to a low of about 227,000 inhabitants in 1990 (Shoemaker 1999, 3). Some tribal groups became nearly extinct; some tribes were so depopulated that they joined other Native groups to survive. Most Native American groups, as a result, found themselves unable to defend themselves and their lands against the ever-increasing advance of the European settlers. Robertson (2001, xi) states, "The white invaders never would have conquered the Americas so readily had they not had a far more lethal weapon than their primitive guns and Old World tactics. European diseases vanquished the New World's natives, not powder and ball." Other factors included personal despair (Duran and Duran 1995) and "military conflict, mistreatment, starvation or malnutrition, depression and loss of vigor or will to live, and exportation into slavery" (Utter 2001, 45).

European technology introduced permanent changes in the economies of most Native groups. The Diné, for example, adopted the newly re-introduced horses and sheep, and many Native groups traded for iron to use as knives and other tools. Guns were also a popular trade item and contributed to heightened warfare between rival Native groups. Because of the popularity of fur in European fashion at the time, Europeans encouraged the development of a continent-wide fur trade that drew many Native American groups away from their traditional economies (horticulture, hunting, fishing, etc.). European sport and food hunting of animals such as the buffalo changed the ecology of whole regions of the continent and depleted Native economies. This led to a dependence on European foods. The removal of Indians to reservations changed Native American economic systems as well, since reservations were usually placed on land inappropriate for traditional economic activities and too poor to farm, even if the group in question wished to. The combination of these factors led to an economic dependency on the colonial governments that continues today (White 1983).

As part of colonization, most Europeans (including Americans after 1776) used ideologies based on social Darwinism and paternalism to justify their treatment of Native Americans. Social Darwinism was the belief that humans were subject to survival of the fittest and that some "subspecies" of human were less fit to survive than others. As Trigger (1985, 16) describes this racist ideology, it "offered a comfortable explanation for the primitive condition of the American Indian and his stubborn refusal to accept the benefits of civilization. White Americans could not be blamed for the tragic failure of natural selection over the course of millennia to produce native North Americans who were biologically able to withstand the impact of Western civilization." Because of their "obvious" superiority, many Europeans believed they had the right to impose their culture, economy, laws, and religion on "inferior" peoples. In gratitude, the "inferior" people were expected to give up their land, economy, beliefs, and sometimes their lives.

In the interests of making Native Americans adopt the "superior" European culture during this era, laws were made forbidding the practice of Native beliefs and ceremonies, and children were taken from their families and communities and placed in European-run schools where they were forbidden to speak their own language and practice their own spirituality. Missionaries played an important role in these efforts to assimilate Native Americans (see for example, Mihesuah 1993). As part of this experience, many children did not learn appropriate parenting, social, and communication skills, an issue that has been passed down generation after generation and has contributed to a wide range of today's social issues such as domestic violence, child abuse and neglect, and substance abuse.

It is important to note that this colonial ideology continues today, but it is now called "racism." This ideology affects how other members of society interact with Native Americans on a daily basis (Mihesuah 1996) and contributes to discriminatory treatment by the criminal justice system and crimes committed against Native Americans, as discussed by some of the authors in their chapters.

Reservations and laws were also designed to protect Native Americans from unscrupulous whites and from themselves, since they were considered to be "like children." Remnants of this paternalism are still found in government policies that refuse Native Americans the right to make decisions about the use of their lands, resources, and funds, and to provide services for themselves. (Cardani in his chapter describes the paternalism in laws currently in place.) Treaties were made between the colonizing powers and Indian tribes. These were legal contracts between nations agreeing to terms of peace, trade, and exchange. Because of differences in conceptualizations of very basic things such as the ownership of land (the Europeans wanted to own it; Native Americans believed it could not be owned, only protected), and because of the greed of speculators, most of the treaties were broken almost immediately by the Europeans (Utter 2001, 84).

Today, relations between the dominant society and Native Americans are still colored by racism and greed among members of the dominant society, but neglect is also a powerful force, with many issues still needing resolution. Ongoing negotiations cover a wide range of issues: education, religious freedom, economic development, and environmental crimes, to name just a few examples. Political rights are a particularly important issue. Indian nations are "domestic dependent nations" that have the right to be protected by the federal government as "distinct political communities" (Utter 2001, 254). This means that they have the right, within limits set by American law, to control their own internal affairs, including the administration of justice. (See the chapter by Cardani for more on this). Sovereignty can be defined as "the inherent right or power of self-government," but, as Utter also states, it "means many things to many people" (Utter 2001, 264). Wilkins and Lomawaima (2001, 4) describe sovereignty as follows: "a sovereign nation defines itself and its citizens, exercises self-government and the right to treat with other nations, applies its jurisdiction over the internal legal affairs of its citizens and subparts . . . , claims political jurisdiction over the lands within its borders, and may define certain rights that inhere in its citizens."

The loss of control of their own societies is one of the main issues that continues to face Native Americans. Native American peoples are still trying to gain more legal and political power to develop and control more of their own social institutions—not just criminal justice but also education, health care, social services, and others. This is what is meant by "self-determination initiatives." A second important issue is the lack of resources available to Native American communities and organizations. Despite the legal obligations of the federal government as outlined in the treaties and several court decisions, the federal and state governments (in PL 280 states) have regularly underfunded and underresourced tribal governments and urban organizations.

The process of colonization has led to Native Americans becoming marginalized; that is, they have been placed at the economic, political, and social edges of American society. A number of examples of their marginalization follow.

Politically marginalized, Native Americans received the right to vote in national elections in the United States in 1924, although some states continued to deny them the right until as late as 1956 in Utah and 1962 in New Mexico (Utter 2001, 248–49). Economically marginalized, about 20 percent of Native Americans live below the poverty line, compared to 7 percent of whites (and 22 percent of African Americans) (U.S. Census 2006, 40). About 14 percent of Native Americans are unemployed, compared to about 6 percent of the white population (U.S. Census 2005, s2301). Native American are less likely to finish high school (24 percent did not), compared to whites (14 percent) and African Americans (21 percent), and have a lower median income than any other group except African Americans ($34,641 for Native Americans, $55,938 for whites, and $34,608 for African Americans) (U.S. Census 2006, 40). They are also more likely to work in lower-income jobs, such as manual labor (Snipp 1989). Related to economic marginalization, Native Americans are more likely to suffer from ill health than white Americans. This is not to say that all Native Americans are disadvantaged; but a greater proportion of them are disadvantaged than the white American population, and a smaller proportion than the African American population (Snipp 1989).[5] Discrimination and stereotyping by members of the dominant society also increase marginalization. Add to these the disruption of traditional justice values and practices, and these conditions are conducive to the development of substance abuse, violent behavior toward self and others, and destabilized families.

Marginalization is often linked to offending and victimization, according to criminological theory. Although there is little or no research to back any of them up, physiological, psychological, cultural deviance, strain, social reaction, social structural, learning, social control, and social reaction theories have all been used at one time or another to explain the causes of Native American crime (Lester 1999). A lack of social integration arising from colonial processes seems to be one of the most promising theories of causation (Frideres and Gadacz 2008, 151). Marginalization factors we have mentioned, such as poverty, social isolation, drug and alcohol abuse, and high rates of unemployment, came about differently for Native Americans than they did for other marginalized groups within the dominant society. Frideres and Gadacz (2008, 151) suggest that Canadian Aboriginal peoples (like Native Americans),

> continue to be marginalized and anomic, their level of integratedness with either their own community or that of the dominant society has decreased over time and continues to block the effects of integration. Aboriginal people have lost their social sense of community . . . the diminishment of the family and group authority on the reserves has created social and economic divisions between individuals and families, and has had a profound impact on the socialization of the young.

Chapters in this volume by Silverman, Meyer (on juveniles), and Tippeconnic Fox offer some insight into Native American crime and its antecedents. It is clear that more scholarly work in this area is desirable.

Roles in the Criminal Justice System

In addition to the factors mentioned above, some Native American offenders also face special problems in dealing with the criminal justice system because of marginalization:

- They may not be familiar with Euro-based laws and justice;
- they may lack education about the criminal justice system;
- they may have language difficulties;
- they may not know about legal assistance;
- they may lack money to pay lawyers, fines, or bail;

- they may lack knowledge of resources to help with criminogenic conditions such as alcoholism and unemployment; or
- they may be discriminated against at one or more levels of the criminal justice system from arrest to parole (an area that needs more research).

Native people are also victims of crime. In 1999, the Bureau of Justice Statistics reported that Native Americans experience rates of violent victimization that are "more than twice those of the U.S. resident population" and that at least 70 percent of this victimization occurs at the hands of those from other racial groups (Greenfeld and Smith 1999, v, vi). A 2004 Bureau of Justice Statistics study by S. W. Perry confirms these high rates of victimization in sampled tribes. Barbara Perry in this volume reports on hate crimes against Native Americans, Hamby reports on sexual victimization, and Robyn reports on corporate crime committed against Native Americans.

Native people are not only offenders and victims; they are active service providers working to improve the effectiveness of criminal-justice-system services to Native victims and offenders, as well as to ameliorate the poor socioeconomic conditions that lead to crime. As they do this, they are also working to increase self-determination for Native Americans. Native Americans are active both on and off reservations, and in the provision of Euro-model criminal justice services as well as modified traditional justice services. Most on-reservation services, with some exceptions, operate on Euro-based justice models, including police departments, courts, corrections, and treatment programs for both adults and juveniles. As described by Cardani later in this book, there are legal limitations on the extent of these services. The Diné courts, for example, can hear only misdemeanor cases and tribal law infractions. Most Native American police departments have the right to carry arms, but not all do.

Not all reservations are large enough or well-resourced enough to develop and operate their own criminal justice systems. Some tribes have cooperated to form, for example, intertribal courts as a solution (see Zion in this volume) or have cross-deputization agreements with local municipal or state police forces (see Luna-Firebaugh in this volume). Also, not all reservations want to operate their own services. Where possible, many

Euro-based programs try to integrate aspects of traditional justice practices and values.

Traditional justice-based services also operate separately on reservations. Traditional justice is both the oldest and the newest area of service provision. Many of the traditional justice practices of Native groups were driven underground by the assimilationist laws mentioned earlier but were not forgotten. The traditional mechanisms included counseling and mediation by community elders and leaders, enforcement of good behavior by police societies, and informal control mechanisms such as gossip, teasing, and banishment (Dumont 1993). In recent years there have been a number of "new" initiatives developed that are based on some of these strategies. The Navajo Peacemaker program, for example, uses community members to settle disputes and arrive at peaceful resolutions (see Nielsen and Zion 2005, and Meyer's chapter). Some of these traditional practices have also been incorporated into urban programs.

Native Americans work as service providers off-reservation in two capacities: as members of the dominant justice system and as the designers and operators of "pan-Indian" justice organizations. Native Americans working within the dominant society's criminal justice system may be police officers, probation supervisors, correctional officers, lawyers, or judges; that is, they may fill any role normally found within the system. Native Americans are, on the whole, underrepresented as service providers and decision makers in the criminal justice system. Very few studies have been done about the reasons for this, although one study by Moras (1998) confirmed this underrepresentation in all aspects of the criminal justice system in Alaska. Another by Riley (2000) focuses on the obstacles to recruiting Alaskan Natives to work in the criminal justice system, especially in correctional work: the job is not seen as helping others, there is a perceived lack of workplace harmony, and it prioritizes rigid time commitments over family obligations.

Native Americans may also design and operate urban criminal justice services for Native people. As mentioned earlier, the majority of Native Americans live in urban areas, and these urban dwellers face many of the same social problems as do those living on reservations but do not have the assistance of reservation-based services. American Indian Centers and Native American medical clinics provide a wide variety of free or low-cost services to all people of Native ancestry, including: educational upgrading programs and medical treatment, health education programs, substance-abuse prevention programs, mental health counseling, crime prevention, Native language classes, legal education programs, and workforce development programs. The holistic nature of these programs addresses some of the marginalization issues that have developed from colonization and thereby helps to prevent crime.

One successful example in Arizona is Native Americans for Community Action, which was started in 1971 and offers substance abuse counseling and mental health programs, in addition to its Family Health Center and other preventative health programs. NACA also had a GED program, but it is no longer offered.

It is unfortunate that there has been so little publicly accessible research on the unique aspects or effectiveness of Native American programs, although there has been related research in other colonized countries. Nielsen (2003), for example, found that a Canadian healing lodge, a type of correctional facility focused on treatment and rehabilitation for Aboriginal peoples, had a 3.5 percent recidivism rate—a sure sign of success, when many American prisons have recidivism rates of over 70 percent.

Some of the chapters in this book describe or mention a few of these successful programs (see, for example, Luna-Firebaugh on policing, Meyer on peacemaking, Archambeault on corrections). In terms of program uniqueness, Nielsen (1998) and Redpath and Nielsen (1997) found that Indigenous justice organizations were flatter in structure than similar Euro-based organizations, had more informal communication, and had administrators who were more likely to use a new management style. They had developmental ideologies that focus on marginalization, sovereignty, and ineffectiveness of Euro-based programs; and they differed most in the practices and values used by staff in providing client services, and in the kind of staff they employed. For example, wherever possible they incorporated Indigenous practices such as counseling by elders, addressing heritage and culture, and using healing ceremonies. They hired qualified Indigenous staff or trained non-Indigenous staff about Indigenous practices and values.

The involvement of Native Americans as service providers in the criminal justice system is important, because they have a better understanding of the issues and problems faced by their Native American "clients."

They understand the socioeconomic conditions that may contribute to their clients' personal problems. They are aware of the resources, both Native American and non-Native American, that are available to their clients in the community. They know that there are minority groups within Native American groups. Native American women, Native American young offenders, and members of small tribal groups may have different needs than other Native American groups (see the chapters by Fox, Meyer [on juveniles], and Hamby). They are also contributing to self-determination for their Nations through providing access to resources and opportunities, providing leverage and brokering external resources, creating or reinforcing community identity and commitment, fostering the development of human resources, and supporting community advocacy and exertion of power (Nielsen 2004).

The potential that these programs have for contributing to the welfare of the entire population—Native American and non–Native American—is profound. There is a movement in the dominant criminal justice system to develop new services that are more effective in preventing offenses and in keeping offenders from reoffending. The "new" concepts being used by non-Native American society—restorative justice, diversion, community ownership, community responsibility—are old ideas in Native American communities. In reviving and modifying their traditional services to fit contemporary problems, Native Americans are well ahead of the dominant society's leading-edge reformers. Of course, they need more resources and more control of their own decision making to do this. Undoubtedly, Native American communities and the dominant society alike have a great deal to gain from these groundbreaking Native American programs.

References

Alaska Justice Forum. 1999. Growth in corrections. *Alaska Justice Forum* 15, no. 4. http://justice.uaa.alaska.edu/forum/15/4/winter1999/a_growth.html (accessed 10/19/2006).

Bachman, Ronet, Alexander Alvarez, and Craig Perkins. 1996. Discriminatory imposition of the law. In *Native Americans, crime and justice*, ed. Marianne O. Nielsen and Robert A. Silverman, 197–208. Boulder, CO: Westview.

Blaut, J. M. 1993. *The colonizer's model of the world: Geographical diffusionism and Eurocentric history.* New York: Guilford Press.

Deloria, Vine Jr., and Clifford Lytle. 1983. *American Indians, American justice.* Austin: University of Texas Press.

Dumont, James. 1993. Justice and Aboriginal people. In *Aboriginal peoples and the justice system,* ed. The Royal Commission on Aboriginal Peoples, 42–85. Ottawa: Canada Communication Group.

Duran, Eduardo, and Bonnie Duran. 1995. *Native American postcolonial psychology.* Albany: SUNY Press.

Frideres, James S., and René R. Gadacz. 2008. *Aboriginal peoples in Canada,* 8th ed. Toronto: Pearson/Prentice-Hall.

Garrett, Michael T., and Eugene F. Pichette. 2000. Red as an apple: Native American acculturation and counseling with or without reservation. *Journal of Counseling and Development* 78:3–13.

Greenfeld, Lawrence A., and Steven K. Smith. 1999. *American Indians and crime.* Washington, DC: U.S. Department of Justice (NCJ 173386).

Hagan, William T. 1993. *American Indians.* 3rd ed. Chicago: University of Chicago Press.

LaPrairie, Carol. 1990. The role of sentencing in the overrepresentation of Aboriginal people in correctional institutions. *Canadian Journal of Criminology* 32:429–40.

Lester, David. 1999. *Crime and the Native American.* Springfield, IL: Charles C. Thomas.

Mihesuah, Devon A. 1993. *Cultivating the rosebuds: The education of women at the Cherokee female seminary, 1851–1909.* Urbana: University of Illinois Press.

———. 1996. *American Indians: Stereotypes and realities.* Atlanta: Clarity Press.

Moras, Antonia. 1998. Native employment in the Alaska justice system. *Alaska Justice Forum* 15, no. 2. http://justice.uaa.alaska.edu/forum/15/2summer1998/a_native.html (accessed 10/19/2006).

Morse, Bradford W., ed. 1989. *Aboriginal peoples and the law: Indian, Métis, and Inuit rights in Canada,* rev. 1st ed. Ottawa: Carleton University Press.

Nielsen, Marianne O. 1998. A comparison of Canadian Native youth justice committees and Navajo peacemakers: A summary of research results. *Journal of Contemporary Criminal Justice* 14(1):6–25.

———. 2003. Canadian Aboriginal healing Lodges: A model for the United States? *Prison Journal* 83(1):67–89.

———. 2004. A comparison of community roles of Indigenous-operated criminal justice organizations in Canada, the USA and Australia. *American Indian Culture and Research Journal* 28:57–75.

Nielsen, Marianne O., and James W. Zion. 2005. *Navajo Nation peacemaking: Living traditional justice.* Tucson: University of Arizona Press.

Perry, Steven W. 2004. American Indians and crime: A BJS statistical profile, 1992–2002. Washington, DC: Bureau of Justice Statistics (NCJ 203097).

Redpath, Lindsay, and Marianne O. Nielsen. 1997. A comparison of Native culture, non-Native culture and new management ideology. *Canadian Journal of Administrative Sciences* 14(3):327–39.

Riley, John. 2000. Obstacles to minority employment in criminal justice: Recruiting Alaska Natives. *Alaska Justice Forum* 16, no. 4. http://justice.uaa.alska.edu/forum/16/4wonter2000/a_obstacles.html (accessed 10/19/2006).

Robertson, R. G. 2001. *Rotting face: Smallpox and the American Indian.* Caldwell, ID: Caxton Press.

Shoemaker, Nancy. 1999. *American Indian population recovery in the twentieth century.* Albuquerque: University of New Mexico Press.

Snipp, C. Matthew. 1989. *American Indians: The first of this land.* New York: Russell Sage Foundation.

Trafzer, Clifford E. 2000. *As long as the grass shall grow and rivers flow: A history of Native Americans.* Fort Worth, TX: Harcourt.

Traisman, Ken. 1981. Native law: Law and order among eighteenth-century Cherokee, Great Plains, Central Prairie and Woodland Indians. *American Indian Law Review* 9:273–287.

Trigger, Bruce G. 1985. *Natives and newcomers.* Kingston: McGill-Queen's University Press.

U.S. Census Bureau. n.d. *American Indians by the numbers.* http://www.infoplease.com/spot/aihmcensus1.html (accessed 11/29/2006).

———. 2002. *The American Indian and Alaska Native population: 2000.* Washington, DC: U.S. Department of Commerce.

———. 2004–2005. American Indian, Alaska Native tables. *Statistical abstract of the United States, 2004–2005: The national data book.* http://factfinder.census.gov/home/aian/index.html (accessed 10/22/2006).

———. 2005. American factfinder: S2301: Employment status. http://factfinder.census.gov/servlet/STTable?_bm=y&-geo_id=01000US&-qr_name=ACS (Accessed 9/19/2006).

———. 2006. *Statistical abstracts of the United States: 2006.* http://www.census.gov/prod/www/statistical-abstract.html (Accessed 10/22/2006).

Utter, Jack. 2001. *American Indians: Answers to today's questions,* 2nd ed., rev. and enl. Norman: University of Oklahoma Press.

Westerfelt, Alex, and Michael Yellow Bird. 1999. Homeless and Indigenous in Minneapolis. In *Voices of First Nations people,* ed. Hillary Weaver, 145–62. New York: Haworth Press.

White, Richard. 1983. *The roots of dependency: Subsistence, environment, and social change among the Choctaws, Pawnees, and Navajos.* Lincoln: University of Nebraska Press.

Wilkins, David E., and K. Tsianina Lomawaima. 2001. *Uneven ground: American Indian sovereignty and federal law.* Norman: University of Oklahoma Press.

Wright, Ronald C. 1992. *Stolen continents: The "New World" through Indian eyes.* Boston: Houghton-Mifflin.

Zion, James W. 1983. The Navajo Peacemaker Court: Deference to the old and accommodation to the new. *American Indian Law Review* 11:89–109.

2

Patterns of Native American Crime, 1984–2005

Robert A. Silverman

IN 1996 I published an article describing Native American crime patterns from 1987 through 1992. The major finding of that article had nothing to do with the patterns I discerned for the years under review. Rather, the major finding was that the high rates of Native American crime (often above those of any other racial group) revealed in most of the early literature were actually an artifact of a measurement error. In particular, the denominator in the equation that produces rates (the population) was wrong. It seems that for many years Native Americans did not cooperate with the Census Bureau officials who collect population data, with the result that the Native American population was under-reported and undercounted in the census. In effect, the mathematical division that generates a rate was being performed with a denominator that was too small. In the same article, I also argued that the numerator (the number of arrests) was not very accurate either.

Other findings from that study included the following:

- While the Native American crime rate was lower than earlier studies had indicated, it was higher than crime rates for all Americans and for whites. Their rates were, however, substantially lower than rates for African Americans.
- In the case of violent crime, the Native American rate paralleled the overall crime rate in the United States but was higher than that for whites.
- Native American property-crime rates were higher than those for whites, and property-crime rates for all Americans, but were substantially lower than those for African Americans.
- For murder and non-negligent manslaughter, Native American rates were below the national average, above whites, and below African Americans.

- For liquor law violations, drinking while intoxicated, and drunkenness, Native Americans had higher rates than any other group.
- During the period under review, the crime rates displayed were relatively stable. There were slight upward trends in some of the offenses. While Native Americans had, by far, the highest rates of drunkenness arrests, there was a significant decline in those rates during the six-year period reviewed.

In this chapter I will examine Native American crime trends over a longer period of time—from 1984 through 2005. The object of the chapter is to provide the reader with a grasp of Native American involvement in crime (as measured by national-level arrest rates).

Methodological Notes

In the United States and in many other countries, the "crime rate" is measured using arrest data. Arrest data do not provide an accurate indicator of the total volume for most kinds of crime, as there are far more crimes committed than there are offenders arrested. There are a variety of reasons for this underreporting, but that is a subject for other texts. The FBI has created a "crime index" that consists of crimes that are considered more serious and/or better reported. These include: murder and non-negligent manslaughter, forcible rape (very serious but very poorly reported), robbery, aggravated assault, burglary, larceny-theft, motor vehicle theft, and arson.

The FBI's Uniform Crime Reports provide national-level arrest statistics on an annual basis. The data come from police jurisdictions that report directly to the FBI. The program is voluntary, but coverage is generally good. Coverage as it relates to smaller population groups (such as Native Americans) can be tricky, depending on a variety of factors, such as geographical distribution of the population. Calculation of rates is based on two factors—either of which can distort the picture of crime—the population base and the number of arrests. A typical crime rate is calculated by dividing the numbers of arrests made in a particular year by the population of the group under discussion.

In 2005, for instance, 10,189,691 arrests made in the United States were reported to the FBI. The U.S. population was estimated to be

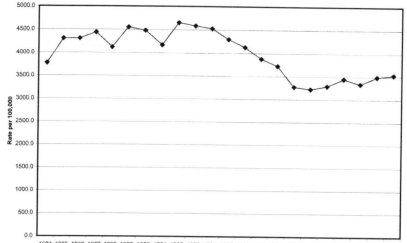

CHART 2.1 All crime, 1984–2005

288,378,137. Dividing the first number by the second and multiplying by 100,000 gives us a crime rate of 3,533 arrests per 100,000 people living in the United States in 2005. Chart 2.1 shows arrest rates in the United States for the whole population for the twenty-one-year period under consideration.[1] It is striking that the crime rate in the United States drops by about 30 percent between 1992 and 2000. There have been several attempts to explain this drop (For examples, see Blumstein and Wallman 2006; Farrington, Langan, and Tonry 2004; Conklin 2003). In the charts that follow, you will see that there is often a drop in crime rate for each racial group examined over the twenty-one years. The explanations generated by criminologists for the kinds of drop you observe include demographic changes, longer prison terms, changes in drug markets, changes in policing, and success of rehabilitation programs. Few of these "causes" have been proven with any certainty. The cause of drops in the arrest rates for Native Americans has not been specifically analyzed, though for particular offenses I speculate on possible explanations. It is worth noting that drops in crime rates over the last decade or more are global phenomena—at least for industrialized countries.

In this chapter I examine all crime and summary measures of index crimes in some depth. Specific index crimes are also described. Alcohol offenses are reviewed because of the literature linking alcohol to both crime commission and Native American offenders. Drug abuse is used as a contrasting crime. For purposes of calculating rates, all population data are census data (or estimates), and all crime data are FBI Uniform Crime Report data.

Before examining the data, a few more cautions are in order. With regard to Native American arrest rates, several problems have been identified. As noted, the FBI arrest data do not provide 100 percent coverage. The data are likely to favor urban over rural areas, and Native Americans often live in rural areas. There is, of course, a problem with "race" as a category. It is unlikely that this variable is recorded consistently. Some recording will be simple observation by a police officer, while others will involve asking the alleged offender his or her race. Evidently, in some jurisdictions "Native American" is not a category on the police form, so there will be no record linking race to arrest.

In spite of these problems, the FBI data are the best we have when we want to examine offenders. We are likely getting a good idea of offense patterns, if not volume. It will be noted in the charts that follow that Native American arrest rates are more likely to "bounce around" than are rates for other groups. The reason for this is population size. Because Native Americans are a relatively small portion of the total population and the population of offenders, small changes in either the arrest numbers or the population base make a larger difference in the rate.

The last paragraph deals with the numerator in the calculation of a rate. There are also problems with the denominator. The major finding in my earlier research pinpointed problems with the denominator. Certainly, the 1990 and 2000 censuses obviated some of the problems of the earlier census. However, there are still counting issues related to Native American populations. For instance, between the 1980 census and the 2000 census, the U.S. population grew by about 24 percent; the comparable percentage for whites is 12 percent, and for African Americans 30 percent. But the Native American population is shown to have grown by 74 percent. That "growth" is an artifact of reporting of population and does not represent a real increase in the numbers of people in the subpopulation. Further, the growth is greater between 1980 and 1990 than between 1990 and 2000. This may provide some evidence that to some extent, the problems identified in the 1996 article were still operant between 1980 and 1990. The later numbers are likely to be far more accurate, as the U.S. Bureau of the Census made real efforts to reach Native Americans and other ethnic groups to convince them that accurate reports are important to their well-being. Having said that, it is obvious that the numbers in the denominator of the equation for rates will have a significant effect. Downward trends will likely be, in some part, a result of the reporting issues. That is, as the population gets bigger (for whatever reason) but the number of crimes does not increase in the same way, rates will decline.

Finally, the literature that analyzes victims rather than offenders often generates different findings than the literature on offenders. For instance, when examining victimization, Perry (2004) echoes an earlier study by Greenfeld and Smith (1999) when he reports that "American Indians experience a per capita rate of violence twice that of the U.S. resident population" (2004, iv)—quite a different pattern than you will see in chart 2.3. It is important as you read on to remember that I am dealing only with arrest rates.

Patterns of Crime

All Crime, Violence, and Property Offenses

Chart 2.2 shows the arrest rates for all Americans, Native Americans, whites, and African Americans for the years 1984–2005. The peak year for arrest rates was 1992–4,652 per 100,000 for all Americans, 3,975 for whites, 11,637 for African Americans, and 6,340 for Native Americans (1985 and 1987 were actually a little higher for this group). The lowest rates occur in 1999 or 2000. The drop is over 30 percent for all Americans, 25 percent for whites, 28 percent for Native Americans, and an astounding 39 percent for African Americans. Johnson et al. (2006) offer an explanation for the drop that is bound up with crack cocaine markets and the way they changed during the 1990s. Given the participation of African Americans in that trade, this argument makes some sense (though it is not the full explanation). If one looks only at the total for all Americans, whites, and Native Americans, we find that crime during the entire period has a downward trend, leveling off after 2000 and perhaps even starting to rise again in the last two years. Native Americans more or less parallel whites and all Americans for the entire twenty-one-year period.

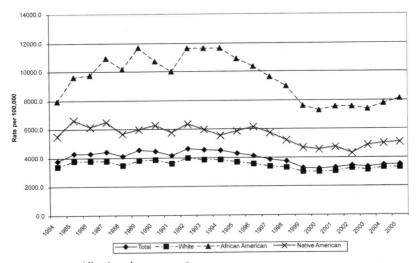

CHART 2.2 All crime by race, 1984–2005

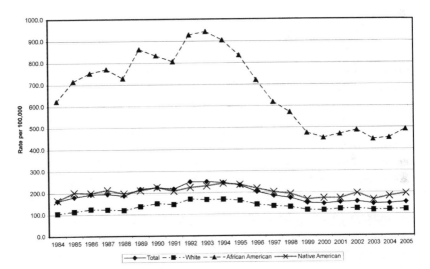

CHART 2.3 Violent crime by race, 1984–2005

The violent crime (chart 2.3) is even more dramatic. Again, 1992 or 1993 are the peak years, and 2000 is the lowest in terms of violence rates in the United States. The high rate for all Americans is 251 per 100,000; for whites it is 170, for Native Americans it is 242, while for African Americans the rate is 929 per 100,000—almost four times that of all Americans and Native Americans. The decline to 2000 is 23 percent for Native

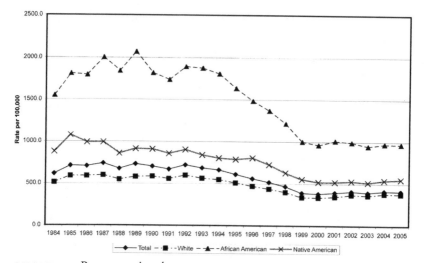

CHART 2.4 Property crime by race, 1984–2005

Americans, 41 percent for all Americans, 31 percent for whites, and 51 percent for African Americans. Again, one can probably link the decline in violent crime to a direct relationship with the drug trade. African Americans involved in the drug trade had very direct links to gun possession and to the violence that goes along with that. It is more difficult to try to explain the declines in the other groups. Native American arrest rates for violent crime more or less parallel those for all Americans.

Chart 2.4 shows the same years for property crime. The trend lines are not as dramatic, but the downward trend (and leveling off after 2000) persists, and there is much less of a buildup to a peak than was the case for violence. Again, African American rates are most prominent. Here, Native Americans clearly have rates above the national average and above that for whites (consistent with my earlier findings). During the peak years, the African American rate is about double that of Native Americans, while the Native American rate is about 50 percent higher than that for whites. The decline can probably be partially explained by the link between property crime and drug use. There is a great deal of theft associated with generating funds to purchase drugs.

In charts 2.2, 2.3, and 2.4, Native American arrest patterns follow those indicated in the earlier article (Silverman 1996). Essentially, the patterns mimic those of all Americans and of whites. For property crimes

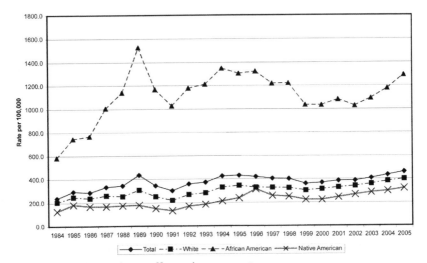

CHART 2.5 Drug abuse offenses by race, 1984–2005

their rates are above those for the other two groups, but the pattern is consistent with that of the others. For violence their rates are virtually the same as the national average, while they are greater than that for whites. Finally, when all reported arrests are considered, Native American rates parallel the patterns for all Americans and whites but are higher than those of either of those two groups.

Drugs and Alcohol

Chart 2.5 indicates that the patterns for drug abuse offenses do not follow those for the crimes discussed above. African Americans are the most involved in this crime, while Native Americans are the least likely to be arrested. In general, there is a slight upward trend between 1984 and 2005. In fact, between 1984 and 2005, the rates for all Americans and for whites increase by over 90 percent, while African Americans' rates increase by 120 percent, and Native Americans by 155 percent (though they have the lowest rates throughout the period). Given the explanations offered for the overall decline in arrest rates, this finding may be surprising, but one should keep in mind that this chart does not indicate the kinds of drugs being used. It has been argued that marijuana has become the drug of choice as crack cocaine has gone out of favor.

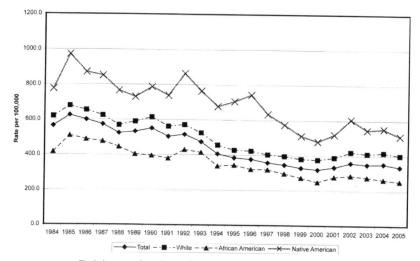

CHART 2.6 Driving under the influence by race, 1984–2005

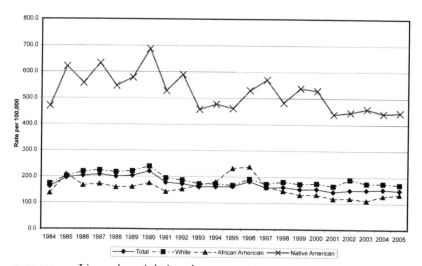

CHART 2.7 Liquor law violations by race, 1984–2005

Driving-under-the-influence (DUI) offenses (chart 2.6) decline rather steadily during the entire period. In terms of race, African Americans have the lowest rates, while Native Americans have the highest rates. There is no obvious reason for the decline. Liquor law violations (chart 2.7) also decline somewhat, though the curves are flatter than those for DUI offenses. In fact, it seems that arrests for this offense have been pretty

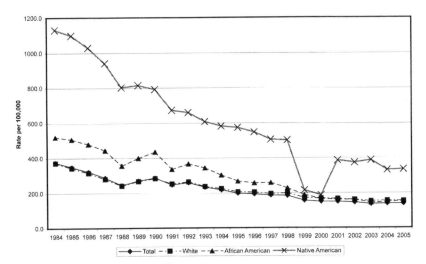

CHART 2.8 Drunkenness offenses by race, 1984–2005

consistent for twenty-one years. Again, Native Americans have the highest rates by a substantial margin.

On the topic of substance abuse, the most interesting finding is shown in chart 2.8.[2] The offense of drunkenness declines for all groups but does so most dramatically for Native Americans. For African Americans and Native Americans, the rate of drunkenness in 2005 is 30 percent of the rate in 1984. Throughout the period, Native Americans continue to have the highest rate for this kind of offense. While the lines in the chart look dramatic, it is worth noting that in 1984 the Native American rate was three times the average rate for all Americans, while in 2005, the Native American rate was still 2.4 times that of the average for all Americans.

It seems that alcohol-related arrests remain a problem for Native American populations, but they are declining. It is worth noting that the patterns seen in charts 2.4 through 2.8 are not like those seen for violent or property offenses. With the exception of drug offenses, all of these indicate substantial declines in arrest rates—the most dramatic being that for drunkenness.

This finding cries out for an explanation. Of course, the arrest rate could represent a real drop in drunkenness behavior. It is known that Americans drink less than they did in the 1980s (Greenfield and Kerry 2003). However, none of the literature during this period has suggested that drinking is less of a problem for Native Americans than it has been in the past (Snipp 1992; French 2000; White 2003; Shore et al. 2006). The best explanation seems to involve the decriminalization of drunkenness and an increase in the use of police discretion (National Institute of Justice 1996; Clews 1990) when they encounter public drunkenness. In essence, informal methods rather than formal methods are applied to public drunkenness. Increases in the use of tribal courts, drug courts, and alcohol detoxification programs could also provide partial explanations. If the decline between 1984 and 2005 seen in chart 2.8 represents discretion, the gradual way it has evolved is interesting. There is no place where the lines in the graph take a precipitous fall. Instead, there is a steady decline. If one examines linear trend lines for these groups, one finds that the slope for Native Americans is the steepest. The decline in African American rates is less steep but steeper than that for either total crime or for whites. Again, if the discretion explanation is correct, the trend means that the effect on Native Americans was greatest over that period. The explanation for the decline need not be the same for all of the groups. There may, of course, be a demographic effect on the decline for any or all of these groups—that is, they should be examined by age group (Fox 2006a). However, for the moment, these remain as hypotheses.

Other Index Crimes

Homicide is of interest as it usually provides a reliable measure of all violent crime committed (Fox 2006b). It is, by far, the most reliably measured offense. The pattern of homicides in the United States is very much like the pattern shown for violent offenses (chart 2.3). Native American homicide rates have been relatively stable, have paralleled that of all homicide offenders in the United States, and are higher than rates for whites. Between 1991 (the peak year for Native American homicide) and 2005, there is about a 40 percent drop in the rate.

In the case of robbery, the Native American rate parallels the rate for all Americans and is below that for both African Americans and whites. It seems to be a crime in which Native Americans do not participate as much as others. The drop in crime rates in the 1990s that we have come to expect from the charts shown earlier is also evident for robbery.

As one might expect, aggravated assault follows the pattern illustrated by the total amount of violent crime. The trend for Native Americans is slightly different than that for any other racial group. In general their pattern parallels that for whites and all Americans but is at a slightly higher level, while they are substantially below the rates for African Americans. The difference comes in the last few years, when there seems to be a slight increase in aggravated assault arrests for Native Americans, while the rates for all Americans and for whites has, more or less, remained flat.

Rape is the last of the violent index crimes to be considered. Data regarding rape are notoriously poor because of reluctance to report the crime (for a variety of reasons). According to the 2003 National Crime Victimization Survey, only 39 percent of rapes were reported. As a result, interpreting the police data is often difficult. In general, the data show a declining trend over the twenty-one years. The Native American rate drops from a high of 15 per 100,000 in 1994 to a low of 8.3 in 2005 but tends to be higher than the national average.

Property index crimes include larceny-theft, motor vehicle theft, burglary, and arson. In each of these cases, the Native American rates parallel those for whites and all Americans but are somewhat higher. In the case of larceny-theft, they are significantly higher than those groups. The patterns are slightly different than those for violent crimes and, instead, are more like the patterns identified for all property crime (chart 2.4).

Interestingly, the pattern for motor vehicle theft is different than the other three offenses. For this offense, there is a discernible peak, between 1993 and 1995 for whites, all Americans, and Native Americans; but in 1988 for African Americans. Native Americans tend to be close to the national average for this crime.

Conclusion

The patterns of arrest for Native Americans are similar to the patterns observed in my 1996 study. For the most part, the pattern of Native American crime follows the pattern for all Americans. Certainly, there are deviations from the pattern but, for most crimes, the lines for the two groups look very similar.

If we define being above the national average as defining a crime problem in terms of arrest rates, then Native Americans have had a persistent problem over the twenty-one years investigated in this chapter. The data show that Native American arrest rates are above the national average when all crimes are considered. In fact, their rate is almost one and a half times the national average and has been at that level for virtually the whole period.

Native American arrest rates have tended to be right on or very close to the national average for violent crimes. The rates for the last few years seem to be rising. They tend to be around the average rate in terms of homicide commission and below the national average for robbery. For aggravated assault and rape, their rates are above the national average.

For property crimes, over the twenty-one years, Native Americans have had rates 1.2 to 1.5 times higher than the national average. They are more or less on the national average for arson, motor vehicle theft (with some variation), and burglary. In terms of larceny-theft, Native Americans are arrested almost 50 percent more often than the average for all Americans.

For drug offenses, Native Americans are below the national average and below the rates for whites throughout the period. However, for alcohol offenses, their rates are substantially above that for the other groups observed. Native American rates are usually more than three times that for all Americans for liquor law violations. DUI arrests for Native Americans are one and a half to two times that of the national average. And, as reported earlier, drunkenness offenses remain substantially higher than for other groups, despite their decline over the twenty-one years.

In sum, arrests of Native Americans, as a measure of involvement in crime, have declined in the same way that arrests for all Americans have declined.[3] However, for many crimes, arrest rates for Native Americans have remained above the national average. Victimization data produce an even more grim picture (Greenfeld and Smith 1999; Perry 2004).

Arrest rates are, of course, only one measure of social disorganization and social problems, but they often reflect other social issues. They do not give us a lot of confidence in the efficacy of programs aimed at alleviating the social ills linked to Native American life.

References

Blumstein, Alfred. 2006. Disaggregating the violence trends. In *The crime drop in America*, rev. ed., ed. Alfred Blumstein and Joel Wallman, 13–44. Cambridge: Cambridge University Press.

Blumstein, Alfred, and Joel Wallman. 2006. *The crime drop in America*, rev. ed. Cambridge: Cambridge University Press.

Clews, Thomas. 1990. Alcohol, the law and police discretion. In *Alcohol and crime: Proceedings of a conference, 4–6 April, 1989*, ed. Julia Vernon. Canberra: Australian Institute of Criminology.

Conklin, John E. 2003. *Why crime rates fell*. New York: Pearson Education.

Farrington, David, Patrick Langan, Michael Tonry, eds. 2004. *Cross-national studies in crime and justice*. Washington, DC: Bureau of Justice Statistics.

Fox, James Alan. 2006a. Demographics and U.S. homicide. In *The crime drop in America*, rev. ed., ed. Alfred Blumstein and Joel Wallman, 288–317. Cambridge: Cambridge University Press.

———. 2006b. *Homicide trends in the United States*. Washington, DC: Bureau of Justice Statistics.

French, Laurence. 2000. *Addictions and Native Americans*. Westport, CT: Praeger.

Greenfeld, Lawrence A., and Steven K. Smith. 1999. *American Indians and crime*. Washington, DC. Bureau of Statistics (NCJ 173386).

Greenfield, Thomas K., and William C. Kerr. 2003. Tracking alcohol consumption over time. *Alcohol Research and Health* 27:30–38.

Johnson, Bruce, Andrew Golub, Eloise Dunlap. 2006. The rise and decline of hard drugs, drug markets, and violence in inner-city New York. In *The crime drop in America*, rev. ed., ed. Alfred Blumstein and Joel Wallman, 164–206. Cambridge: Cambridge University Press.

National Institute of Justice. 1996. Law enforcement in a time of community policing. Summary of a study by Stephen D. Mastrofski. *National Institute of Justice, Research Review*. Washington, DC: National Institute of Justice.

Perry, Steven W. 2004. *American Indians and crime: A BJS statistical profile, 1992–2002*. Washington, DC: Bureau of Justice Statistics (NCJ 203097).

Shore, Jay, Janette Beals, Heather Orton, and Dedra Buchwald. 2006. Comorbidity of alcohol abuse and dependence with medical conditions in two American Indian reservation communities. *Alcoholism: Clinical and Experimental Research* 30:649–55

Silverman, Robert A. 1996. Patterns of Native American crime. In *Native Americans, crime, and justice*, ed. Marianne Nielsen and Robert A. Silverman, 58–74. Boulder, CO: Westview.

Snipp, Matthew, C. 1992. Sociological perspectives on American Indians. *Annual Review of Sociology* 18:351–71.

White, William L. 2003. Native American addiction: A response to French. *Alcoholism Treatment Quarterly* 21:93–97.

3

Ha'áłchíní, haadaah náásdah / *"They're Not Going to Be Young Forever"*

JUVENILE CRIMINAL JUSTICE

Jon'a Meyer

WHILE A GOOD deal of writing describes the experiences of Native Americans in the federal, state, and tribal justice systems, very little has been written about the situation faced by Native American juvenile delinquents. Part of the paucity may stem from the maze that is often navigated by youthful Native American delinquents and which often takes paths that lead out of Indian country entirely.

In describing Native American youth, Congress has said, "there is no resource that is more vital to the continued existence and integrity of Indian tribes than their children" (Indian Child Welfare Act, 1978). Native Americans across the continent agree with that sentiment, describing their children as cherished treasures from their Creator; the Lakota word for *children*, for example, is *wakanyeja*, which translates literally to "sacred beings." When a child commits a delinquent act, Native Americans tend to eschew mainstream notions of punishment, preferring instead that wayward youth participate in restorative justice programs, seek healing through traditional ceremonies, or obtain mentoring from respected elders (e.g., Armstrong, Guilfoyle, and Melton 1996, 49; Donelan 1999, 68; Patterson 2000, 824). The goal is to reintegrate juvenile delinquents into society and mold them into productive citizens and future role models.

Unfortunately, this reintegrative goal is not always met in Indian country, due to fiscal realities and federal legislation. This chapter will discuss the intertwining of these two obstacles to justice for Native juveniles by considering the adjudication of off-reservation delinquents, serious juvenile offenders, moderately serious offenders, and the far more common nonserious delinquents. Due to the interplay between the federal and tribal justice systems, one must examine both when describing the experiences of Native Americans in the juvenile justice system.

Off-Reservation Native American Delinquents: "What Happens in Vegas Stays in Vegas"?

The treatment of off-reservation Native American delinquents is the most straightforward situation. Because tribal courts do not have jurisdiction over juveniles who engage in delinquency off their respective reservations, those youth are adjudicated in whichever local or state court has jurisdiction over the type of acts alleged to have been committed (e.g., *State ex rel Elmer 1999*, 177–78). If off-reservation tribal youth happen to violate a federal code, of course they would be adjudicated in the federal courts, but otherwise, the same local and state courts that adjudicate non-Indian delinquents govern their criminality.

At least one scholar feels this situation should be changed to allow tribes to decide the fates of their delinquents much as they now decide the adoption placements for Native American children. Polashuk (1996, 1226) argues that state courts should transfer cases involving Native American juvenile defendants back to their reservation justice systems: "I suggest that all offenses committed by Indian juveniles, whether in Indian country or outside its boundaries, are presumed to be adjudicated in the tribal court of the Indian juvenile." Polashuk (1996, 1210, 1214) notes that tribal courts are in the best position to understand the juvenile's specific needs and how best to proceed with the case while still honoring their tribal traditions.

While other scholars may not specifically advocate for the transfer of off-reservation cases to the tribal courts, they do view tribal courts as best able to adjudicate cases involving Native youth. Patterson (2000, 825), for example, notes that tribal youth "must be . . . disciplined in the traditions of the[ir] culture," to maintain and empower Native American culture and communities. Though a number of scholars note the importance of tribal courts in maintaining culture, it is unlikely that federal law will ever be revised to compel local jurisdictions to send tribally affiliated delinquents to their home reservations for adjudication. The current situation is somewhat akin to what would happen if a citizen of the United States committed an offense in a foreign country; to borrow an idea from a popular tourism campaign, what happens in a foreign country stays in the foreign country. Absent extraordinary circumstances, American citizens, even juveniles, who commit crimes abroad cannot expect to be repatriated for trial. Similarly, Native American juveniles cannot expect to be repatriated to their tribes for adjudication.

Serious Juvenile Offenders in Indian Country: Too Often Making a Federal Case out of It?

Serious juvenile offenders are relatively rare in Indian country, but their treatment by the justice system has attracted a great deal of attention and criticism. Nearly two-thirds (61 percent) of juveniles held in federal detention are Native American (Scalia 1997, 3). This is due, in part, to the Federal Juvenile Delinquency Act (1938), the Major Crimes Act (1885) and other related legislation, which automatically transfers jurisdiction over serious felonies from Native American tribes to the federal government (Polashuk 1996, 1207–08). Thus, tribal youth aged fifteen or older who commit serious crimes such as murder, rape, or robbery in Indian country fall under the purview of the federal courts, as do youth aged thirteen and fourteen whose tribes consent to the transfer (Standefer 1999, 483).

In 1995, the only recent year for which statistics have been published, a total of 122 youth were adjudicated in the federal courts, and "many" of those were Native American (Scalia 1997, 1). Though the published data fail to note exactly how many Native American youth were adjudicated that year or whether any of them had committed off-reservation federal crimes (meaning they had not been processed under the guidance of the Major Crimes Act), it is clear that tribal defendants form the majority of the federal juvenile court caseload. Unfortunately, there is no "separate" juvenile justice system at the federal level, so the only real differences between the adult and juvenile systems are that federal juvenile proceedings are closed without juries (Scalia 1997, 1) and that the sanctions are governed by the Federal Juvenile Delinquency Act, discussed below.

The lack of a separate system geared specifically toward the needs of young offenders poses some problems for juvenile justice. Owing in part to their reduced numbers, and also the typical case type (usually quite serious for non-Native American youth) that is processed at the federal level, the federal system has not kept pace with the state courts in terms of developing rehabilitative programming. The sorry situation led one scholar to comment that agents of the federal justice system, from pretrial services staffers to judges and beyond, "lack the expertise and infrastructure necessary to provide channels of restorative justice for youth in the federal system" (Langley 2005, 6).

In fact, the Federal Juvenile Delinquency Act acknowledges the paucity of programming available for federally prosecuted juveniles by limiting transfers of cases into the federal system from state courts to those that have met one of three conditions (18 U.S.C. § 5032). The first two conditions are designed to ensure better services than some resource-poor jurisdictions can provide: the state court must either (1) not have or refuse jurisdiction over the youth, or (2) not have adequate programming or services at its disposal for juvenile offenders. The third condition that merits a transfer into the federal system from a state court occurs when "the offense charged is a crime of violence that is a felony or an offense described in [certain specified federal drug or firearms laws] and that there is a substantial Federal interest in the case or the offense to warrant the exercise of Federal jurisdiction" (18 U.S.C. § 5032). If none of the three conditions applies, the juvenile is to remain in the state system. From these conditions, it is clear that Congress intended for only the worst of the worst or youth who could not be better served by their resource-poor or overwhelmed jurisdictions to end up on the federal docket.

The three conditions do not seem to apply if the juvenile is a Native American who commits certain crimes in Indian country, however. Instead, Native youth are automatically transferred from their tribal justice systems even if the tribal court wants jurisdiction and has adequate programming at its disposal, and the juvenile is not alleged to have violated any of the enumerated drug or firearm laws. At first confusing, the reason is neatly tucked away in the first condition, because tribal courts do not have jurisdiction over federal-eligible offenses committed by adults or juveniles. Enacted in 1885 in the political fallout and aftermath of the Crow Dog decision by the U.S. Supreme Court (which supported tribal sovereignty in justice decisions), the Major Crimes Act transferred jurisdiction over seven serious offenses from tribal justice systems to the federal courts (see also Cardani in this volume). The list has now been extended to include fifteen offenses: murder, manslaughter, kidnapping, maiming, federally regulated sex offenses, incest, assault with intent to commit murder, assault with a dangerous weapon, assault resulting in serious bodily injury, assault against a person under the age of sixteen, felony child abuse or neglect, arson, burglary, robbery, or felony theft (18 U.S.C. § 1153). Because the federal-eligible list includes several property crimes, Native American youth who commit only moderately serious offenses can easily find themselves ushered into the federal system. The process that is designed to keep most juveniles in their local courts, then, does not apply to Native American delinquents.

While the federal courts must process Native American juveniles over the age of fifteen who commit any of the offenses enumerated in the Major Crimes Act, they appear ill-prepared to do so. Because the Bureau of Prisons (BOP) does not operate facilities for juveniles, federally adjudicated youth are housed in state facilities under federal contract (Scalia 1997, 3); for this reason, the BOP cannot control the type or quality of programs to which the juveniles are exposed. One of the specific purposes of the Federal Juvenile Delinquency Act is to be "helpful and rehabilitative rather than punitive" whenever appropriate (18 U.S.C. § 5032), but the federal courts recognize that facilities under the BOP "offer little in way of programs for [certain] juveniles" (*United States vs. Juvenile No. 1* 1997, 310), and many scholars feel the federal courts cannot fulfill this significant mandate (e.g., Langley 2005, 10). These unfortunate realities combine to create a system that cannot function as it was created to do, which leads to an additional problem associated with addressing delinquency in the federal courts: because the Federal Juvenile Delinquency Act limits incarceration terms to five years and does not have adequate rehabilitation programs at its disposal, waiver or certification to the federal adult system is probable whenever it is authorized as a possible course of action. (Three groups of delinquents may be certified to the adult system: those [1] aged fifteen or older who are charged with violent or drug trafficking/importation offenses, [2] aged 13 or older who possessed a firearm during the commission of a violent offense, or [3] those with prior violent or drug-related felonies).

The problems do not end there. Another major weakness of the federal system as a venue for adjudicating juvenile delinquency is the lack of aftercare or parole, which was abolished during the move toward federal sentencing guidelines. Aftercare has long been recognized as necessary to help ensure that juveniles who have been incarcerated eschew criminality when they are ultimately released. One scholar properly noted that jailing juveniles is unproductive without suitable aftercare: "Incarceration is only as effective as the reintegration services that are available to support these youth when they return home" (Conward 2001, 2462). The absence of aftercare for federally adjudicated delinquents means that those youth may be more likely to reoffend. Native youth, who are more likely than other juveniles to fall under the purview of the federal justice system, are disproportionately deprived of the rehabilitative programming offered to off-reservation delinquents.

Due in part to worries about reoffending resulting from inadequate rehabilitation options at the federal level, the situation involving certification into the adult system has become critical. Very few, between 1 and 2 percent of juveniles processed in the state courts, are waived to the adult system (Puzzanchera et al. 2003, 28; Scalia 1997, 2). At the federal level, however, 134 juveniles were adjudicated in 1994, and an additional 65 were transferred to the adult system in the year preceding September of 1994 (Scalia 1997, 2), meaning that approximately one-third of juveniles in the federal courts are waived into the adult system. The huge disparity in likelihood of certification may stem from the fact that the Federal Juvenile Delinquency Act has failed to keep up with social changes that favor retribution in light of concerns about high-profile violent youth, so it continues to limit incarceration to five years or until the juveniles reach age twenty-one, whichever comes first (unless adjudicated after their eighteenth birthdays, in which case they may be incarcerated for five years). When faced with situations involving teens who are nearing the age of majority, judges may fear that the ineffectual rehabilitation options available to federally adjudicated juveniles require more than a few years to make a real difference in the lives of detained youth, and grant waivers to the adult system (e.g., Standefer 1999, 473).

Once in the adult federal system, juvenile delinquents face a host of issues. First, delinquent youth in the adult courts are exposed to harsher sanctions than those who remain in the juvenile system (e.g., Burnstein 1999, 880). While those who retain their juvenile status are only half as likely as adults to be sent to prison (Scalia 1997, 1), those who are sentenced as adults receive the same sentences as their adult counterparts

(Standefer 1999, 482). Federal sentences tend to be twice as long as those imposed in state courts (Standefer 1999, 474); and unlike youth adjudicated in the state-level adult courts, who can earn significant amounts of good time toward an early release or bank on parole to get them out of detention earlier, delinquents serving terms in the federal system must serve nearly all of their sentences under federal sentencing guidelines.

Some scholars complain that transferring juveniles to the adult courts due to real and perceived weaknesses in the federal juvenile system is wrongheaded and smacks of racism, because the policy disproportionately applies to Native Americans (e.g., Standefer 1999, 475, 495). Among the suggested remedies to this thorny problem are including age as a legal factor under the sentencing guidelines, so that juveniles can receive shorter sentences, and creating a "youth discount" that would allow juveniles to serve a smaller proportion of their sentences than is currently required (Standefer 1999, 490, 500–501). Such a youth discount combined with restoring parole for juveniles could go a long way toward improving the situation experienced by Native American youth sentenced in the federal courts.

While support has swelled within Congress regarding increasing the number of juveniles adjudicated in the federal courts since gang violence associated with the 1990s drug wars gripped the nation (Langley 2005, 1), most scholars argue against mandatory transfer to federal court for Native American youth. They worry that separating juveniles from the more effective state and tribal rehabilitative programming will have negative results for Native youth.

Moderately Serious Juvenile Offenders in Indian Country: To Detain or Not, That Is the Question

Despite widespread worries about gangs and murderous teens in Indian country (e.g., Donovan 1997; Weyermann 1998), we know that very serious offending is relatively uncommon on tribal lands; otherwise, the federal juvenile caseload would be far higher than the hundred or so tribal youth now processed per year. Yazzie and Zion (1995, 72), for example, report that only around one-fifth of the juvenile offenses on the Navajo reservation for 1993 had some element of violence, including assault or battery cases (13 percent), resisting arrest (3 percent), and weapons offenses (3 percent), and that an additional one-eighth were relatively serious property crimes, including theft (8 percent) and burglary (4 percent). While a few of those cases ended up on the federal docket, the vast majority were left to other venues. Those delinquents and others like them who engage in delinquency in Indian country that does not warrant automatic transfer to the federal system can find themselves on either the tribal or the federal docket, depending on their tribal affiliation and the severity of their acts.

Tribes have jurisdiction over acts committed by Native youth on their reservations, as long as the crimes are not governed by the Major Crimes Act or the General Crimes Act (1817), which transfers Native Americans who commit crimes against non-Native victims into the federal system (Standefer 1999, 488). Under the Federal Juvenile Delinquency Act, a tribe could technically surrender jurisdiction over a particular juvenile who was not subject to automatic transfer to the federal courts, saying either that jurisdiction was refused (somewhat akin to modern-day banishment) or that the tribe's resources were inadequate to serve the juvenile's needs. These cases appear to be quite rare. Instead, tribes seek to maintain jurisdiction over their juvenile delinquents even if the tribe does not have adequate resources to deal with the particular youth.

Jail space is very limited in Indian country, especially for juveniles. In 2003, 278 juveniles were held in Indian country facilities (Minton 2005, 1). According to recent statistics, the Gila River Nation in Arizona has the largest juvenile facility, which has a rated capacity of 106 youth; not surprisingly, it is also the newest facility mentioned in the report, having been built in 2003 (Minton 2005, 3–4). Another comprehensive report (Greenfeld and Smith 1999, 32–33) provides extensive data on juvenile detention capacity: while many tribes have no juvenile detention space (thirteen tribes were listed as having adult but not juvenile space, and many tribes were not included in the write-up because they do not have any form of detention facilities), the rated capacity for other juvenile facilities in Indian country was four or fewer youth (eighteen tribes), five to ten juveniles (ten tribes), eleven to twenty youth (eight tribes), and more than twenty (eight tribes). The data make it clear that the vast majority of America's more than five hundred federally recognized tribes have inadequate detention space for juveniles (or adults).

The widespread lack of jail space leads to a heavy reliance on probation (e.g., Yazzie and Zion 1995, 76) and other community-based sanctions for juveniles, even those adjudicated for moderately serious offenses. The Mashantucket Pequots, for example, use home confinement as an alternative to detention for serious juvenile offending (Miller 1995, 1); because the tribe does not have juvenile space of their own, home confinement allows delinquents to remain on their reservation, surrounded by their families, while preventing the tribe from having to place the youth in off-reservation sites. Tribes without juvenile detention facilities of their own must lease space from other tribes or from a state-run facility.

Typically, tribes prefer their own facilities, but that goal is unattainable without significant federal assistance, due to the tremendous expense associated with building and maintaining a juvenile detention center. The second-best choice is to lease space in another tribe's facility if it has space. For example, the Sac and Fox Nation Juvenile Detention Facility is rated for an occupancy of sixty youth but housed only sixteen delinquents at midyear in 2003 (Minton 2005, 7), meaning it had space to lease out to other tribes. Only a few tribal youth facilities have space to lease, however, due to the relatively tiny sizes of the typical facility in Indian country. The least desirable choice is to lease space in a state-run facility, both because of the expense and because of the potential loss of sovereignty that results from placing tribal youth in off-reservation facilities.

Fiscal exigencies have forced many tribes to transfer their delinquents to the state justice system, due to their lack of appropriate resources such as placements for youth in need of supervision; this occurs "across the United States" (Patterson 2000, 801, 815). Tribes are wary of state placements following the Elmer case, in which a Menominee youth was placed in a state facility by his tribe, then arrested and processed in the state courts after he attacked a staff member (*State ex rel Elmer J. K.* 1999). Elmer's tribe tried to get him repatriated back to their reservation courts for adjudication on the new crime, but the Wisconsin Court of Appeals ruled that since Elmer committed the assault off his reservation, he was subject to state prosecution. Tribal delinquents who are placed in state facilities may be able to take advantage of the superior rehabilitative programming available in those facilities (Langley 2005, 3–4), but they are subject to state adjudication for any misbehavior that occurs while they are housed there.

In a few cases, tribes that are unable to pay state fees to house offenders find that they must release even violent youth (e.g., Patterson 2000, 816). This situation results in dangerous youth being sent home or sentenced into community corrections, for which they are inappropriate given the danger they pose to their communities. Due to their growing numbers and the danger they pose to society, tribal youth who commit moderately serious offenses are most in need of change in how they are handled by the justice system.

The Far More Common Nonserious Delinquents in Indian Country

The vast majority of juvenile delinquency in Indian Country would be classified as nonserious acts. Though much more research is needed to fully describe the nature and type of crimes committed by Native American juveniles in Indian Country, the few available studies have been consistent in their findings. Poupart's 1995 review of four studies detailing arrests of Native American juveniles in Indian country, for example, revealed that the most common arrests were for drunkenness and other liquor violations, public disorder, vagrancy, and status offenses. Similarly, Yazzie and Zion (1995, 72) report that at least one-third of juvenile offenses on the Navajo reservation for 1993 were similarly mundane, tied to alcohol for the most part, though an additional 12 percent of youth had been arrested for possession of marijuana. Even among youth who are incarcerated, relatively petty offenses seem to be the norm. More than half (56 percent) of youth admitted to the Gila River Indian Community youth detention facility between 1990 and 1997, for example, had some sort of substance abuse charges, mostly underage consumption of alcohol, possession of marijuana, or inhaling toxic vapors (U.S. Congress 1997a, 75).

The high number of alcohol-related offenses is not surprising, given the harsh social realities on reservations, which include high rates of unemployment, poverty, alcoholism, and criminal victimization (e.g., Donelan 1999, 68). Some families on reservations actually provide young children with alcohol, further fueling the pervasive spiral of alcoholism (e.g., Yazzie and Zion 1995, 72). One Gila River probationer referred by the court for alcohol and substance abuse was just six years old, and he was not the only kindergartner with those problems (U.S. Congress 1997a, 16). Alcohol and other substance abuse by Native youth do not seem to be problems that will soon be eradicated.

For these and other relatively minor offenses, community corrections are appropriately the norm. Probation coupled with mentoring by elders is commonly used with tribal delinquents (e.g., Abrams 1994; Armstrong et al. 1996, 49). Community service and restitution, too, appear to be rather routine sanctions in tribal courts, with youth sometimes asked to perform tasks for elderly tribal members or attend or serve at tribal events/ceremonies (e.g., Abrams 1994; Miller 1995). Gila River delinquents, for example, grow fruits and vegetables in a community garden for the local elderly (U.S. Congress 1997a, 16). Restitution is also imposed with some regularity (e.g., Lowery 1993, 401). The tribal preference for restorative justice with delinquents is not unforeseen, given the emphasis by Native Americans on reintegrative sanctions and the "flurry" of restorative programs being developed for juveniles both on and off reservations (McCold 1996, 89).

Peacemaking (discussed more fully in chapter 12) has been successfully implemented at the juvenile level. The Navajo Nation, for example, operated the Yaa Da'Ya peacemaking program for juveniles between 1993 and 1997 and still welcomes youthful offenders into their mainstream peacemaking program. Yaa Da'Ya was unique in that the process was tailored for young participants and the program staff worked with the delinquents to get them back into school and reintegrated into their families, from whom some had become estranged (Meyer 2005). In an era of high recidivism, very few youth referred into Yaa Da'Ya were arrested or detected using alcohol or drugs after becoming involved with the program (Meyer 2005, 134). Other tribes also use peacemaking as a tool in their fight against juvenile crime, and criminal justice practitioners who support peacemaking feel the process is very effective with juveniles (e.g., Gould 1997, 12, 16; Meyer 2006).

Programs like peacemaking and other innovative approaches may help turn the tide of juvenile delinquency in Indian country. Labeled "perhaps the most serious threat to the future prosperity of Indian communities" in 1997 (U.S. Congress 1997b), juvenile crime can be addressed by Native American communities given adequate support. Even the most effective community corrections programs cannot run themselves and require funding for effective operation if they are to serve juveniles for whom they are appropriate. Indeed, the sad reality is that many tribes are handicapped in their pursuit of justice by a lack of facilities and personnel for dealing with juvenile crime. Funding lapses may be the greatest determinant of whether justice can be achieved for both Native youth and their communities.

It is important to note that some tribal programs are effective in reducing juvenile offending. Such initiatives integrate culturally sensitive anticrime efforts into a comprehensive system of justice that combines restorative-justice-inspired sanctions, persuasive healing approaches, and tribal knowledge and traditions, where appropriate, to reintegrate delinquents back into society. Six model tribal youth programs, for example, were recently discussed at a conference dedicated to addressing juvenile delinquency (Office of Juvenile Justice and Delinquency Prevention 2003); all were among the many initiatives funded by the Office of Juvenile Justice and Delinquency Prevention between 2000 and 2003. The Navajo Nation's Hozhooji Youth Diversion Project couples culturally relevant counseling with traditional activities, such as sweat lodges, to help first-time delinquents remain crime-free. The Choctaw Nation's Project Free Mental Health Program serves juvenile delinquents who are in need of mental health services. The Cherokee Nation's Cherokee Challenge program helps combat delinquency by teaching Cherokee youth their traditions and utilizing peer mediators to help resolve disputes. The Healing Lodge of the Seven Nations was created by seven affiliated tribes as a way to serve their youth locally rather than sending them to state-run facilities; the culturally sensitive residential program addresses alcohol and substance abuse among teens. The Eastern Shoshone and Northern Arapahoe Tribes' Wind River Youth Justice Project attempts to create a sense of accountability through peacemaking and other services. Finally, the Tanana Chiefs Conference (a grouping of Alaskan villages) initiated culturally relevant youth courts in fourteen tribal villages in Alaska.

The goal of these and other tribal programs is to reduce the deleterious effects of juvenile delinquency and save future youth from the downward spiral of crime. Much more investment is needed in supporting Indian nations in developing innovative juvenile programs such as these and the infrastructures needed to support them. Tribes feel they have to protect both their futures and their youth, because as one Navajo peacemaker pointed out, "*Ha'álchíní, haadaah náásdah* (they're not going to be young forever)," (personal interview with peacemaker #63 1997). Let's hope they succeed.

References

Abrams, Joan. 1994. Who's the law of the land? Jurisdiction on Indian reservations is confusing, even for the experts. *Lewiston Morning Tribune* (Idaho), November 26.

Armstrong, Troy L., Michael H. Guilfoyle, and Ada P. Melton. 1996. Traditional approaches to tribal justice. In *Native Americans, crime, and justice*, ed. Marianne O. Nielsen and Robert A. Silverman, 46–51. Boulder, CO: Westview.

Burnstein, Florence B. 1999. Juvenile law. *Denver University Law Review* 76:877–902.

Conward, Cynthia M. 2001. Where have all the children gone? A look at incarcerated youth in America. *William Mitchell Law Review* 27:2435–64.

Donelan, Brenda. 1999. The unique circumstances of Native American juveniles under federal supervision. *Federal Probation* 63:68–71.

Donovan, Bill. 1997. Shiprock dubbed as homicide capital. *Navajo Nation Times*, August 14.

Federal Juvenile Delinquency Act. 1938. (18 U.S.C. § 5032).

General Crimes Act. 1817. (18 U.S.C. 1152).

Gould, Larry A. 1997. The dilemma of the Navajo police officer: Traditional versus European-based means of social control. Unpublished manuscript in the possession of the author.

Greenfeld, Lawrence A., and Steven K. Smith. 1999. *American Indians and Crime.* Washington, DC: Bureau of Justice Statistics.

Indian Child Welfare Act. 1978. (25 U.S.C. § 1901–63).

Langley, Laura K. 2005. Giving up on youth: The dangers of recent attempts to federalize juvenile crime. *Journal of Juvenile Law* 25:1–15.

Lowery, Daniel L. 1993. Developing a tribal common law jurisprudence: The Navajo experience, 1969–1992. *American Indian Law Review* 18:379–438.

Major Crimes Act. 1885. (18 U.S.C. § 1153).

McCold, Paul. 1996. Restorative justice and the role of community. In *Restorative justice: International perspectives*, ed. Burt Galaway and Joe Hudson, 85–101. Monsey, NY: Criminal Justice Press.

Meyer, Jon'a F. 2005. *Bił_háí'áázh* ("I am his brother"): Can peacemaking work with juveniles? In *Navajo Nation peacemaking*, Marianne O. Nielsen and James W. Zion, 125–42. Tucson: University of Arizona Press.

———. 2006. Peacemaking as viewed by criminal justice professionals. Paper presented at the Western Social Science Association, April, Phoenix.

Miller, Julie. 1995. Expanding system metes out Mashantucket justice. *New York Times*, July 30.

Minton, Todd D. 2005. *Jails in Indian country, 2003.* Washington, DC: Bureau of Justice Statistics.

Office of Juvenile Justice and Delinquency Prevention. 2003. Juvenile justice partners convene in Indian Country. *OJJDP News @ a Glance* 2(4). http://www.ncjrs .gov/html/ojjdp/news_at_glance/201242/1_conference.html (accessed October 7, 2006).

Patterson, Sarah M. 2000. Native American juvenile delinquents and the tribal courts. *New York Law School Journal of Human Rights* 7:801–33.

Polashuk, Stacie S. 1996. Following the lead of the Indian Child Welfare Act: Expanding tribal court jurisdiction over Native American juvenile delinquents. *Southern California Law Review* 69:1191–1231.

Poupart, Lisa M. 1995. Juvenile justice processing of American Indian youths. In *Minorities in juvenile justice*, ed. Kimberly K. Leonard, Carl E. Pope, and William H. Feyerherm, 179–200. Thousand Oaks, CA: Sage.

Puzzanchera, Charles, Anne L. Stahl, Terrence A. Finnegan, Nancy Tierney, and Howard N. Snyder. 2003. *Juvenile court statistics 1998*. Washington, DC: Office of Juvenile Justice and Delinquency Prevention.

Scalia, John. 1997. *Juvenile delinquents in the federal criminal justice system*. Washington, DC: Bureau of Justice Statistics.

Standefer, Amy J. 1999. The Federal Juvenile Delinquency Act: A disparate impact on Native American juveniles. *Minnesota Law Review* 84:473–504.

State ex rel Elmer J.K., III v. Elmer J. K., II, 591 N.W. 2d 176 (Wisc. 1999).

U.S. Congress. Senate. Committee on Indian Affairs. 1997a. *Hearing on Juvenile Justice in Indian Country*. Statement of Mary Thomas, Governor, Gila River Industry Community. 105th Cong., April 8, 1997.

———. 1997b. *Hearing on Juvenile Justice in Indian Country*. Statement of Thomas LeClaire, director, Office of Tribal Justice. 105th Cong. April 8, 1997.

United States v. Juvenile No. 1, 118 F.3d 298 (1997).

Weyermann, Debra. 1998. And then there were none: On the Navajo reservation, a passion for blood sport. *Harper's Magazine*, April 1998.

Yazzie, Robert, and James W. Zion. 1995. "Slay the monsters." In *Popular justice and community regeneration*, ed. Kayleen M. Hazlehurst, 67–87. Westport, CT: Praeger.

Criminal Justice Challenges
for Native American Women

Mary Jo Tippeconnic Fox

NATIVE AMERICANS are victims and offenders in crime-related activities more often than their population numbers would predict. Native American women, both on and off the reservation, suffer disproportionately in this regard. This chapter focuses on Native American women and criminal justice by first examining the historical context in which they find themselves, then examining the impact of victimization and incarceration on their families, traditions, and culture. Finally, some successful programs and interventions are highlighted, and suggestions for the future are offered. Criminal activity, per se, is not a focus of this chapter.

Historical Context

To fully understand Native American women and crime, a historical context is helpful. Colonization in the United States was a turning point in Native American history. (See Nielsen in this volume for a discussion of colonization.) In Indian country, the past truly affects the present and the future. Violence against Native women was not a common occurrence in most traditional Native American tribes before contact with Europeans. When violence did occur, Native nations had systems in place to deal with the transgressions of tribal members based upon their own traditions, philosophies, and standards. The core of Native American justice was usually restitution, which involved mediation, compensation, and recuperation to restore harmony (Ross 1998). These codes of conduct were usually passed to each generation by oral traditions. Each of the approximately 550 current tribal nations in the United States dealt with crimes in their own particular way, which generally reflected their unique culture.

While there was wide variation in the way codes were implemented, in most cases this meant immediate relief for victims and no escape from penalties for the offender. Violence against Native American women had harsh consequences, including, in some cases, banishment or death. As noted, culture was a major factor in the specific ways of handling the offense. The Cherokee and the Pueblos provide contrasting examples. One important role of the Cherokee matrilineal clan was arbiter of justice (Perdue 1998). Retaliation was the principle; if one Cherokee killed another, the clan kin avenged the death, and the matter was settled. Clan vengeance rested with the family, not with other leaders of the community. On the other hand, the Pueblos were peaceful people, and violent crime was rare; most conflicts and disputes were settled through mediation and arbitration. The goal was "to cure and cleanse the offender of the bad thoughts that caused negative behavior" (Melton 2006, 190).

Colonization destroyed many of the tribal systems and traditions in place to protect women from rape, sexual assault, and other violence. During American colonization and reservation periods, Native American women were often raped and otherwise sexually assaulted by non-Native frontiersmen, settlers, cavalrymen, military men, or reservation personnel. Most of this was not reported or was dismissed by non-Native law enforcement and judiciary (Native American Circle [hereinafter, NAC] 2002). The Europeans and later Euro-Americans systematically oppressed Native cultures. The introduction of alcohol proved to be particularly devastating. The correlation between alcohol use and violent crimes is well known (National Sexual Violence Resource Center 2000). To combat violence, some Native nations are trying to revitalize some of the old traditions in conjunction with modern paradigms of justice. This is often difficult, as Native American justice is often based on holistic philosophies (see Archambeault in this volume) and worldviews, whereas Western justice is more vertical (Melton 2006, 180–96).

Compounding difficulties for Native American women is negative stereotyping (Lujan 2006, 130–39; Perry in this volume). Non-Natives often characterize Native American women as prostitutes, squaws, or drunks. When these stereotypes are held by police or judges, discrimination can be the result. There is little doubt that these stereotypes also affect Native American women's self-image. This in itself can result in not reporting crime victimization. Obviously, there is fallout from stereotyping that affects families of the victims.

Native American Women as Crime Victims

From 1992 to 2001, the annual violent victimization rate for all Americans was 41 per 1,000 individuals twelve years of age or older. For American Indians the rate was 101—the highest rate among all races. "American Indians were twice as likely to experience rape/sexual assault (5 per 1000 persons age twelve or over) compared to all races (2 per 1000)" (Perry 2004, 5). In the same period, the annual average violent victimization rate was 35 per 1,000 females (all races), while for Native American women, it was 86 per 1,000, or two and a half times that for all females and substantially higher than the rate for any other racial group (Perry 2004, 7). Further, other research shows that Native American females are more likely to report rape or sexual assault than other groups and that they are more likely to report being victims of stalking (Stalking Resource Center 2006). Some research data show that Native American couples may generate more violence toward each other than do couples from some other racial groups (Bachman 1992, 99–101).

Perry (2004) analyzed data for three specific tribes—the Confederated Tribes of the Umatilla Indian Reservation (CTUIR), the Southern Ute Indian Tribe (SUIT), and the Zuni Pueblo. While the numbers are small, each case provides striking examples of female American Indian victimization. In the case of CTUIR, 66 percent of the 88 reported cases of violent victimization were against women. Most of these were nondomestic violent crimes such as assault, sexual assault, battery, and threats and intimidation. Similarly, in the SUIT case, 70 percent of the violent victimizations reported (106 crimes) were against women. Again, in the Zuni Pueblo, most "of the reported violent victimizations were against women" (Perry 2004, 40). Regardless of the age of the victim, females made up a higher proportion of assault victims than did men. "Of those responding to the question, about 30 percent indicated they were the victims of emotional, physical and/or sexual abuse at the hands of someone they lived with. More victims of sexual abuse reported being emotionally or psychologically abused (44 percent) than physically abused (38 percent) by someone whom they lived with during the past 12 months"

(Perry 2004, 40–41). Alcohol or drugs were a factor in three of five cases of domestic assault at the Zuni Pueblo.

The most prevalent crimes against Native American women are domestic violence, sexual assault, and stalking. Each will be briefly addressed.

Domestic Violence

The Office on Violence Against Women (OVW 2006) defines domestic violence as a pattern of abusive behavior in any relationship that is used by one partner to gain or maintain power and control over another intimate partner. Domestic violence can be physical, sexual, emotional, economic, or psychological abuse, including behaviors that intimidate, manipulate, humiliate, isolate, frighten, terrorize, coerce, threaten, blame, hurt, injure, or wound someone. Native American women suffer a disproportionate level of intimate-partner violence and assault, according to the Bureau of Justice Statistics (Perry 2004).

The National Violence Against Women Survey (Tjaden and Thoennes 1998a) found that American Indians/Alaskan Native women were more likely to report rape and physical assaults than were women of other racial/ethnic backgrounds. While there are clear differences among groups with regard to prevalence and reporting of rape and other assaults, the study is not able to show how race and ethnicity might intersect with social, environmental, and demographic variables to produce the differential. Native American women may be revictimized and their rights affected when police and courts ignore cases of violence due to confusion regarding legal jurisdiction. (See Cardani in this volume.) Law enforcement officials and even attorneys are often unfamiliar with jurisdiction issues. Further, institutionalized racism can result in delays in response time or court proceedings when Native Americans are not trusted by those charged with enforcing the law. Some Native American women still mistrust white systems as a result of colonization (Bhungalia 2001).

In cases of domestic violence, Native American women may face the risk of losing their children to their husbands, relatives, or the courts. This creates a stressful and painful situation for both the mother and her children. This is the reason why some Native American women stay with abusive husbands or partners (Bhungalia 2001). Domestic violence affects everyone associated with it, and children witnessing this behavior may consider violence a normal way of life, leading to another generation of victims and abusers (Office on Violence Against Women [hereinafter, OVW] 2006).

Sexual Assault

According to the Office on Violence Against Women, sexual assault is any type of sexual contact or behavior that occurs without explicit consent of the recipient of the unwanted sexual activity. Sexual assault includes forced sexual intercourse, sodomy, child molestation, incest, fondling, and attempted rape. The offender, by way of violent behavior, threats, coercion, manipulation, pressure, or tricks perpetrates sexual assault. Extreme cases may involve physical violence, display of a weapon, or immobilization of the victim (OVW 2006).

Native Americans are more likely to be victims of assault and rape/sexual assault committed by a stranger or an acquaintance than by an intimate family member, and approximately 78 percent of victims described the offender as white (Perry 2004). As noted earlier, in the period 1992–2001, Native Americans were twice as likely to experience rape/sexual assault compared to all races—5 rapes or sexual assaults per 1,000, compared to 2 per 1,000 for whites and blacks (Perry 2004). It is common for victims of rape and sexual assault not to report the crime to anyone, including the police. The 2005 National Crime Victimization Survey states that only 38 percent of the rapes and sexual assaults were reported (Catalano 2006). In fact, some individuals with experience and knowledge of tribal histories and cultures suggest the violence reported by Native American women accounts for only a fraction of the rapes and sexual assaults perpetrated against them (NAC 2002). It is especially difficult for them because of social and personal oppression, a high level of mistrust from non-Native agencies, fear of being ostracized by their families, and disincentives and difficulties associated with the legal system. In essence, there are cultural factors at work among Native American women who are victims that are not present (or are present to a different degree) among other groups. (See Hamby in this volume for a thorough examination of these crimes.)

Sexual assault for Native American women often results in severe trauma, and many victims report crying spells, nausea, depression, nightmares, insomnia, fear, anger, and self-contempt. A victim may turn to alcohol or drugs to help her cope with the anguish and shame, or she may even become suicidal. The victim may be unable to work, missing days on the job, which can financially impact her family and children, especially if she is the primary wage earner. Few victims have the skills to cope with sexual assault alone, and recovery requires counseling, a good support system, and time to heal (NAC 2002). Of course, similar reactions are possible for any women who are victims of these crimes, but the cultural and environmental circumstances can be quite different. The culture one lives in shapes one's reaction to sexual assault and determines the form of healing. For Native American female victims to confront and heal from rape/sexual assault, culturally appropriate measures must be taken that can vary from tribe to tribe. Crisis advocates assisting Native American women with sexual assault must understand the importance of culture to the situation. Cultural, historical, and jurisdictional issues often discourage Native American women from reporting sexual assault (NAC 2002).

A recent Amnesty International USA report (2007) on sexual violence against Indigenous women in the United States concludes Native American/Alaskan Native women often do not get timely—or any—response from police, may not get forensic medical examinations, or may never see their cases prosecuted. The report, to some extent, motivated the U.S. Congress to propose additional funding to protect Native American women who suffer disproportionate levels of rape and other sexual abuse (Lobe 2007).

Stalking

Legal definitions of stalking vary from one jurisdiction to another. However, stalking is a crime in all fifty states, the District of Columbia, and federal jurisdiction. The Office of Violence Against Women (2006) defines stalking as a pattern of repeated and unwanted attention, harassment, contact, or any other conduct toward a specific person that could cause reasonable fear. Stalking can include repeated unwanted communications by phone, mail, or e-mail; leaving the victim unwanted items; following the victim; making direct or indirect threats to harm the victim; threatening to damage the victim's property; harassing, spreading rumors, and obtaining personal information about the victim. The working definition by the Stalking Resource Center (2006) is "a course of conduct directed at a specific person that would cause a reasonable person to feel fear." Fear experienced by the victim is the key concept in all definitions.

Native American women are twice as likely to report being stalked as any other racial group—17 percent are stalked in their lifetime, compared to 8.2 percent for white women and 6.5 percent of African American women (Hally 2002). It should be noted that this finding is based on a very small sample of Native American women, which means that the results cannot really be generalized (National Violence Against Women Survey, as reported in Tjaden and Thoennes 1998b). Stalking among Native American women needs further study to determine why there is a variance between the rates in comparison to women of different races and ethnicity, the influence of demographic, social, and environmental factors, and stalking prevalence among the different tribal groups (Tjaden and Thoennes 1998b).

Stalking can have an impact on both the victim and her family. Victims of stalking take measures to protect themselves as drastic as relocating, missing or quitting work, and seeking counseling. The psychological effects can result in anxiety, insomnia, social dysfunction, and severe depression. For women as a whole, a link between stalking and other violence in intimate relationships is strong, and most stalking involves perpetrators and victims that know each other. Women, including Native American women, are stalked by intimate partners (current or former spouses, current or former cohabitants, or current or former boyfriends or girlfriends), and the majority (87 percent) of the stalkers are male (Tjaden and Thoennes 1998b).

In tribal communities, urban and rural, Native American women being stalked may be reluctant to contact authorities or other support services, out of shame or fear that the stalker will find out, or the knowledge that the stalker has friends or relatives in law enforcement. Other obstacles may be the limited access to phones, transportation, emergency services, and shelters, and the isolated locations of some tribal residences (Luna-Gordinier 2004).

The U.S. Department of Justice Violence Against Women Office funded initiatives in 2001 to assist tribes with developing interventions, services and community responses to stalking crimes. There are very few tribes that list legal codes that cover stalking, and even fewer have developed formal criminal justice protocol to effectively respond to those crimes (Hally 2002). "The reasons for these problems are many and are as uniquely varied as the cultures, customs and traditions of the more than 500 federally-recognized American Indian and Alaska Native tribes" (Hally 2002, 1). There are substantial jurisdictional issues that affect the quality and type of victim response. Needless to say, available financial resources are another complicating feature of the problem (Hally 2002). Native nations with tribal courts and police forces can have difficulty holding offenders accountable without tribal legal codes that address stalking as a stand-alone crime. When the stalker is a non-Native in Indian country, tribes have no criminal jurisdiction and non–PL 280 (see Archambeault, Cardani, and Luna-Firebaugh in this volume) states do not have jurisdiction over crimes in Indian country against Native Americans. The prosecution of misdemeanor domestic violence and stalking offenses in federal court must involve serious bodily injury or death. The Violence Against Women Act II, signed into law on November 1, 2000, resulted in some clarification of public policy, especially as it pertains to non-Natives, but barriers still exist.

Incarceration of Native Women Offenders

With regard to incarceration, specific data on Native American female offenders are sparse and difficult to discern, because much of the information is lumped into the general categories of American Indians, women, or "other." This situation points to the need for further analysis of the data and more research on the topic.

The information on women offenders, in general, indicates women are more likely to commit minor offenses, and female criminal behavior is usually perceived as less serious than male criminal behavior. However, nationally, the percentage of female offenders is rising, with more women participating in violent crimes (National Criminal Justice Reference Service 2006). In 2002 at year's end, 26,300 female prisoners were in state prisons for violent crimes, which accounted for 33 percent of all female prisoners under state jurisdiction. Growth in the number of women offenders is seen in each component of corrections, with 103,910 women under state and federal jurisdiction on June 30, 2004, a 2.9 percent increase from June 30, 2003. In 1999, one in ten female offenders belonged to a race other than white (other), including American Indians, Aleuts, or Inuit. During this time, women offenders accounted for one in fifty violent sex offenses, including rape and sexual assault, one in fourteen robberies, one in nine aggravated assaults, and one in six simple assaults (Greenfeld and Snell 1999).

Of the 1,745 inmates in Indian country jails in 2004 at midyear, 324 were adult females, and 74 juvenile females. Offenses were reported for 1,428 inmates, male and female, of which 39 percent were violent offenses: 18 percent domestic violence, 13 percent aggravated or simple assault, 2 percent rape or sexual assault, and 6 percent other violent offenses. Another 14 percent of the inmates were held for DWI/DUI, and 7 percent for drug law violations. Among the 1,540 inmates in Indian country jails in midyear 2004, 88 percent were being held for misdemeanors, down from 1,700 at midyear 2003. The number of inmates held for felony increased to 110, compared to 58 at midyear 2003. In addition, 94 inmates were held for other reasons, including protective custody, court-ordered treatment, detoxification, public intoxication, and other status offenses (Minton 2006).

In 2001, state and local law enforcement made approximately 433,764 arrests for the violent crimes of murder/non-negligent manslaughter, forcible rape, robbery, and aggravated assault; Native Americans accounted for about 1 percent (4,354) of these arrests. Arrest for violent crimes among Native Americans increased 1.7 percent from 2000 to 2001, and arrest rates for alcohol violations among Native Americans were double the national rate (Perry 2004). In midyear 2005, women comprised 7.0 percent of all state and federal inmates, up from 6.1 percent at midyear 1995 (Harrison and Beck 2006). Of all women in state prisons, 64 percent are women of color (Snell and Morton 1994, cited in Ross 1998).

Women prisoners are treated mainly as a homogeneous group, without references to race/ethnicity and class, and most studies reflect this (Ross 1998). Of the women in state prisons, 60 percent committed nonviolent crimes, and over 32 percent are imprisoned for violent offenses. Fifty percent of the violent offenses are homicide or manslaughter, with 32 percent perpetrated against a relative or intimate partner (most likely a male) (Snell and Morton 1994, cited in Ross 1998). The number of women in state prisons grew by 75 percent between 1986 and 1991 and accounted for 5.2 percent (approximately 39,000) of all prisoners in 1991 (Snell 1994).

For most Native Americans, it is not uncommon to either have been incarcerated or know someone who is or was incarcerated (Ross 1998). Until Luana Ross's landmark research on Native American women in prisons in Montana, the first study conducted on the topic, little was known about this population of women, even though Native Americans are disproportionately imprisoned. By documenting their experiences in prison, Ross gave Native American women in prison a voice (Ross 1998). Luana Ross states, "In sum, Native women face overwhelming odds at every stage of the criminal justice system" (Ross 1998, 79). Her research indicates that race, gender, and class influence not only incarceration rates but also the treatment received in prison. While Native Americans composed about 6 percent of the state population in 1990–92, Native American men accounted for 20 percent of the Montana prison population, and Native American women composed about 25 percent. The profile of the Native American woman was thirty years old, landless, single or divorced, with two children. Prior to being incarcerated, she experienced violence in her life, was unemployed, and had an eighth-grade education. Native American women were convicted of murder, robbery, assault, and escape (crimes more often associated with males). Sentences ranged from five to sixty years, with the average time served being 19.1 years. Crimes committed by Native American women were often alcohol- or drug-related. Ninety percent of imprisoned women studied were victims of prior abuse, usually by a family member (Ross 1998)—a finding consistent with that of Perry (2004) reported earlier. In comparison, the profile of the white incarcerated female in Montana (Ross 1998, 88–89) was thirty years old, likely divorced with two or three children, completed high school or had a GED, experienced violence in her life prior to prison, and if employed, held a low-level, low-paying position. Her crime was alcohol/drug-related, she was convicted of a female-type crime, and the sentence length ranged from five to twenty years, with the average being 9.0 years. In comparing Native American women with white women in her study, Ross (1998, 89) states, "Thus, there is a qualitative difference in crime type that makes comparisons difficult. Despite this, sentence disparity warrants an immediate investigation; because when the crimes are the same, Native women receive longer sentences than white women."

As mothers, incarcerated Native American women face emotional and legal challenges. These include (but are not limited to) the stress of the separation, placement and custody of children, visitation arrangements, and readjustment problems after release. Adding to this pressure is the stereotypic image of imprisoned mothers being "unfit." How Native American women and white women deal with separation from children differs. Native American women find comfort in uniting together in cultural activities such as spiritual prayer groups, while white mothers tend to isolate themselves (Ross 1998).

In her study, Ross (1998) found that few of the women placed their children in foster care or adoptive homes, and of those that did, more were white and non-reservation (landless) Native American mothers. Imprisoned mothers in general want to place their children informally with relatives, to ensure contact through visitation, phone calls, and letters. Incarcerated mothers often fear that their children will forget them or think they are not loved. Even though imprisoned Native American mothers had less contact with their children than did white mothers, in spite of reservation status, reservation and off-reservation Native American mothers were usually more satisfied with the qualify of care their children received regardless of placement type than were non-reservation or white mothers. It is the extended family that often helps the imprisoned reservation Native American woman deal with issues pertaining to her children. Native American female prisoners are closer emotionally to their extended families, even when they are dysfunctional, than are white women. Native American women have a community rather than a nuclear family to call home, and they will be welcomed back into their tribal community upon release unless they are banished for a violent crime (Ross 1998).

Incarcerated Native American women cannot always practice tribal customs, traditions, and spirituality in prison. Prison officials' lack of understanding of Native cultures often hinders Native American women prisoners from getting the culturally appropriate services to assist with rehabilitation and survival. Access to Native American counselors, spiritual leaders, and culturally specific treatment programs is what Native American women prisoners, reservation and non-reservation, often ask for. For unidentified reasons, Native American men in prisons seem to be more successful at securing culturally appropriate services than are Native American women (Ross 1998; and see Archambeault in this volume).

Programs/Interventions

In Indian country, there is a wellness movement occurring, often led by Native American women, which stresses healing from personal and historical abuse. An open discussion of violence (crimes) against Native American women is taking place to break down barriers to healing. Native Americans and their communities cannot undermine the lingering effects of colonization until they address gender violence (Smith 2005, 63–76). Today, there are numerous initiatives happening in Indian country, including the following selected examples.

Culture and traditions are being used to address crimes against women in many tribal nations. For example, mediation, which involves talking things out among victims, offenders, and relatives, occurs in Navajo Nation peacemaking. Peacemaking often occurs before charges are filed, at time of plea, prior to sentencing, and after sentencing. Navajos use peacemaking instead of filing charges for family disputes, alcohol-related offenses, family violence, and even sex offenses (Yazzie 1998). Peacemaking is conducted in Navajo and English and emphasizes harmony and balance using mediation, restorative justice, therapeutic intervention, family counseling, and Navajo cultural beliefs and practices (Lujan 2006, 130–39; see also Meyer in this volume).

In tribal nations, violence against Native American women is being addressed with the establishment of culturally appropriate modes of resolution for stalking, development of mandatory arrest policies in domestic violence legal codes and protocols, use of court protective orders, and a new focus on resolution of domestic violence situations (Luna-Firebaugh 2006, 125–36).

Another effort funded by the Office of Violence Against Women is the Safety for Indian Women Demonstration Initiative, to enhance the response of tribal and federal agencies to the high rates of sexual assault committed against Native American women. OVW awarded over $900,000 to four tribes, Navajo Nation, Hannahville Indian Community, Red Lake Band of Chippewa Indians, and the Rosebud Sioux Tribe (OVW 2006), to address this issue.

Universities and other organizations are also participating in wellness efforts through conferences and gatherings, such as two conferences conducted by the University of Oklahoma, and the gatherings sponsored by the Indigenous Women's Network. These offer opportunities for Native Americans, women and men, to network, to address issues of violence and decolonization, and to heal individually and as a community.

Next Steps

Crime and victimization among Native American women are difficult topics for those of us who are Native Americans to acknowledge and address without feeling anger, hurt, and frustration. This was recently evident in my Native American women's class, where the topic of rape and violence against women was discussed. The Native American students, especially the women in the class, found it almost impossible to talk about this topic. Many of the young women and men knew of cases of rape, sexual assault, stalking, and domestic violence in their communities or families, and they knew many of the victims and offenders. In fact, the students, Native and non-Native, males and females, felt crimes against or committed by Native American women are serious contemporary issues in Indian country, and the situation needs to be acknowledged. It was the consensus of the class that for Native Americans and their communities to heal, go forward, and tackle the situation of Native American women as victims and offenders of crimes, they must recognize the situation, educate themselves on interventions, and look to culturally appropriate strategies to heal and restore harmony and balance.

To address the prevalence of violence in Native communities by and against Native American women, the situation must be viewed in conjunction with historical oppression, an awareness of complicated jurisdictional issues, and complete knowledge of the consequences for women and the community. The challenge for Native Americans is to retraditionalize through cultural beliefs and customs, to regain respect and value for each other as human beings, and to reestablish healthy communities. The following quote from the late prominent Lakota anthropologist, author, and lecturer Dr. Beatrice Medicine (Mankiller 2004, 194) appropriately applies to all Native American nations and their citizens wanting to heal and rid themselves of crime and violence, especially against women. "To be a good Lakota woman and for our brothers to be good Lakota men, we have to help each other; men and women are leaders and I feel strongly that we must maintain respect and honor between males and females and transmit that to our children."

References

Amnesty International USA. 2007. *Maze of injustice: The failure to protect indigenous women from sexual violence in the USA.* New York. http://www.amnestyusa .org?Womens_Human_Rights?Summary/page.do?id=1021170&n1= . . . (accessed September 8, 2007).

Bachman, Ronet. 1992. *Death and violence on the reservation.* Westport, CT: Auburn House.

Bhungalia, Lisa. 2001. Native American women and violence. *National NOW Times.* http://www.now.org/nnt/spring-2001/nativeamerican.html (accessed August 18, 2006).

Catalano, Shannan M. 2006. *National crime victimization survey, criminal victimization, 2005.* U.S. Department of Justice, Office of Justice Programs, Bureau of Justice Statistics (NCJ 214644). http://www.ojp.usdoj.gov/bjs/abstract/cvo5 .htm (accessed November 5, 2006).

Greenfeld, Lawrence A., and Tracy L. Snell. 1999. *Women offenders, special report.* Washington, DC: Bureau of Justice Statistics (NCJ 175688).

Hally, Jo. 2002. Addressing stalking in Native American communities. *Newsletter of the Stalking Resource Center* 2. http://www.ncvc.org/src/main.aspx?db Name= DocumentViewer&DocumentID=37132 (accessed August 18, 2006).

Harrison, Paige M., and Allen Beck. 2006. *Prison and jail inmates at midyear 2005.* Washington, DC: Bureau of Justice Statistics (NCJ 213133).

Lobe, Jim. 2007. Congress moves to protect Native women from assaults. *Truthout Issues.* Inter Press Service, July 26, 2007. http://www.truthout.org/docs_2006/ 072707P.shtml (accessed September 5, 2007).

Lujan, Carol Chiago. 2006. Perpetuating the stereotypes of American Indian nations and peoples. In *Images of color, images of crime,* 3rd ed., ed. Coramae Richey Mann, Marjorie S. Zatz, and Nancy Rodriguez, 130–39. Los Angeles: Roxbury.

Luna-Firebaugh, Eileen. 2006. Violence against American Indian women and the Services-Training-Officers-Prosecutors Violence Against Indian Women (STOP VAIW) Program. *Violence against Women* 12:125–36.

Luna-Gordinier, Anne M. M. 2004. Stalking in Indian Country: Enhancing tribal sovereignty through culturally appropriate remedies. Master's thesis, University of Arizona, Tucson.

Mankiller, Wilma. 2004. *Every day is a good day.* Golden, CO: Fulcrum.

Melton, Ada Pecos. 2006. American Indians: Traditional and contemporary tribal justice. In *Images of color, images of crime,* 3rd ed., ed. Coramae Richey Mann, Marjorie S. Zatz, and Nancy Rodriguez, 180–96. Los Angeles: Roxbury.

Minton, Todd D. 2006. *Jails in Indian country, 2004.* Bureau of Justice Statistics Bulletin. Washington, DC: Bureau of Justice Statistics (NCJ 214257). http://www.ojp.usdoj.gov/bjs/.

National Criminal Justice Reference Service. 2006. Women and girls in the criminal justice system. http://www.ncjrs.gov/spotlight/wgcjs/Summary.html (accessed September 3, 2006).

National Sexual Violence Resource Center. 2000. Sexual assault in Indian Country: Confronting sexual violence. http://www.nsvrc.org/publications/booklets/indian.htm (accessed September 24, 2006).

Native American Circle. (NAC) 2002. *Domestic violence, sexual assault and stalking: Prevention and intervention programs in Native American communities.* Avery, TX: Native American Circle.

Office on Violence Against Women (OVW). 2006. http://www.usdoj.gov/ovw.

Perry, Steven W. 2004. *American Indians and crime: A BJS statistical profile, 1992–2002.* Washington, DC: Bureau of Justice Statistics (NCJ 2030997). http://www.ojp.usdoj.gov/bjs/.

Perdue, Theda. 1998. *Cherokee women: Gender and culture change, 1700–1835.* Lincoln: University of Nebraska Press.

Ross, Luana. 1998. *Inventing the savage.* Austin: University of Texas Press.

Smith, Andrea. 2005. Rape and the war against Native women. In *Reading Native American women, critical/creative representations,* ed. Ines Hernandez-Avila, 63–76. New York: Altamira Press.

Snell, Tracy L. 1994. *Women in prison.* Bureau of Justice Statistics Bulletin. Washington, DC: Bureau of Justice Statistics (NCJ 145321). http://www.ojp.usdoj.gov/bjs/pub/ascii/wopris.txt.

Stalking Resource Center (SRC). 2006. Stalking fact sheet. www.ncvc.org/src.

Tjaden, Patricia, and Nancy Thoennes. 1998a. Prevalence, incidence, and consequences of violence against women: Findings from the National Violence Against Women survey. *National Institute of Justice Centers for Disease Control and Prevention, Research Brief.* Washington, DC: National Institute of Justice (NCJ 172837).

Tjaden, Patricia, and Nancy Thoennes. 1998b. Stalking in America: Findings from the National Violence Against Women Survey. *National Institute of Justice Centers for Disease Control and Prevention, Research Brief.* Washington, DC: National Institute of Justice.

Yazzie, Robert. 1998. The Navajo response to crime. *Justice as Healing* 3, no. 2. http://www.usask.ca/nativelaw/publications/jah/1998/Navajo_Response.pdf.

Finding Their Way

CHALLENGES AND RESOURCES OF AMERICAN
INDIAN VICTIMS OF SEXUAL ASSAULT

Sherry Hamby

SEXUAL VICTIMIZATION is a part of the history of oppression, violence, and maltreatment that American Indians have experienced by the U.S. government and its citizens (Smith 1999). The consequences of this history continue to manifest themselves today, as rates of sexual victimization for American Indian women are higher than for any other U.S. ethnic group (Tjaden and Thoennes 2006). Unemployment, poverty, prejudice, and other problems both increase victimization risk and limit access to victim services. Despite these dark realities, tribal membership also offers resources and benefits, such as access to culturally specific healing practices. This chapter will discuss patterns of sexual victimization among American Indians, and issues related to helpseeking for American Indian victims of sexual assault.

Rates of Sexual Victimization among American Indian Women

Existing data consistently indicate that rates of sexual victimization are very high among American Indian women. According to the National Violence Against Women Survey (NVAWS), American Indian women experience more rape, by both strangers and intimate partners, than other U.S. racial and ethnic groups (Tjaden and Thoennes 2006). In other studies of sexual victimization among American Indian women, most including data specific to one state or one tribe, rates have ranged from 4 percent to 49 percent (Malcoe and Duran in press; Fairchild, Fairchild, and Stoner 1998; Malcoe, Duran, and Montgomery 2004; Walters and Simoni 1999; Yuan et al. 2006).

Rapes involving American Indian women are also often more severe than rapes committed against other women (Bachman 2004). In National Criminal Victimization Survey data, 94 percent of rapes of American Indian women involved physical assault, versus 74 percent of non-Indian women. Half (50 percent) of American Indian women were injured during rape, compared to 30 percent of non-Indian women. More than three times as many rapes of American Indians involved weapons—34 percent compared to 11 percent (Bachman 2004).

Another distinctive feature of sexual crimes against American Indian women is that most perpetrators are non-Indian—at least 86 percent are non-Native, according to U.S. Department of Justice data (Perry 2004). In contrast, 73 percent of white victims are assaulted by white men, and 83 percent of African American victims are assaulted by African American men (U.S. Department of Justice 2005; pooled average for 1996–2005 computed by author). The high rate of victimization by non-Indians is particularly problematic, because reservation police have no jurisdiction over non-Indians, even on Indian land, and so can only refer these crimes to federal, or (in some cases) state authorities, which often impedes arrest and prosecution of these cases.

Antecedents of Sexual Victimization in Indian Country

High rates of rape are part of the legacy of racism and oppression perpetrated against American Indians, which often included sexual victimization as one weapon of war used against Indigenous people (Deer 2005). As recently as the 1970s, many American Indian children were forcibly removed from their homes and sent to boarding schools, where many experienced sexual molestation and other abuse. Further, generations of American Indian youth lost exposure to their tribe's language and traditions. They also lost a normal family and parenting environment, and many show the typical scars of being reared in an institution (Duran et al. 1998). The forced conversion to a cash economy and the forced removal of many tribes to remote areas have contributed to high rates of poverty and unemployment (U.S. Commission on Civil Rights 2003), which are widely acknowledged to contribute to higher rates of violence in Indian country (Hamby 2000). Crime is also associated with other negative effects of the oppression of Indian communities. For example, American Indian victims of violence are more likely to be assaulted by an offender under the influence of alcohol or drugs (Perry 2004). As with other women, a prior history of childhood abuse or neglect is also associated with an increased risk of sexual victimization (Yuan et al. 2006). Despite these common patterns, however, it should also be noted that victimization rates vary significantly across tribes in the United States (Yuan et al. 2006).

Consequences of Sexual Victimization

Many of the consequences of sexual victimization are similar for American Indians and non-Indians. Physical consequences, including rates of injury and sexually transmitted diseases, are high (Bachman 2004; Rosay and Henry 2007). As elsewhere, convictions of offenders are low—14 percent in one study (Rosay and Henry 2007). Although there has been little research on psychological consequences specific to sexual assault of American Indians, depression and posttraumatic stress are common outcomes for American Indian victims of other forms of violence (Hamby and Skupien 1998). This is similar to findings for non-Indians. Research on the broader social effects of victimization, such as on gender roles and family structures, is lacking.

Obstacles to Seeking Help

All rape victims face significant obstacles to helpseeking. As a result, most rape victims, regardless of ethnicity, do not report their rape to police or other authorities (Tjaden and Thoennes 2006). American Indian victims, however, confront many unique obstacles (Hamby 2004). The latest information on the most challenging of these barriers follows.

Victim Blaming and Prejudice

Some residents of one reservation reported negative experiences with health-care providers, stating they showed superior attitudes, used confusing terminology, and avoided the reservation outside of work hours (Fifer 1996). Recent publications on American Indian victims of violence still sometimes include a surprising degree of victim blaming, as for example in a study by MacEachen published in the *Indian Health Services*

Provider, in which she complained about low rates of disclosure and even more startlingly concluded that women might "provoke rape and battery in order to satisfy their needs" in her attempt to explain sexual victimization among AI women (MacEachen 2003, 127). Such harsh views from service providers still constitute an obstacle to helpseeking.

Value Conflicts

Human-service professionals, including rape-crisis advocates, health-care providers, and law enforcement personnel, typically make recommendations based on the cultural values of the majority. These can include encouraging rape victims to have physical exams, get tested for sexually transmitted diseases, take medication to prevent pregnancy, terminate relationships in cases of intimate-partner rape, and legally prosecute perpetrators. At a most basic level, most advocates and providers expect victims to disclose the details of their victimization, often many times in the course of seeking help from different agencies. Many of these interventions have tangible benefits, such as the way forensic "rape kits" can increase physical evidence and thus improve conviction rates. This eventually benefits victims of all backgrounds, who may experience increased justice and safety as conviction rates go up.

Nonetheless, the difficulties of going through a pelvic exam shortly after a sexual assault should not be minimized. A pelvic exam, which typically involves inserting foreign objects into the vagina, may be traumatizing for victims of sexual assault. It is surely not what most victims have in mind when seeking comfort and care from health providers.

Of course, the difficulty of such procedures is not unique to American Indian women, but many American Indians hold values that may make these interventions even more upsetting. Many American Indian cultures highly value privacy regarding sexuality and family problems. Laboratory interventions may seem to distract from spiritual/holistic healing, counter pro-life values, or even cause negative consequences themselves.

Problems with Law Enforcement and the Justice System

Some data suggest that American Indian women's experience with law enforcement is more problematic than it is for other U.S. women.

Secondary analyses of the NVAWS (Hamby in press) showed that American Indian women were more likely to expect that law enforcement wouldn't believe their reports (14 percent versus 7 percent of non-Indians) and were more likely to report that they or their family handled the matter themselves (10 percent versus 4 percent of white women). Unfortunately, the NVAWS data does not directly address the underpinnings for these beliefs, but many problems that contribute to these perceptions have been identified. Some are not unique to American Indians but are found among many U.S. minority groups. These include fear of stigma following public charges, fear of being accused of a crime themselves, and hesitation to accuse a fellow community member and make him confront a racist legal system in addition to his crime.

The complicated relationships among tribal, state, and federal laws create unique issues, however. For example, if the perpetrator is non-Indian and the assault was committed on reservation land, jurisdictional problems arise because reservation authorities cannot prosecute a non-Indian and off-reservation authorities are often reluctant to get involved in all but the most severe reservation crimes (Amnesty International 2007).

Language Barriers

Language influences the way we perceive sexuality and victimization. Victim advocates and prevention specialists tend to use Latin-based words, like *intercourse*. The equivalent term for *intercourse* that derives from Anglo-Saxon is not considered polite.

Not all languages have the potential to shift between polite and vulgar terms for sexual experiences (Tafoya 2000). In one Apache community, for example, outsiders are often told that there are no curse words in Apache. This is true in one sense—there are not separate words for intercourse or other acts that sound vulgar no matter how they are used. On the other hand, there is no "polite" equivalent in Apache either, which relies on context and tone more than English. In cross-cultural communication, it can be hard to communicate information about sexuality in ways that are not offensive.

Modern English has more terms for victimization than most other languages, in part because of the influence of the U.S. social movements against rape and intimate violence. Among the many English terms for sexual victimization are *rape, sexual assault, date rape, sexual abuse, incest,* and *molestation.* For purposes of both intervention and prevention, it can be hard to identify comparable words in other languages. Even English speakers who are not immersed in addressing these social problems may not appreciate the subtle distinctions between these terms.

On the other hand, by no means do these differences imply that American Indian languages are lacking in specificity or subtlety (Manson 2000). There is considerable variability across languages, Indian and non-Indian alike, in the phenomenology and terms for emotion. For example, among the San Carlos Apache, the English word *somehow* is often used to convey a negative mood or irritability, perhaps without immediate apparent cause. The usage does not closely correspond to any majority culture usage of the same word. To provide effective services, one must learn the specific terms used in the community one serves.

Economic and Geographic Barriers

Poverty rates for American Indians are more than twice as high as for the total U.S. population (U.S. Commission on Civil Rights 2003). The forced conversion to a cash economy from hunting, gathering, and farming economies is one major cause of this problem (Chester et al. 1994). Unemployment exceeds 50 percent on many reservations (U.S. Commission on Civil Rights 2003). The U.S. government continues to resist fair compensation for access to reservation resources such as oil (Weiss 2006), helping to perpetuate economic distress.

For victims of sexual assault, poverty means that the services they need are often not readily available. Per capita spending on law enforcement in Native communities is only 60 percent of the overall U.S. rate (U.S. Commission on Civil Rights 2003). Per capita health-care rates, which also directly affect services to sexual assault victims, are also alarmingly low (U.S. Commission on Civil Rights 2004). In fact, "Native Americans receive less funding per capita than any other group for which the federal government has health care responsibilities, including Medicaid/Medicare recipients, veterans, and prisoners" (U.S. Commission on Civil Rights 2004, 13).

Further, because tribes were pushed off desirable lands, many reservations are in rural or geographically remote areas. As with most rural areas, public transportation is typically unavailable and a major barrier to accessing care. There may be fewer programs available, and these programs often have high staff-vacancy rates, because it can be difficult to attract qualified individuals to remote areas (Indian Health Service 2002). Poverty and geographic isolation also contribute to a lack of telephones in many American Indian households (Stoddardt et al. 2000).

The Effects of Small Community Size

Many tribal communities are a fraction of their size before colonization. As in many small communities, people know one another and are often interrelated by blood or marriage. Close-knit communities can offer enhanced support and other advantages, but the reduced privacy can be a problem for stigmatized issues such as sexual victimization. In one study, lack of confidentiality was cited as a major reason for not seeking help for another sensitive issue, drug and alcohol treatment (Duran et al. 2000). Although most advocates attempt to maintain confidentiality, even the perception of limited confidentiality can prevent helpseeking.

Another important and often less-recognized consequence of small community size is the issue of tribal survival. Although more than 4 million people identified themselves as American Indian or Alaska Native on the 2000 U.S. Census, only eleven tribal groups had more than 50,000 members (Ogunwole 2002). Many tribal communities literally face the possibility of extinction. Victims may be unwilling to prosecute male tribal members, because that will take another person out of the community. They may also hesitate to terminate a relationship with a male tribal member, because options for intraracial remarriage are more limited for American Indians than they are for other U.S. ethnic groups (Hamby 2000).

Underfunded Programs

In 2003, Tex Hall, then president of the National Congress of American Indians, testified before the Senate Committee on Indian Affairs regarding President Bush's budget for Indian programs, which included further declines in per capita spending for Indian programs. He stated that "this trend demonstrates the abject failure of the federal government to commit the serious resources needed to fully honor its trust commitment to Indian tribes" (Hall, cited in U.S. Commission on Civil Rights 2003, 16).

Unfortunately, this problem is not new. Considerable data document the longstanding lack of services available to American Indians (for a review, see Manson 2000). More recently, legislation such as Public Law 93–638, which authorizes transfer of IHS functions from federal to tribal administration, was implemented to improve local input and control over health services. Although the long-term effects of such laws are likely to be positive, in the short term they are leading to increased variability in service provision and downsizing of technical assistance, quality control, and long-range planning at the federal level (Manson 2000).

Resources for American Indian Helpseekers

American Indian communities have significant assets, despite the barriers they face and the traumatic history they have endured (Hamby 2004).

Native Healers

American Indian women sometimes have available Native healers. Despite the very different philosophies espoused by Western providers and Native healers, American Indians may feel comfortable seeking both kinds of counsel (Kim and Kwok 1998). A survey of medical patients at a Navajo clinic indicated that 62 percent had seen a Native healer in their lifetime (Kim and Kwok 1998). Those seeking help after victimization may find, as one respondent put it, that "the doctors give me pills for my body, the medicine man gives me songs for my spirit" (Kim and Kwok 1998, 2248). This quote recognizes the focus of Western medicine on the physical body. In contrast, Native healers also focus on the importance of spiritual healing. In many Native traditions, healing of the physical body cannot proceed independent of treatment for the spirit or whole person.

Spirituality and Cultural Resources

Most, if not all, American Indian communities have unique cultural ceremonies that can be important resources for women healing from sexual victimization (Senturia et al. 2000). These include sweat lodges, talking circles, and other ceremonies. Native advocates may be able to offer more support than non-Indians to American Indian women. These ideas were well expressed by one Native woman:

> That helped me a lot, . . . smudging [ritual purifying with the smoke of sacred herbs such as sage] and just doing a lot of different things about being strong and protecting myself, you know. The Native person can teach me how to protect myself in a Native way, like smudging, and not cutting my hair, and just leaving it on the ground so someone can stomp on it! And you know, just things like that, little things. And the music, powwow music was a big healing for my heart and made my heart strong again. (Senturia et al. 2000, 114–15)

Tribal Justice Forums

The justice traditions of some tribes were radically different from U.S. laws. Sarah Deer has researched the first recorded laws of her tribe, the Muscogee (Creek) Nation. In 1824, the rape law included in the original codification of their laws read: "And be it farther enacted if any person or persons should undertake to force a woman and did it by force, *it shall be left to woman* what punishment she should satisfied with to whip or pay *what she say it be law*" (Waring, cited in Deer 2005, 464; emphasis added by Deer).

The law is very victim-centered and clearly indicates that sexual violence against women is wrong. The language indicates the assault was considered a crime against the woman, rather than her father or husband. These features stand in stark contrast to many laws of the time in the United States and elsewhere, and even some today. Unfortunately, later revisions of the Muscogee legal code were more similar to U.S. law, but this document remains a striking example of early tribal justice.

Many tribal nations have resumed justice forums that provide an alternative to standard U.S. jurisprudence. These forums emphasize restorative and reparative approaches to justice rather than the adversarial system found in U.S. courts (Melton 2002). Often called "peacemaking courts," many tribal nations operate them, such as the Navajo (Zion 1998). Although safety must be protected, these forums are often more focused on the needs of victims and community members and may offer a useful resource to some women seeking justice for sexual victimization. Traditional punishments such as banishment and time-limited expulsion are often used in these courts.

Free Western-Style Health Care

Members of federally recognized Indian tribes are eligible for services funded by the Indian Health Service. IHS services are most easily accessed for American Indians who live on or near reservations, but some facilities serve urban areas (Indian Health Service 2002). Unfortunately, many IHS facilities do not have specific programs for sexual victimizations, but American Indian women can get treatment for injuries, sexually transmitted diseases, pregnancy, and other consequences of sexual victimization with fewer financial concerns than some U.S. women. American Indian women also have access to free psychotherapy, if they can locate an IHS therapist with expertise in dealing with sexual victimization.

Outreach

Some advocates and organizations make consistent efforts to be respectful and culturally sensitive (Fifer 1996). These can include working toward creating an ethnically representative staff, providing literature appropriate for all community members, and collaborating with organizations frequented by members of all ethnic groups (Donnelly, Cook, and Wilson 1999).

Financial Assistance

Many tribes offer financial assistance to members. Housing assistance is probably one of the most common benefits (although there may be a waiting list). Some tribes also offer educational grants and may have discretionary funds available for emergency travel or other needs.

Federal Funds

Federal agencies sometimes earmark funds specifically for American Indian tribes. Although these funds are allocated in part to redress generations of federal neglect, tribes may still find them helpful. The most recent reauthorization of the Violence Against Women Act includes several provisions to enhance tribes' abilities to respond to sexual and domestic violence, such as a large study of violence against American Indian women and the creation of a national tribal registry of sex offenders (National Task Force to End Sexual and Domestic Violence Against Women 2005).

Implications for Prevention and Intervention

The unique obstacles and resources of American Indian victims need to be considered to create effective services and prevention efforts. There are several ways that an understanding of these issues can enhance services and help eliminate violence against future generations of American Indian women.

Incorporate Culturally Congruent Processes into Services and Programs

Community stakeholders need time and resources to establish viable working approaches in each Native community. Members of the Sault Sainte Marie tribe of Chippewa Indians recently used talking circles in a federally funded project as a key part of decision making and consensus building (McBride 2003). Talking circles allow each member of a group to speak uninterrupted, guided by a facilitator such as an elder or other important person. Talking circles, ceremonies, and the involvement of elders or traditional healers may not be typical components of many federally funded projects, but they can be crucial for developing culturally congruent programs in Native communities. Illustrated materials, including videos and pamphlets, should be culturally congruent and not simply include tacked-on images of Native women.

Although cultural congruence is important, communities should also have access to service and prevention models developed for other groups. Tribal communities need not start from scratch in some outsider's interest of developing a "Native" approach. Taking the time to develop an entirely new program instead of adapting an existing one may seem like a luxury that can be afforded only by people of privilege (Hamby 2000).

People working with American Indian victims may choose to borrow from existing programs.

Make Services and Programs Accessible to Community Members

Programs need to address logistical issues such as transportation, meals, and child care (McBride 2003). Thorough dissemination of information is also important. The best way to disseminate information will vary, but local cable-access channels, local radio stations, bulletin boards in frequented offices and stores, parent–teacher meetings at schools, public restrooms, pow-wows, and other community events are good places to advertise. Although victims may not approach advocates in such public settings, these strategies raise awareness. Home visits, approached in a manner sensitive to local cultures, are also an important component of many successful programs. Agencies and programs should have community members and survivors as part of their staff.

Adapt Language and Communication Styles to the Audience

Advocates and prevention specialists should avoid the use of jargon when possible and clearly explain all specialized terms. Providers should also learn any terms or phrases unique to the community they serve, especially those related to victimization, health, or psychological states. Storytelling or other Native traditions may enhance communication.

Offer Choices to Protect Confidentiality and Reduce Stigma

American Indian women should have options to seek services where they choose. Some may prefer to seek help from outside of the community to protect confidentiality. Victims from reservations may find it convenient to use services both on and off the reservation. For example, they may rely on reservation services for emergency health care but may choose to seek support or counseling elsewhere.

Implications Regarding Law Enforcement and Criminal Justice

Law enforcement personnel can make sure they are empowering victims to make their own choices about involvement of the legal system, and are being honest about the pros and cons of different choices. Advocates and prevention specialists can also work toward improving relationships with law enforcement and empowering victims to understand the law enforcement system and make informed choices about it. Promoting alternative-justice forums and evaluating their appropriateness for cases of sexual victimization are also important goals. Political efforts to extend full faith and credit recognition for tribal orders of protection on nontribal lands, and to clarify jurisdictions, are steps towards improving law enforcement. Many American Indians would like to see full tribal jurisdiction on tribal lands for both Indians and non-Indians.

Funding Issues

Political activism may be the best way to ensure better funding for American Indian victims and to ensure that tribal members are receiving all resources to which they are entitled. Although gambling has had both positive and negative effects on Native communities, Indian gaming earns more than $10 billion in annual net revenues (Gonzales 2003). Although some of this money has gone to programs for victims, advocates and survivors could lobby for more to be directed toward social programs.

Make Use of Community Strengths

Much of the literature about American Indians focuses on deficits and problems, but there are many strengths in these communities. The strengths addressed thus far—Native healers, American Indian spirituality, alternative tribal justice forums, free Western-style medical care, housing and other financial assistance, and federal funds earmarked for tribal efforts to reduce violence against women—are not exhaustive. Individual communities have unique strengths that will best be appreciated by those living and working in those communities.

Conclusion

Many outsiders think that the mistreatment of American Indians is entirely historical, but the reality is that many institutions still perpetuate the problems of most American Indian communities and tribal members (Duran et al. 1998). Yet the enduring spirituality and traditions of many

American Indian communities offer the potential to help victims heal and for communities to move toward greater balance and the elimination of sexual victimization.

References

Amnesty International. 2007. *Maze of injustice: The failure to protect indigenous women from sexual violence in the USA*. New York: Amnesty International.

Bachman, Ronet. 2004. Using Justice Department data to analyze nature and extent of sexual assault against Native American women. Presentation to the U.S. Dept. of Justice Federal-Tribal Working Group on Sexual Assault. Washington, DC, July 12, 2004.

Chester, Barbara, Robert W. Robin, Mary P. Koss, Joyce Lopez, and David Goldman. 1994. Grandmother dishonored: Violence against women by male partners in American Indian communities. *Violence and Victims* 9:249–58.

Deer, Sarah. 2005. Sovereignty of the soul: Exploring the intersection of rape law reform and federal Indian law. *Suffolk University Law Review* 38:455–66.

Donnelly, Denise A., Kimberly J. Cook, and Linda A. Wilson. 1999. Provision and exclusion: The dual face of services to battered women in three Deep South states. *Violence against Women* 5:710–41.

Duran, Bonnie, Marc D. Bulterys, Jon Iralu, Cheryl Graham, Ahmed Edwards, and Melvin Harrison. 2000. American Indians with HIV/AIDS: Health and social service needs, barriers to care, and satisfaction with services among a western tribe. *American Indian and Alaska Native Mental Health Research* 9:22–35.

Duran, Eduardo, Bonnie Duran, Wilbur Woodis, and Pamela Woodis. 1998. A postcolonial perspective on domestic violence in Indian country. In *Family violence and men of color: Healing the wounded male spirit*, edited by Ricardo Carillo and Jerry Tello. New York: Springer.

Fairchild, David G., Molly W. Fairchild, and Shirley Stoner. 1998. Prevalence of adult domestic violence among women seeking routine care in a Native American health care facility. *American Journal of Public Health* 88:1515–17.

Fifer, Susan. 1996. Perceptions of caring behaviors in health providers. *Indian Health Service Primary Care Provider* 21:89–95.

Gonzales, Angela A. 2003. Gaming and displacement: Winners and losers in American Indian casino development. *International Social Science Journal* 55:123–133.

Hamby, Sherry L. 2000. The importance of community in a feminist analysis of domestic violence among American Indians. *American Journal of Community Psychology* 28:649–669.

———. 2004. *Sexual victimization in Indian country: Barriers and resources for Native women seeking help*. VAWnet. http://www.vawnet.org/SexualViolence/Research/VAWnetDocuments/AR_SVIndianCountry.pdf (accessed October 5, 2005).

————. In press. The path of helpseeking: Perceptions of law enforcement among American Indian victims of sexual assault. *Journal of Prevention and Intervention in the Community.*

Hamby, Sherry L., and M. B. Skupien. 1998. Domestic violence on the San Carlos Apache Indian Reservation: Rates, associated psychological symptoms, and current beliefs. *Indian Health Service Primary Care Provider* 23:103–06.

Indian Health Service. 2002. *Indian Health Service fact sheet.* http://www.ihs.gov/ PublicInfo/PublicAffairs/Welcome_info/ThisFacts.asp. Accessed November 16, 2003.

Kim, Catherine, and Yeong S. Kwok. 1998. Navajo use of Native healers. *Archives of Internal Medicine* 158:2245–49.

MacEachen, Joan. 2003. The community context of domestic violence: The association of pecking order violence with domestic violence. *Indian Health Service Primary Care Provider* 28:125–29.

Malcoe, Lorraine Halinka, and Bonnie Duran. In press. Intimate partner violence and injury in the lives of low income Native American women. In *Violence Against Women and Family Violence: Developments in Research, Practice, and Policy Conference Proceedings,* edited by B. Fisher. Washington, DC: National Institute of Justice, U.S. Department of Justice.

Malcoe, Lorraine Halinka, Bonnie M. Duran, and Juliann M. Montgomery. 2004. Socioeconomic disparities in intimate partner violence against Native American women: A cross-sectional study. Review of reviewed item. *BMC Medicine* (20), http://www.biomedcentral.com/1741-7015/2/20/abstract.

Manson, Spero M. 2000. Mental health services for American Indians and Alaska Natives: Need, use, and barriers to effective care. *Canadian Journal of Psychiatry* 45:617–26.

McBride, Beverly A. 2003. Aspects of community healing: Experiences of the Sault Sainte Marie Tribe of Chippewa Indians. *American Indian and Alaska Native Mental Health Research* 11:67–83.

Melton, Ada Pecos. 2002. *National Victim Assistance Academy textbook: Tribal justice.* National Victim Assistance Academy, U.S. Department of Justice. http://www .ojp.usdoj.gov/ovc/assist/nvaa2002/toc.html (accessed March 1, 2004).

National Task Force to End Sexual and Domestic Violence Against Women. 2005. *The Violence Against Women and Department of Justice Reauthorization Act of 2005: Summary.* http://nnedv.org/VAWA/VAWA2005Summary.PDF. Accessed March 19 2006.

Ogunwole, S. U. 2002. The American Indian and Alaska Native population: 2000. Washington, DC: U.S. Census Bureau.

Perry, Steven W. 2004. *American Indians and crime: A BJS statistical profile, 1992–2002.* Washington, DC: Bureau of Justice Statistics.

Rosay, André B., and Tara Henry. 2007. Descriptive analysis of sexual assault nurse examinations in Anchorage: 1996–2004. Anchorage: University of Alaska.

Senturia, K., M. Sullivan, S. Cixke, and S. Shiu-Thorton. 2000. *Cultural issues affecting domestic violence service utilization in ethnic and hard to reach populations.* National Criminal Justice Reference Service. http://www.ncjrs.org/pdffiles1/nij/grants/185357.pdf. Accessed February 15 2004.

Smith, Andrea 1999. Sexual violence and American Indian genocide. *Journal of Religion & Abuse* 1:31–52.

Stoddardt, Martha L., Betty Jarvis, Beverly Blake, Richard R. Fabsitz, Barbara V. Howard, Elisa T. Lee, and Thomas K. Welty. 2000. Recruitment of American Indians in epidemiologic research: The strong heart study. *American Indian and Alaska Native Mental Health Research* 9:20–37.

Tafoya, Terry. 2000. Unmasking Dashkayah: Storytelling and HIV prevention. *American Indian and Alaska Native Mental Health Research* 9:53–65.

Tjaden, Patricia, and Nancy Thoennes. 2006. Extent, nature, and consequences of rape victimization: Findings from the National Violence Against Women Survey. Washington, D.C.: National Institutes of Justice.

U.S. Commission on Civil Rights. 2003. *A quiet crisis: Federal funding and unmet needs in Indian country.* http://www.usccr.gov/pubs/na0703/na0204.pdf (accessed October 15, 2005).

———. 2004. *Broken promises: Evaluating the Native American health care system.* http://www.usccr.gov/pubs/nahealth/nabroken.pdf (accessed January 26, 2006).

U.S. Department of Justice. 2005. *Table 42: Percent distribution of single-offender victimizations, based on race of victims, by type of crime and perceived race of offender, 1996–2005.* Bureau of Justice Statistics. http://www.ojp.usdoj.gov/bjs/pub/pdf/cvus/previous/cvus42.pdf (accessed September 10, 2007).

Walters, Karina L., and Jane M. Simoni. 1999. Trauma, substance use, and HIV risk among urban American Indian women. *Cultural Diversity and Ethnic Minority Psychology* 5:236–48.

Weiss, Eric M. 2006. At U.S. urging, court throws Lamberth off Indian case. *Washington Post*, July 12.

Yuan, Nicole P., Mary P. Koss, Mona Polacca, and David Goldman. 2006. Risk factors for physical assault and rape among six Native American tribes. *Journal of Interpersonal Violence* 21:1–25.

Zion, James W. 1998. The dynamics of Navajo peacemaking. *Journal of Contemporary Criminal Justice* 14:58–74.

6

"It's Just the Way Life Is Here"

HATE CRIME AGAINST NATIVE AMERICANS

Barbara Perry

SCHOLARLY ATTENTION has largely been devoted to the historical and contemporary victimization of Native Americans as nations. Equally important is the corresponding victimization of Native Americans as individual members of those many nations. A review of the literature on Native Americans and criminal justice, and even a similar review of the narrower literature on hate crime, reveals virtually no consideration of Native Americans as victims of racially motivated violence (Levin and McDevitt 1993; Jenness and Broad 1997; Nielsen 1996, 2000). Bachman's (1992) examination of violence on Native American reservations is silent on the question of intergroup violence. Nielsen and Silverman's (1996) anthology on Native Americans, crime, and justice likewise makes no mention of Native Americans as victims of racially motivated crime. Barker's (1992) journalistic account of the murders of Native Americans in Farmington, New Mexico, touches on the issue of hate crime but provides no concrete data or analysis. It is this void that this chapter begins to address. What I offer here are observations about the dynamics of hate crime against Native Americans in three distinct regions: the Four Corners area, the Great Lakes, and the northern plains. In particular, I argue that such violence is so pervasive that it has come to be seen by many Native Americans as normative. Additionally, I highlight the cumulative impacts of the experience of both direct and vicarious victimization. I begin, however, by considering the contexts that condition the environment for hate crime to emerge.

The Context for Anti-Indian Violence: Native Americans and the "Five Faces of Oppression"

Exploitation, from Iris Marion Young's (1990) perspective, refers to processes that transfer "energies" from one group to another in such a way as to produce inequitable distributions of wealth, privilege, and benefits. While typically understood in class terms, the notion of exploitation can also be extended to racial and ethnic relations. Historically, people of color, including Native Americans, have been relegated to the categories of "menial laborers" or even servants. Racialized job segregation persists to this day. When employed, Native Americans continue to be overrepresented in menial and low-paying jobs, and dramatically underrepresented in the professions.

Beyond the exploitation associated with underemployment, there is a lengthy history of resource exploitation (Osborne 1995; Fixico 1998). Native Americans have lost over 95 percent of their land base. What is left is indeed resource-rich. However, consecutive abrogations of treaty rights with respect to mineral resources (Churchill and LaDuke 1992), water (Guerrero 1992), and fishing (Institute for Natural Progress 1992) have largely ceded control of resources to governments and corporations, at the expense of Native economies.

Related to the exploitation of Native Americans and their lands is the *marginalization* of Native Americans—the process of pushing them to the political and social edges of society. More so than other minority groups, Native Americans have even been geographically marginalized, first through expulsion into the "frontier," and subsequently by "relocation" onto reservations or into fragmented urban communities (Bigfoot 2000; Stiffarm and Lane 1992). Concomitant with this physical separation have been myriad practices intended to expel them from "useful participation" in the economic and political life of society (Nielsen 1996; Jaimes 1995). Economically, Native Americans are among the most impoverished, with 23 percent of all Natives living below the poverty line, as compared to 12 percent of the general population. This is even more pronounced on reservations, where poverty rates may go well over 50 percent (Housing Assistance Council 2002). They also experience elevated rates of unemployment. At a time when national unemployment rates reached lows of less than 5 percent, the rate of unemployment for Native Americans was well over 40 percent (Centre for Community Change 2005). Similar patterns of disadvantage are apparent in the area of educational attainment, wherein Native Americans continue to experience high rates of early school dropout, and low levels of participation in postsecondary education. The cumulative impact of these multiple forms of marginalization is evident in dramatically heightened rates of alcoholism, malnutrition, infant mortality, suicide, and early death by accident and disease (Bachman 1992; Beauvais 1996; Jaimes 1992).

The marginality of Native Americans renders them relatively *powerless* within the context of structural and institutional relationships. Most pressing is the ongoing loss of autonomy of Native Americans (Robbins 1992; Snyder-Joy 1996). By virtue of being a colonized people, Native Americans were very early stripped of their right to control their own destinies. The attempt to eliminate Native sovereignty was exacerbated by the Major Crimes Act of 1885, for example, which extended federal jurisdiction over felonies to Indian territories. This was followed by over 5,000 additional statutes that extended federal control to Native jurisdictions (Robbins 1992, 93). This political disempowerment, coupled with their economic marginalization, leaves Native Americans with limited power with which to exercise the right to freely determine their own political, economic, and social directions.

The federal state's rejection of Native Americans' traditions of governance is but one symptom of *cultural imperialism*. Specifically, this dimension of oppression refers to the ways in which "the dominant meanings of society render the particular perspective of one's own group invisible at the same time as they stereotype one's group and mark it out as "Other" (Young 1990, 58–59). Since first contact, Europeans and then Euro-Americans have engaged in this process of deculturating Native Americans, and simultaneously representing them as inferior beings (Stannard 1992; Mihesuah 1996; Jaimes 1995). It is the long-lasting images of Native Americans as "savages," as "backward," as "uncivilized," or as "unintelligent" that have facilitated the injustice and oppression experienced by Native Americans (Riding In 1998). With missionary zeal, Euro-Americans have persisted in "saving" Native Americans "from themselves" by repressing traditional folkways and attempting to assimilate them into the dominant culture.

The structural constraints on Native Americans, together with their construction as the deviant Other, provide the context for anti-Indian *violence*. The former makes them vulnerable targets; the latter makes them legitimate targets. As noted previously, the collective victimization of Native Americans is well documented. Stannard's (1992) work is an encyclopedic survey of the atrocities perpetrated against the Indigenous peoples of the Americas. Similarly, the extensive works of Churchill frequently return to the theme of Native American genocide (see Churchill 1994), as does the more recent work of Andrea Smith (2005). What these accounts fail to address, however, are the "mundane" experiences of "unprovoked attacks on their person or property, which have no motive but to damage, humiliate or destroy the person" (Young 1990, 61).

It is the latter element of oppression—otherwise known here as hate crime—that is at the core of this chapter. It is important to recognize that hate crimes are not simply individual acts, motivated by individual prejudices. Rather they are systemic; they are embedded in the broader power relations within a given culture (Young 1990; Bowling 1993). Similarly, the victim of hate crime is not restricted to the individual who might have been assaulted. Rather, the harm and the message extend to the victim's community. So, for example, vandalizing the home of one Native American family is intended to send the message to all Native Americans that they are not welcome in the neighborhood. Moreover, hate crimes are not solitary events; they are typically part of a broader pattern of social oppression. Thus, the term calls for a similarly dynamic definition.

Legal definitions of hate crime have followed the lead of the Hate Crime Statistics Act, which states that they are "crimes that manifest evidence of prejudice based on race, religion, sexual orientation or ethnicity." Yet such a definition says nothing about the power relations endemic to the act. Consequently, I have developed the following definition of hate crime, which has come to be widely cited in the sociological literature:

> It involves acts of violence and intimidation, usually directed toward already stigmatized and marginalized groups. As such, it is a mechanism of power, intended to reaffirm the precarious hierarchies that characterize a given social order. It attempts to recreate simultaneously the threatened (real or imagined) hegemony of the perpetrator's group and the "appropriate" subordinate identity of the victim's group. (Perry 2001, 10)

What is especially useful about this definition is that it recognizes that hate crime is a structural rather than an individual response to difference. Moreover, by emphasizing both violence and intimidation, it allows us to consider the continuum of behaviors that might constitute hate crime. According to the legal definitions, hate crime involves an underlying violation of criminal law or some other statute. From a sociological perspective, this is not very satisfying. It neglects legal forms of violence that nonetheless cause harm to the victim and his or her community. The literature on violence against women, for example, has long argued for a broader understanding of what constitutes violence, and indeed crime. Thus, it is important to keep in mind that the violence to which I refer runs the continuum from verbal harassment to extreme acts such as assault, arson, and murder. Clearly, not all incidents that fall within this definition will be "crimes" from a legal perspective. Yet they do constitute serious social harms regardless of their legal standing. Indeed, as the interviews revealed, by their very frequency and ubiquity, some of the most minor types of victimization—name calling, verbal harassment, and the like—had the most damaging effects.

Normative Violence

The analysis offered in this chapter is largely informed by a long-term project in which I conducted the first large-scale empirical exploration of hate crime against Native Americans. The project has consisted of three legs of research: a 1999 pilot study undertaken in the Four Corners region (funded by the Office of Intramural Grants at Northern Arizona University [NAU]); a campus hate crime survey of Native American students at NAU; and a 2002–2003 study in the Great Lakes and the northern plains region (funded by USDA). In total, I have interviewed approximately 280 Native Americans from seven states (Colorado, New Mexico, Arizona, Utah, Wisconsin, Minnesota, Montana), representing a minimum of seven Native American nations.

The majority of Native Americans that I interviewed told tales of exactly those daily onslaughts referred to above. Most had either themselves been victim or knew of someone close to them who had been victim of some form of hate crime—ranging from verbal harassment to pushing and shoving to brutal assaults with knives and lighter fluid. By far the most common incidents were various types of name calling and verbal harassment on the street and in commercial establishments. Nonetheless, there were also a small number of physical and property offenses.

Among the most vicious attacks were two cases in which perpetrators bit their victims. In one of these cases, a small piece of the victim's ear was bitten off; in the other, the tip of the victim's tongue was lost. Some participants further reported that they had been victimized by police officers, which might help to explain why so few victims in general reported their experiences.

For the Native American community, nothing in recent years compares to the harassment and violence they experienced at the Wisconsin boat landings in the closing years of the twentieth century. Participants shared some remarkable tales of their experiences at the time:

> I was out by the boat landing one night where there was over a thousand people chanting racial things. . . . The stories that came out of that, especially the ones . . . how people would prepare themselves to be there at night. There was spear guns, there was pipe bombs, there was air guns, there was slingshots. One day we were setting the nets and they were throwing rocks and they were shooting, shooting wrist rockets, slingshots with ball bearings. One hit Sarah in her side, and knocked her to the bottom of the boat. I got hit too. (Wisconsin, female)

> We had people chase us, we had people follow us. We had threats, we had people pushing. When we would stand at the landings they would come up behind us and they would push the backs of our knees, and they would throw lit cigarettes at us. They would spit on us, throw rocks. Death threats. My son—nuts were loosened on his tires on his van. He was coming home and he thought he had a flat tire, because his car started wobbling. So he stopped and all the lug nuts were loose. A lot of them too were slashed at the landings. (Wisconsin, female)

While the tension around spear fishing has subsided, the violence and harassment has not disappeared. Rather, it continues and, to those with whom I spoke, it seems unremarkable. Racial violence and the potential for racial violence is in fact normative in Native American communities and reservation border towns. It has become an institutionalized mechanism for establishing boundaries, both social and physical. Violence is one means by which to remind Native Americans where they do and don't belong. As one Montana man says of it, "The Crow people have it in their heart that just by walking down the street, or seeing him in the wrong place, if they're alone especially and don't know anyone, or if they've been drinking or whatever, and they see Anglos that have been drinking, they don't know if there's going to be violence. They always have it in their heart that there just might be."

This observation cuts to the heart of the paramount theme that emerged over the course of the interviews. Regardless of the region, or town, or tribal community, there was a very strong sense among participants that racial violence—hate crime—was endemic. That violence permeates the lives of Native Americans is, first, evident in that most complained of multiple victimizations over the course of their lives. Rarely did they describe violent victimization as something that touched them once and never again. There was always the sense, the fear, the expectation, that in the presence of non-Native Americans, they were vulnerable to harassment and attack. One Minnesota male told me, "It's always there. I don't want to say it's a norm, but we get so used to it, we never know what's coming next, or where it's coming from. That's what it's like to be an Indian around here."

Ironically, so common is the violence and harassment perceived to be that many claim to have ceased to pay attention: "We get so used to it—some of us, most of us, just ignore it, let it wash away" (Montana, male). "You don't really notice it, it's so common. It's like an itch that's always there. After a while, it's just another irritation" (Montana, male). Perhaps one of the most telling statements in this context comes from a Lame Deer resident who observed that he is "so used to it, when it's absent you don't know how to act. You are so used to the harassment and name calling being around, you don't notice it until it is gone." He described for me his experiences in towns and cities away from the reservation, away from the state, where his reception was much warmer than in nearby border towns. He explained that he didn't feel the same animosity; how he was able to relax without fear of harassment. It was in those situations, he claimed, that he realized how bad things were on the reservation and local communities. His story is especially revealing. It highlights how incessant and oppressive the reservation and border climate must be for so many Native Americans. While seemingly minor, the very pervasiveness of those petty actions—name calling, being followed, and so forth—is experienced as a violent form of oppression. Moreover, it is not readily apparent which of these acts might be the prelude to a more serious assault or beating.

It is also important that the significance of harassment and violence be seen through the prism of Native Americans' social and individual histories. For them, any one incident of hate crime adds to the ledger of racism (Varma-Joshi, Baker, and Tanaka 2004, 191). As Varma-Joshi and colleagues (2004, 191) describe it, Indigenous peoples experience racist harassment and violence within the context of the history of colonization and segregation, and within the context of their own lifelong experiences of similar incidents. The combined personal and cultural biographies cultivate a sense of intergenerational grief and trauma that, according to Bubar and Thurman (2004, 74), is the "psychological fallout from federal policies that demeaned Native culture and used violence to force assimilation." It is, moreover, the correspondence of the individual and the collective experience that makes the treatment problematic, while at the same time rendering it normative.

To those with whom I spoke, the violence seems unremarkable. Often, when asked if they perceived racial violence to be a problem in their communities, participants would respond with an almost dismissive, "Oh, yeah. Of course." One participant responded to the question, saying, "Yeah, racial attacks are common in Indian country, and of course Indian people have become calloused over the years, and when it happens, they don't think anything of it. It's just the way life is here" (Wisconsin, male). This is eerily reminiscent of Trask's (2004, 10) observation that "the natural, everyday presence of the 'way things are' explains the strength and resilience of racism. Racism envelops us, intoxicating our thoughts, permeating our brains and skins." Consequently, racial attacks are dismissed, rendered meaningless by their very pervasiveness. "The paradox," writes Scheper-Hughes (1996, 889), "is that they are not invisible because they are secreted away and hidden from view, but quite the reverse." They are invisible because they are sewn into the fabric of daily life. To say that this is "everyday violence" is not to diminish its importance. Rather, it is to highlight the ubiquity and taken-for-grantedness of victimization:

Anyway, I think race-motivated violence in the Native Americans is common in the community, so I'm not sure it's unusual, there's a lot of, there's a lot of Indian bashing. I just think that, um, I think people get used to it, so they don't say anything. I think I've, and all my friends and family and kids, we've all got lots of stories. You don't think about it, 'cause it's normal, you don't think about it until somebody like you comes, and you ask us. (Minnesota, female)

What's the Harm?

Not surprisingly, the cumulative effect of anti-Indian activity takes its toll. Those I have interviewed describe an array of individual and collective reactions, many of which were indicative of the aggregate impact of normative, systemic victimization. One participant stated the impact very simply: "A lot of it is petty stuff. But it's the petty stuff that gets to you after a while, because it's all the time." This corresponds to Feagin's (2001, 196) observation that "for any given individual, repeated encounters with white animosity and mistreatment accumulate across many institutional arenas and over long periods of time. . . . The steady acid rain of racist encounters with whites can significantly affect not only one's psychological and physical health, but also one's general outlook and perspective."

Among my Native American participants, there were many whose stories supported Feagin's contention, especially with respect to "outlook and perspective." Indeed, there was a generalized sense of feeling weighed down, oppressed by the ongoing threat of harassment and other racist actions:

> You just get tired. You don't want to have to face it anymore. After a while, you hate to go into town, 'cause ya know as soon as you cross that line, somebody's gonna do something—yell at ya, curse ya, maybe chase you back across the river. Sometimes it's just too much.

> It wears us down, ya know? We don't have to do anything. We're just there and someone calls us a "lazy Indian," or an "Indian whore," and maybe they throw stuff, or one time someone spit on me—I didn't do anything! It's that stuff everyday or every week that gets to me. I just don't wanna have to face any white people. (Minnesota, female)

The perception of recurrent threats and harassment leaves its victims feeling disempowered. It is, as many expressed it, "overwhelming," or "tiring, or "wearing." Even those who try to ignore or deny their daily realities feel embattled by that effort. For some, the constancy of the fear is almost paralytic. At the very least, it limits their desire to interact with white people. For others, it limits their movements and their perceived options, resulting in withdrawal. It creates "more borders," said one participant, in that people become fearful of moving out of the relative safety of the reservation. They "stay here for all their lives, because they're afraid to go 'out there' because of what's going on, for all of these reasons." Very similar sentiments were expressed by others: "That's why people don't leave, why they don't go into the towns to look for a job. They're afraid to go there, so they stay inside. They know—from their experience, or their family's, or their friends'—what can happen. There's too much risk out there" (New Mexico, female).

For too many Native Americans, the perception, if not the reality, of what's "out there" has its intended effect of keeping people in their place. It reinforces the boundaries—social and geographical—across which Native Americans are not meant to cross. It contributes to ongoing withdrawal and isolation; in short, it furthers historical patterns of segregation. Through violence and the threat of violence, or even through the malevolent gaze, Native Americans are daily reminded that there are places in which they are not welcome:

> There were places you just didn't want to go. Like Mercer and all— that's where the head of the Ku Klux Klan lives. That's only fourteen miles from here. There's just places you don't wanna go, you don't feel safe. Really you don't feel safe when you go off the rez. (Wisconsin, female)

> There is just places where you get in, you know you are not supposed to be in there. I guess there is, there's a kind of sense, places—for Indians and non-Indians in the communities around here—there is an idea that Indians have a certain place; that there is a certain way that they are supposed to behave when they are in the communities. And like in the South compared to this area is the deep North, you know. The whole sense of maintaining one's place and one's position in society is the kind of feeling that Indian people get around here. (Wisconsin, male)

Another damaging cumulative effect of the daily threat of harassment is the cultivation of anti-white sentiment, and ultimately, anti-white violence. Several participants spoke of the way that their harassment exacerbates anger toward and distrust of whites. For example, one Montana female said, "I just get so mad sometimes. Why do they have to do that? Why do they follow me and call me names? Or try to scare me? It makes it so I don't want to have nothin' to do with them. Why would I? They hate me, so I kinda feel the same way."

For some, the anger spills into action. Some reported hearing of, witnessing, or engaging in retaliatory violence against whites. Again, it was the daily barrage of insults, slights, harassment, and surveillance that engendered bitterness that some were unable to contain: "For many of the Native people, we hit a boiling point of pent-up frustrations and anger at the racism and ignorance and the fact that we feel powerless to fight, and we explode" (Minnesota, male). One Minnesota educator described her perception of retaliatory violence in the schools:

It goes both ways. The Indian kids come here, maybe from the reservation schools, or at least from the reservation. And they're already angry when they get here, so it doesn't take much for them to react when someone calls them "Chief," or tells them to go back to the reservation, or bumps into them—intentionally or not—in the hall. These kids live with it every day, and at some point, some of them turn around and give some back.

A mother tells the story of how her daughter "gave some back:"

My kids are going through the same thing, just like I did. . . . My daughter got in a fight last week, and she ended up leaving because that's what the guy said, kept saying, "ya Indian, ya fuckin' Indian," "You girls are nothin' but Indian whores," "You need to go back to your reservation where you belong," "I wish you were all dead." She just went off. She ended up fighting with him, and then I had to go to the school, and she ended up being suspended. I had to take her out of that school because this is happening all the time. (Minnesota, female)

Not surprisingly, many of the reactions to the normative violence described by participants are negative. That is, they are characterized by withdrawal, anger, or even retaliation. However, there are those who react in a constructive manner. Some use harassing moments as opportunities to educate. One student in a campus hate crime survey tells this tale: "The first incident was in a class with a professor who did not know I was Native American and made some condescending remarks about Native Americans. I immediately raised my hand and told him that I had a 4.0 GPA, was in the Honors program, never drank, smoked, or had sex, and I did not appreciate his stereotype. That was the only comment he ever made" (Arizona, female).

Other examples of people standing up to and correcting bigotry were plentiful. A particularly memorable one occurred on a bus trip:

> This lady was sitting in back of the bus driver, and I was sitting in the other front seat. And they started to talk about things, and the subject of spearing came up, and about *all* those fish that are thrown in the dump and why do they take them. And he was kinda half-agreeing with her. After they got through talking, I said, "Can I interject something here?" And I told them, "I don't know if people realize it or not, but those aren't fish that are thrown in the dump. It's the hide and the skeleton of the fish. The meat is taken out of it." "Oh," he says, and she didn't say nothin'. She got off in Minocqua! It's all these misconceptions, and lies—they're just ignorant. (Wisconsin, female)

Most remarkable, perhaps, is the strength and resilience of Native Americans in the face of the everyday violence described here. In fact, they currently enjoy a resurgence of numbers and of nationalist identity. As Frideres (1993, 508) puts it, "with the emergence of Native identity, the sense of alienation experienced by many Natives has been dispelled by a new sense of significance and purpose." The activism that has been at the root of so much violence, and the backlash associated with it, has engendered a renewed pride in Native American identity, and with it, a recognition of the need to pursue that which is theirs by right. In short, it has mobilized Native Americans around their cultural identity and political sovereignty.

A lot of people—this has been my experience anyway—even among Indian people there were people saying "Don't!" Because when you're told you're bad for doing something, and told a thousand times, sometimes you start to believe it. And there were others that weren't quite sure but became supportive. People who don't go to meetings were coming to meetings. People who went about their lives, they wanted—they really needed to learn—what are these treaties about, how did they occur, you know. And they developed the sense that it was a birthright for future generations. That was exciting. That was a very positive outcome of the conflict that will have contributions for years to come. (Wisconsin, male)

It is these sorts of reactions to the normativity of violence that will ultimately present the greatest defense. To use the moment of victimization to confront and challenge oppression speaks volumes. In particular, it says to the perpetrator that Native Americans refuse to "stay in their place" but will instead fight for a reconstructed definition of what that place is. Moreover, such resistance also sends a powerful message of strength and solidarity to Native American communities as well.

References

Bachman, Ronet. 1992. *Death and violence on the reservation.* New York: Auburn House.

Barker, Rodney. 1992. *The broken circle.* New York: Simon & Shuster.

Beauvais, Fred. 1996. Trends in Indian adolescent drug and alcohol use. In *Native Americans, crime and justice,* ed. Marianne Nielsen and Robert Silverman, 89–95. Boulder, CO: Westview.

Bigfoot, Dolores Subia. 2000. *History of victimization in Native communities.* Oklahoma City: Center on Child Abuse and Neglect.

Bowling, Benjamin. 1993. Racial harassment and the process of victimization. *British Journal of Criminology* 33(2):231–50.

Bubar, Roe, and Pamela Jumper Thurman. 2004. Violence against Native women. *Social Justice* 31:70–86.

Center for Community Change. 2005. *Native American background information.* http://www.cccfiles.org/issues/nativeamerican/background (accessed August 15, 2006).

Churchill, Ward. 1994. *Indians are us?* Monroe, ME: Common Courage Press.

Churchill, Ward, and Winona LaDuke. 1992. Native North America: The political economy of radioactive colonialism. In Jaimes, ed., 241–66.

Feagin, Joe. 2001. *Racist America: Roots, current realities and future reparations.* New York: Routledge.

Fixico, Donald. 1998. *The invasion of Indian country in the twentieth century.* Niwot: University Press of Colorado.

Frideres, James. 1993. *Native peoples in Canada: Contemporary conflicts.* 4th ed. Scarborough, ON: Prentice Hall.

Guerrero, Marianna. 1992. American Indian water rights: The blood of life in Native North America. In Jaimes, ed., 189–216.

Housing Assistance Council. 2002. *Taking stock of rural people, poverty, and housing for the 21st century.* Washington, DC: HAC.

Institute for Natural Progress. 1992. In usual and accustomed places: Contemporary Native American fishing rights struggles. In Jaimes, ed., 217–40.

Jaimes, Annette. 1992. Introduction: Sand Creek: The morning after. In Jaimes, ed., 1–12.

———. 1995. Native American identity and survival: Indigenism and environmental ethics. In *Issues in Native American cultural identity*, ed. Michael Green, 273–96. New York: P. Lang.

Jaimes, Annette, ed. 1992. *The state of Native America: Genocide, colonization, and resistance.* Boston: South End Press.

Jenness, Valerie, and Kendal Broad. 1997. *Hate crimes: New social movements and the politics of violence.* New York: Aldine de Gruyter.

Levin, Jack, and Jack McDevitt. 1993. *Hate crimes: The rising tide of bigotry and bloodshed.* New York: Plenum.

Mihesuah, Devon. 1996. *Native Americans: Stereotypes and realities.* Atlanta: Clarity Press.

Nielsen, Marianne. 1996. Contextualization for Native American crime and justice. In *Native Americans, crime and justice*, ed. Marianne Nielsen and Robert Silverman, 10–19. Boulder, CO: Westview.

———. 2000. Native Americans and the criminal justice system. In *Investigating difference: Human and cultural relations in criminal justice*, ed. Criminal Justice Collective, 47–58. Needham Heights, MA: Allyn & Bacon.

Nielsen, Marianne, and Robert Silverman, eds. 1996. *Native Americans, crime, and justice.* Boulder, CO: Westview.

Osborne, Stephen. 1995. The voice of the law: John Marshall and Indian land rights. In *Issues in Native American Cultural Identity*, ed. Michael Green, 57–74. New York: P. Lang.

Perry, Barbara. 2001. *In the name of hate: Understanding hate crimes.* New York: Routledge.

Riding In, James. 1998. Images of Native Americans: Native Americans in popular culture: A Pawnee's experiences and views. In *Images of color, images of crime*, ed. Coramae Richey Mann and Marjorie Zatz, 15–29. Los Angeles: Roxbury.

Robbins, Rebecca. 1992. Self-determination and subordination: The past, present and future of Native American governance. In Jaimes, ed., 87–122.

Scheper-Hughes, Nancy. 1996. Small wars and invisible genocides. *Social Science and Medicine* 43:889–900.

Smith, Andrea. 2005. *Conquest: Sexual violence and Native American genocide.* Boston: South Side Press.

Snyder-Joy, Zoanne. 1996. Self-determination and Native American justice: Tribal versus federal jurisdiction on Indian lands. In *Native Americans, crime, and justice*, ed. Marianne Nielsen and Robert Silverman, 38–45. Boulder, CO: Westview.

Stannard, David. 1992. *American holocaust.* New York: Oxford University Press.

Stiffarm, Leonard, and Phil Lane. 1992. The demography of Native North America. In Jaimes, ed., 23–54.

Trask, Haunani K. 2004. The color of violence. *Social Justice* 31:8–16.

Varma-Joshi, Manju, Cynthia Baker, and Connie Tanaka. 2004. Names will never hurt me? *Harvard Educational Review* 74:175–209.

Young, Iris Marion. 1990. *Justice and the politics of difference.* Princeton, NJ: Princeton University Press.

7

Native Americans and Uranium Mining as State-Corporate Crime

Linda Robyn

PAUSE FOR JUST a moment and consider what immediately comes to mind when you think of the word *crime*. Many people think of "common" crimes like murder, rape, robbery, aggravated assault, burglary, larceny, car theft, arson, kidnapping, drug dealing, gang activity, prostitution, and a seemingly endless list of aberrant behaviors. What we normally do not think of are crimes being committed by people who are engaged in legal business practices and have acquired high status in the community and a high level of trust and respectability. People in these positions who act outside established legal boundaries have not traditionally been the focus of law and justice, for the most part. And, most often, people in these positions who are involved in these types of violations are said to have committed various types of "white-collar crime."

White-collar crime, in all its forms, as a rule is less visible than conventional crime. Conventional crimes are more apt to come to the attention of the police because victims and witnesses report it, and the police may even observe some of it directly. White-collar crime tends to occur out of sight of law enforcement, and many of its victims may not even be aware that a crime has been perpetrated against them. A person aware of this type of crime may be intimidated and confused as to what action to take. As far as law enforcement is concerned, most agencies (i.e., police departments) are not organized to monitor and respond to such crimes, as they are with conventional crimes. Further, most people are far more fearful of conventional crimes than they are of possible white-collar transgressions.

Historically, whistleblowers and journalists have periodically exposed the wrongdoing by the powerful and privileged. Reports of political and corporate corruption began during the 1902–12 time frame. Historically, workers have been among those who have suffered most from certain forms of white-collar crime, especially those that fall under the corporate heading. Labor unions emerged during the nineteenth century and exposed unsafe working conditions, exploitation of workers by managers, wage issues, and the right to strike. More so than journalists or academics, workers in labor unions have been a critical component in revealing white-collar crime (Friedrichs 2007, 23–27).

Where do corporate and government crimes come from? Political institutions are the source of major forms of corruption and illegal activity. Friedrichs (2007, 27–28) writes that government officials and politicians are typically the products of the same broad segment of society that produces white-collar criminals, and that politicians often have close ties with corporations and businesspeople. Sometimes politicians must expose corporate illegalities, but usually they call for "getting tough on crime," and "law and order" regarding street crimes, rather than attack the crimes of powerful corporations that may be among their biggest financial supporters.

How is white-collar crime defined and studied? When we study white-collar crime in all its forms, and disseminate this information through writing and teaching, we must understand that those who read our work will be exposed to many assertions and claims. On what are these claims based? Why do we consider these actions to be criminal? Is it because an actual law has been broken? Or could it be that these actions can be considered criminal because people have been harmed, even though no actual law has been broken? One book chapter does not adequately afford the space needed to explore all of the philosophical issues that emerge from this type of study, but a short explanation can be offered here.

To begin, a positivistic approach is used by some scholars to look at all types of white-collar crime (of which state-corporate crime is a hybrid) as violation of a written law. These types of crimes are explored through scientific observation and measurement through quantitative analysis, leaving out any sort of subjective approach. Another way to explore this type of crime, which is just as valid, is through a humanistic or social harms perspective, which generally puts much less emphasis on traditional scientific methods as appropriate for the study of the human realm. This approach focuses on the social construction of the meaning of white-collar crime. Scholars utilizing this approach believe this type of crime can best be studied through interpretive observation and qualitative methods.

When Edwin Sutherland first coined the term "white-collar crime" in 1949, he suggested criminologists should use an expanded definition of crime based on behavior prohibited either by criminal law or by regulatory law (Beirne and Messerschmidt 1995, 17). Sutherland makes the argument that any *illegalities* that cause social harm should be criminalized, but some radical criminologists (Reiman cited in Beirne and Messerschmidt 2006; Michalowski cited in Beirne and Messerschmidt 2006) argue that *any behavior* should be criminalized if it causes social harm or "*analogous social injury.*" According to Michalowski, analogous social injury refers to "legally permissible acts or sets of conditions whose consequences are similar to those of illegal acts (Michalowski cited in Beirne and Messerschmidt 1995, 17). This, of course, has far-reaching implications and explains the way this chapter is written.

However, I am not suggesting that all collaborations of economic and political interests cause social harms. Throughout modern history, the government and corporations have worked together to produce tremendous material and social benefits. In all this there is a fine line, sometimes, separating what is and what is not a corporate–government transgression. There is no actual precision in measuring these types of crime from this perspective. The only precise observation to this is that, from my perspective, we cannot allow the material advancements of our society to blind us to the fact that in many cases, these material gains came about through great suffering on the part of marginalized people. From a social harms perspective, these transgressions are crimes if people are harmed in the process. Michalowski writes that the costs borne by those less powerful came about "because business and government, with their combined power, very often protected each other from ever having to answer the question: 'what is the least harmful way we can advance the human project?'" (Michalowski and Kramer 2006, 3).

To explain by example, multinational corporations have a tremendous amount of capital to work with. Executives in these corporations know full well the desperation for economic enterprise not only on Native American lands but in third-world countries as well. In many of these nations, there is an absence of regulatory controls. Multinational corporations and transnational corporations operating in third-world countries can get away much easier with hazardous working conditions in industrial facilities; exportation of unsafe products (often banned in developed countries); dumping of toxic wastes and other forms of environmental destruction (as on the Navajo Nation); bribing and corrupting politicians; tax evasion by shifting profits to subsidiaries in countries with favorable corporate tax policies; and a wide range of human rights violations. People in these countries, and Native Americans as well, may gain some economic benefits from doing business with these corporations, but many times they are also clearly exploited and pay a high price, especially in terms of harm to health and the environment (see Friedrichs 2007). Some tribes may very well have more stringent environmental regulations than either states or the federal government, but those regulations are often glossed over or outright ignored by the corporations exploiting resources on Native lands.

One very important variable to note is that many of these corporate transgressions are harmful but not necessarily against any written law. Even though multinational corporations have formidable political power, they are relatively free of accountability and traditionally have been able to conceal much of their power-wielding activity. On all levels of government, powerful corporations play an important, if not always fully visible, role. In other words, to quote Nikos Passas and Neva Goodwin on corporate activities, "It's legal, but it ain't right" (see Friedrichs 2007, 58).

White-collar, corporate, and state-corporate crimes occur in all areas of the business world, but we seldom think of these types of crimes being committed on Native American reservations. It is important to explore this type of criminality on reservations, because the U.S. government and multinational corporations have attempted to appropriate just about every resource Native Americans have ever had, including knowledge and artistry. However, the most common and most serious form of corporate and state-corporate crime (subheadings of white-collar crime) involves direct assault on the environment and Indian tribal sovereignty. Now at a time when the United States seems to be running out of everything, reservations are of strategic importance to the government and multinational corporations, because of the vast mineral wealth on Indian lands. Given that many reservations are poor, the prospect of large corporations bringing jobs and money to a depressed area makes it very easy to exploit marginalized groups of people.

For clarification, we will examine two areas of white-collar crime: corporate crime, and its hybrid, state-corporate crime.

Corporate Crime

Corporate crimes are different than some of the crimes we think of as white-collar crime, in that corporate crimes are not committed for personal gain, even though certain individuals directly benefit from them. Beirne and Messerschmidt define corporate crimes as "illegal and/or socially injurious acts of intent or indifference that occur for the purpose of furthering corporate goals and that physically and/or economically abuse individuals in the United States and/or abroad" (Beirne and Messerschmidt 2006, 194). Some elite executives working in high-ranking offices of multinational corporations, whom we would never consider as criminal, commit offenses for the corporation itself. Even though harmful and reprehensible acts may be committed by corporate executives in the course of their occupation, these acts may not be prohibited by law. There are some who believe that the only responsibility a corporation has is to make money for its stockholders, but others make the argument that corporations are responsible for the physical, emotional, and environmental damages caused by unsafe business practices; and even though the damages perpetrated by corporations may not technically be illegal, these actions should be considered crimes because they hurt people.

When we think about the positive role corporations play in our society, "the very notion of corporate crime is jarring and disconcerting to many people, for it challenges a widely projected image of beneficence" (Friedrichs 2007, 56). So, in light of the above explanation, when we look at corporate ownership and corporate-generated wealth being concentrated in the hands of relatively few people with the means to take advantage of marginalized people, the relationship between these huge multinationals and exploitation is very clear. How do we know this? Because about 1 percent of the population owns about half of the outstanding stock and trust equity in the United States, and two-thirds of the financial securities. The wealthiest 10 percent own some 90 percent of the stock (Wolff 2007, 57). When we link the offenses committed by corporations with agencies of the state, the relationship to Indian nations becomes even more refined as we examine the concept of state-corporate crime. Let's look back at treaty rights for a clear, brief explanation.

Treaty Rights and the Loss of Indian Lands

Historically, treaties were deceptively and unethically created to remove Indian people from land the government wanted to obtain and control. This process of Indian relocation caused great social harm and therefore, under the social harms definition, can be considered a state crime. For the most part, treaties were contracts signed with tribes living in areas where whites wanted to settle. About one-third of treaties were made to help keep peace, and the rest were for land cession. In addition to the state crime of coercively and deceptively using treaties to remove Indian tribes from lands desired by whites, American government (state and federal) has also violated the treaties themselves to advance the economic interests of large corporations. These violations have most often occurred when multinational corporations desire to extract scarce resources from Indian reservations. In this instance, the use of state power, in violation of treaty rights, to assist the corporate plunder of Indian lands is an early type of state-corporate crime.

These state-corporate crimes take several forms. Take, for example, the American Indian Movement during the 1970s when the Lakota Sioux people were trying to keep their corrupt tribal chairman from leasing away tribal lands to the U.S. government and various multinational corporations for strip-mining operations. In an effort to lease tribal lands, the U.S. government began a paramilitary operation to eliminate the American Indian Movement, which was a threat to corporate activity (see Baer 1991; Michalowski and Kramer 2006).

We are a neocolonial society in which state and multinational corporations are skilled at setting one group against another to advance their interests. In the case above, the Lakota believed the land upon which they live is their land, based on the Fort Laramie Treaty of 1868. Since the early 1970s, the federal government argued that under the Homestead Act of 1868, this land is "white" land, and it told both the Indians and the whites that the other was trying to take their land. Both Indian and white people began pointing accusing fingers at each other over who owned the land and who was trying to take the land. Meanwhile, multinational corporations quietly came into the region and claimed the area for themselves. Multinational corporations that arrived in the early 1970s include Union Carbide, Exxon, Westinghouse, Burlington Northern, Chevron, Conoco, and Decker Coal (Ellison interview in Baer 1991).

To give you an example of the magnitude of the profits to be gained and why this particular example constitutes state-corporate crime, it is important to note that approximately four million acres could be mined in the Black Hills of South Dakota. Brohm Mining Company was one of the companies that came to strip-mine the northern hills region. This company requested an expansion of 800 acres onto Forest Service land. According to corporate records and announcements, this 800-acre expansion could yield approximately $3.5 billion of gold in a relatively short period of time. If a mere 800 acres of the Black Hills can yield these huge profits, consider the enormous profit potential from gaining access to the entire Black Hills gold country. The incentive to displace Indians from this land is enormous. This reality explains why the Pentagon (i.e., the government), in conjunction with the multinational corporations, became directly involved with an isolated area of the country inhabited by a small group of impoverished people—people whom corporate interests recognize as a threat to their multibillion-dollar operations. This is a very clear example of a social harms definition of state-corporate crime. These were corporate transgressions, some of which were illegal, but all of which caused pain and suffering to the Indian people living there.

State-corporate actors and their interactions with Indian tribes are historically situated in colonial-style treaties. The psychological impact of the wording of treaties, which fostered removal of Indian people from their homelands and placed them on reserves in particular groups, became a mode of domination. People who grew up on reservations many years ago had unequal access to political power. The generations who followed are changing that unequal balance today, but unequal access to power, which kept Indian people in a subordinate position for many decades, allowed those privileged by power to engage in colonial-type practices that continue to this day, as the example above explains. Today, as Indian people increase their base of knowledge, they are becoming more powerful and are challenging the power structures of state-corporate entities (Robyn 2006).

As corporations continue their operations on a global level, we most certainly can expect to see more cases similar to this one. Market shares are more of a concern than preventing social harms of this nature. Current research in the area of state-corporate crime indicates that much harm has been created through regulatory neglect of corporate activities, and in most instances, corporations are not held legally accountable for their transgressions, whether or not those transgressions are actually against the law.

State-Corporate Crime on the Navajo Reservation

State-corporate crime is a hybrid of white-collar crime, because it has attributes of corporate and government crime. Many of the crimes committed by the government are interlocked with corporations in the private sector. There are many links between corporate "power elites" and the government on all levels. Kramer and Michalowski (cited in Friedrichs 2007) developed the concept of state-corporate, where the interests of corporations and governments intersect. They define this type of crime as follows: "State-corporate crimes are illegal or socially injurious actions that occur when one or more institutions of political governance pursue a goal in direct cooperation with one or more institutions of economic production and distribution."

State-corporate crime focuses on how public and private entities cooperate to further the goals of each of their institutions. This cooperation then leads to "death, injury, ill health, financial loss, and . . . cultural destruction, all the while being insulated from the full weight of criminalization for these actions" (Kramer, Michalowski, and Kauzlarich, cited in Friedrichs 2007, 145). With this information in hand, we will now turn to a case-specific examination of uranium.

In the United States, a large share of energy and mineral resources is found on American Indian reservations. Gedicks (1993, 40) writes that Indian reservations are of strategic importance to corporations and the government because they constitute one of the largest and least known mineral repositories on the continent—nearly 5 percent of the U.S. oil and gas, one-third of its strippable low-sulfur coal, and one-half of its privately owned uranium.

Being able to exploit indigenous groups of people is one of the hallmarks of state-corporate crime, and one common thread that runs through many of the 562 federally recognized Indian nations is that they are poor. Unemployment, substandard health care, education, and substance abuse are but a few of the enormous problems that face Indian nations in the United States. Given these sets of circumstances, large corporations, sometimes in cooperation with public agencies, are well positioned to exploit indigenous peoples who are on the frontline of contemporary colonial struggles. Even though desperately poor people living on Indian reservations in this country may well initially receive some economic benefits from multinational intrusion on their lands, they are also clearly exploited and pay a high price, especially in terms of harm to health and the environment, for these benefits.

While not all people living on the Navajo Nation experience poverty, those living in the former Bennett Freeze area give us an example of the magnitude of poverty and desperation experienced by many tribal members. As Cyndy Cole noted in an *Arizona Daily Sun* article on August 6, 2006, the Bennett Freeze was partly the result of an 1882 presidential order that established a reservation for Hopis and "such other Indians" . . . ignoring who lived where. Bennett's order was an intentional move on the part of the government to cause such hardships on both sides that the tribes would find a way to settle disagreements quickly. By 1966, the boundaries of each tribe's land were still in dispute.

So, for the last forty years, Navajos living in this area have lived involuntarily cut off from power, running water, and adequate housing. They sleep two and three families to a house, on average, in hogans, shacks, and travel trailers. More than two-thirds of these homes lack running water and plumbing. Seventy-four percent have been deemed unfit for human habitation, according to congressional testimony. Before the land dispute was resolved in 2007, the Bureau of Indian Affairs prohibited even minor home repairs, all new construction, and other modernization. It will take astronomical amounts of money, work, and political support to afford them access to the basic necessities most of the population in the United States takes for granted (Cole 2006, A1, A11).

Corporations are well aware of the living conditions on the Navajo Nation, as well as other extremely poor Indian reservations throughout the United States, and they are also aware that approximately 25 percent of the U.S. mineral wealth is located on Indian lands (Gedicks 1993, 41). Given these sets of circumstances, it becomes abundantly clear why the government and giant multinational corporations would have a keen interest in Indian lands that contain a wide variety of valuable resources needed for industrial and military development.

The preceding example of the Navajo people gives us an idea of how and why corporate pursuit of enormous profits on a worldwide scale takes precedence over all other considerations of the people and environment being exploited. Because multinational corporations have such tremendous wealth, they also have great influence over politicians, law-making, and key environmental issues; thus, they play a major role in shaping society to fit their needs. Such enormous power and ties to the government and military allow corporate actors to move freely, without much fear of accountability. The interlocking ties between huge, vastly powerful corporations and the government on all levels as they pursue goals in direct cooperation with one another constitute state-corporate crime.

With this information in hand, we will now turn to a case-specific examination of uranium mining on the Navajo Nation. To better explain this case, we will begin by examining some of the differences between the ways Native Americans think and the Western way of looking at the world.

Traditional Thinking in a Linear World

Empirical thought is subject to verification by observation or experiment. In the Western world, thought processes travel on a more empirical linear line from point A to point B. There is a difference between the mind of a Native American raised in a traditional way and the Western mind of empirical evidence. There is a complexity of the American Indian mind in its traditional cultural and natural environment, and an adaptation of thinking to adjust to the American mainstream (Fixico 2003, xii). Because of differences in socialization and culture, for many Native American people, thinking is a way of "seeing" things from a perspective emphasizing circles and cycles. There is a relationship and value system that guides the behavior of many Indian people in accordance with what they refer to as natural law.

Native peoples have always used sophisticated empirical traditional knowledge. The diversity of Native cultures and kinds of social organizations that developed through time represent a high degree of sociopolitical complexity (Robyn 2002b). For thousands of years, Native Americans maintained a sustainable way of life based on the concept of reciprocity or reciprocal relations based on natural law, defining the relationship and responsibility between people and the environment (LaDuke 1993, i). Seeing things within a reality that includes the physical and metaphysical world, while no less empirical, is a different perspective from the American mainstream that is based on the Western mind believing in empirical evidence (Fixico 2003, 2).

Louise Grenier writes that the empirical method of indigenous knowledge

> refers to the unique, traditional, local knowledge existing within and developed around the specific conditions of women and men indigenous to a particular geographic area. . . . The development of IK [indigenous knowledge] systems, covering all aspects of life, including management of the natural environment, has been a matter of survival to the peoples who generated these systems. Such knowledge systems are cumulative, representing generations of experiences, careful observations, and trial-and-error experiments. (1998, 2)

This is important to the concept of Native Americans and state-corporate crime, because until recently, those seeking to exploit Indigenous lands did not consider drawing upon the vast wealth of Indigenous knowledge. Specifically within the United States, Native Americans experienced loss of power and autonomy through the process of colonialism. The legacy of seventeenth-century European colonial domination placed Indigenous knowledge in the categories of primitive, simple, "not knowledge," or folklore. Through the process of colonization, indigenous knowledge and perspectives have been ignored and denigrated in the past by the vast majority of social, physical, biological, and agricultural scientists, and governments using colonial powers to exploit indigenous resources (Robyn 2002b, 201).

The relationship of Navajo people to ecology and the environment is defined by their culture. Mining uranium on the Navajo Nation depicts the human and ecological results of a conflict in ecological perceptions (or different ways of thinking) between the U.S. government, specifically the Bureau of Indian Affairs, and the Navajo people. In this context, the imbalance and hierarchical social structure produced by the expansionary needs of capitalism is, to many Native Americans, highly destructive to their perception of the need for balance between physical and metaphysical worlds. Leonard Peltier (cited in Robyn 2002a, 89) expressed the American Indian point of view well when he stated,

> Today, what was once called worthless land suddenly becomes valuable as the technology of white society advances. White society would like to push us off our reservations because beneath the barren land lie valuable mineral and oil resources. It is not a new development for white society to steal from nonwhite peoples. When white society succeeds it's called colonialism. When white society's efforts to colonize people are met with resistance it's called war. But when the colonized Indians of North America meet to stand and resist we are called criminals.

The sharp contrast between Western, mainstream linear thinking and circular thinking contributes to misunderstandings between state-corporate actors and many Native Americans. These differences also begin to describe the state-corporate relationships with the Navajo today regarding uranium mining and the physical, emotional, and environmental damage they have endured as a result.

Uranium Mining on the Navajo Nation

Churchill and LaDuke (1992, 243) describe the United States as being one of the most comprehensive systems of imperialism that has ever existed, and that it is fueled by nuclear capabilities fed by uranium. Therefore, the relationship of Indian reservations to that uranium becomes abundantly clear, especially when we consider that roughly half of the recoverable uranium within the United States lies in New Mexico, and about half of that is on the Navajo reservation.

Uranium has been mined on the Navajo Nation since the 1940s. In the race to create and increase nuclear weapons in the United States, a steady supply of uranium ore was required. The Four Corners area of the Southwest, and the Colorado Plateau, held massive supplies of the mineral that the U.S. government wanted. The U.S. government ensured uranium production by giving the mining companies large financial incentives, by knowingly allowing miners to work in unsafe conditions, and by keeping them uninformed about the dangers of exposure to uranium. Believing that the nation's security was at stake, Indian men dug the ore that was crucial to the stockpile of nuclear weapons in the United States (Eichstaedt 1994, xv).

Eichstaedt (1994, xv) writes that about a quarter of the men who labored in the uranium mines and processing mills were Navajo. They dug the uranium ore with pick and shovel in small mines or blasted rocks with dynamite, breathing radon gas and silica-laden dust. They ate food tainted with uranium oxide and drank the contaminated water that dripped from the mine walls. They carried uranium home to their families on their shoes, clothes, and bodies. Yet, in a classic example of state-corporate crime, mounting evidence of the dangers of uranium and warnings from public health service physicians were not acknowledged by mining corporations and the government. In fact, the companies and the government refused to acknowledge that there was danger and that, in addition to gathering uranium, miners were harvesting their own death by being constantly subjected to small doses of radiation over a sustained period of time.

With the mining of uranium came vast amounts of waste cast aside as mine tailings. Grinde and Johansen (1995, 206) write that one of the mesa-like waste piles grew to be a mile long and seventy feet high. On windy days, dust from the tailings blew into local communities, filling the air and settling on water supplies. The Atomic Energy Commission assured worried local residents that the dust was harmless. Attempts by the public health system to warn officials about the upcoming crises were ignored and allowed to turn into an endless sea of studies and reports. But huge profits were at stake, and the Atomic Energy Commission did not want to hear about health problems in the uranium industry, and neither did the mining companies (Eichstaedt 1994, 67). However, one of the reports issued by the Department of Energy in 1978 stated that people living near the tailings ran twice the risk of lung cancer than did the general population, and a Public Health Service study asserted that one in six uranium miners had died, or would die prematurely of lung cancer (Grinde and Johansen 1995, 208). However, if information on the dangerous conditions detailed in this, and in many other reports, reached miners, the Atomic Energy Commission feared it might cause a general panic that would lead to miners walking off their jobs. Again, huge profits were at stake.

On the advice of the Bureau of Indian Affairs, and corporate promises of jobs and royalties to an economically depressed area, the Navajo Tribal Council approved a mining agreement with the Kerr-McGee Corporation in 1952 (Churchill and LaDuke 1992, 247). Kerr-McGee found the reservation location to be very lucrative—there were no taxes at the time, and labor was cheap. Kerr-McGee employed 100 Navajo men, with wages averaging $1.60 per hour, or approximately two-thirds of the then-prevailing off-reservation rate. The corporation also saved money by not enforcing safety regulations at its Shiprock site. Ventilation units installed as a safety measure were found by inspectors to be inadequate or not working at all. One report, dating from 1959, noted that radiation levels in the Kerr-McGee shaft had been allowed to reach ninety times the "permissible" limit (Churchill and LaDuke 1992, 247).

By 1979 Kerr-McGee had all but exhausted the easily recoverable uranium deposits at Shiprock. Any further profitable mining would be unlikely. The Atomic Energy Commission was also phasing out ore buying, and the Shiprock facility closed in early 1980. When the corporation left, about seventy-one acres of "raw" uranium tailing were simply left at the mining site. These tailings contain waste by-products of uranium ore refinement, but retain 85 percent of the original radioactivity of the ore. Only sixty feet from the San Juan River, radioactive contamination from this huge tailings pile flows downstream to communities that draw upon the river for potable water (Churchill and LaDuke 1992, 248).

Churchill and LaDuke write (1992, 248) that "the price of Kerr-McGee's 'development' at Shiprock, in terms of life lost in this generation and in generations yet to come, cannot be calculated by any financial/economic yardstick. Of the 150-odd Diné miners who worked underground at the Shiprock facility during the eighteen years of its operation, eighteen had died of radiation-induced lung cancer by 1975."

Even though the Navajo were facing extreme health issues from uranium mining, speculators continued to come to the Southwest as arms stockpiling and the anticipated needs of nuclear power plants drove up demand, and the price, for the mineral. By late 1978, more than 700,000 acres of Indian land were under lease for uranium exploration and development around Shiprock and Crownpoint on the reservation in New Mexico (Grinde and Johansen 1995, 209).

The U.S. Geological Survey predicted that the water table at Crownpoint would drop a thousand feet and would not return to present levels for thirty to fifty years after mining ended. What water remained would be contaminated by uranium residue. The Indians were powerless to do anything about this, because even though they owned the surface rights, the mineral rights in the area are owned by private companies such as the Santa Fe Railroad (Grinde and Johansen 1995, 210). In speaking from an Indian perspective about the environmental devastation caused by mining, John Redhouse, associate director of the Albuquerque-based National Indian Youth Council, said that the uranium boom is "an issue of spiritual and physical genocide" (cited in ibid., 210). And Winona LaDuke, of the International Indian Treaty Council said, "Indian people refuse to become the silent martyrs of the nuclear industry. We stand fighting in our homelands for a future free of the threat of genocide for our children" (cited in ibid., 211).

Largest Nuclear "Accident": State-Corporate Crime in the United States

Along with the economic and political dimensions of internal colonialism as is found in this story of mining on the Navajo Nation, there is an environmental dimension that is frequently overlooked. Jerry Mander said it best when he observed that most Indian struggles take place outside the media, "in the central Arizona desert, in the rugged Black Hills, the mountains of the Northwest, or else on tiny Pacific islands, or in the icy vastness of the far north of Alaska. The *New York Times* has no bureau in those places; neither does CBS. . . . As a result, some of the most terrible assaults upon native peoples today never get reported" (cited in Gedicks 1993, 43).

The Church Rock Tailings Dam "accident" (state-corporate crime) on the Navajo reservation is one such example of an environmental catastrophe that received very little media attention. At this site, the biggest expulsion of radioactive material in the United States occurred on July 16, 1978. On that day, more than 1,100 tons of uranium mining wastes slammed through a dam near Church Rock, New Mexico.

Along with the tailings, 100 million gallons of radioactive water poured through the dam before the crack was repaired. The Rio Puerco River became hopelessly contaminated, with readings 6,000 times the allowable standard of radioactivity below the broken dam shortly after it was repaired, according to the Nuclear Regulatory Commission (Grinde and Johansen 1995, 211).

This disaster is the largest one-time release of radioactive wastes ever in the United States, greater than the Love Canal or Three-Mile Island "accidents," yet the media showed very little interest in this catastrophic event. What should have been front-page news in every paper in the country received only small reviews. The *New York Times* mentioned the spill in a short news story twelve days after it happened. The *Los Angeles Times* gave it slightly more coverage, largely because California officials were concerned that Lake Mead, Arizona, which is southern California's main water supply, would be contaminated (Gedicks 1993, 43). Grinde and Johansen (1995, 212) write that along the river "officials issued press releases telling people not to drink the water, but they had a few problems: many of the Navajo residents could not read English and had no electricity to power television sets and radios while other consumers of the water—cattle—don't read."

Even though the Church Rock spill was an enormous disaster, it is but one incident in an internal-colonialism way of life on Navajo lands. Stretching back thirty years, the nuclear-mining legacy lives on in the outlying areas of the Navajo Nation. Still today, when the hot, dry winds blow through the area, radioactive dust from the tops and sides of large tailings piles flies through the air, releasing small, steady doses of radiation into the environment. But is this harmless?

To explain the dangers, Eichstaedt (1994, 47–49) writes,

> As uranium breaks down into other elements, the energy released has three different forms: alpha and beta particles, and gamma rays. Alpha particles are potent but can be stopped easily by such things as a sheet of paper or even human skin. However, this does not mean these little particles are harmless. Once alpha particles are taken into the human body, they lodge in tissues, bones, or organs, and steadily radiate and pelt surrounding cells. Beta particles are very similar but thicker, denser materials are needed to stop them, and . . . once inhaled they

can wreak havoc in the body. Gamma rays are highly penetrating rays that require about an inch of lead or a foot of concrete to be stopped. These rays pass right through the human body. The earth is bombarded constantly by gamma radiation from the cosmos, but intense doses from such earthbound elements as radium can be fatal.

It should be noted that all tribes that produce resources such as timber, oil, hydropower, uranium, or other minerals have different environmental regulations, both among themselves and from the federal government. There is a new piece of federal legislation called the Energy Policy Act of 2005, Title V, Section 1813, Indian Land Rights-of-Way Study, created by the U.S. Department of Energy and the U.S. Department of the Interior. The departments' report to Congress presents a summary of comments received in consultation with interested tribes, energy companies, associations, interest groups, and other governmental representatives in regard to tribal sovereignty, self-determination, rates of compensation to tribes, appropriate standards and procedures for grants, expansions, renewals of energy, and the like. The impact of this legislation is unknown at this time.

Why This Is an Example of State-Corporate Crime

American Indian reservations are geographic entities as well as quasi-sovereign nations. Because of less stringent environmental regulations on some reservations than on those at the state and federal levels, American Indian reservations nationwide have always been prime targets for risky technologies such as uranium mining (Angel cited in Westra and Lawson 2001, 8). The cooperative endeavors of Kerr-McGee, United Nuclear Corporation, et al., merged with the interests of the U.S. government to secure uranium for nuclear power needs.

The mining of uranium by multinational corporations in cooperation with the U.S. government (i.e., the Atomic Energy Commission) has resulted in death, injury, ill health, financial loss, and cultural destruction, with no criminalization for these acts. The mining corporations as well as the U.S. government were made aware of the dangers miners were exposed to, and were adequately informed that these dangers could be lessened with proper safety measures. Scientific evidence of the dangers associated with radiation illness existed after 1949. Still, even with this information, measures to properly ventilate mines where the Navajo worked were never taken, as the government pressured Kerr-McGee and other producers to increase the amount of uranium they were mining. The Public Health Service (PHS) recommended working ventilation in 1952, but the Atomic Energy Commission said it did not have any responsibility for the mines, even though they bought more than three million pounds of uranium from Kerr-McGee in 1954 alone (Baker cited in Grinde and Johanson 1995, 20).

The United Nuclear uranium spill in Church Rock, New Mexico, in July of 1979 can be considered a state-corporate crime because it was a direct result of faulty dam structure known to United Nuclear two months before the dam broke. Even though United Nuclear *knew* the dam was faulty, no repairs were made or even attempted. Seventeen hundred Navajo people were immediately affected, their single water source hopelessly contaminated. More than 1,000 sheep and other livestock that drank from the Rio Puerco water after the spill, died (Churchill and LaDuke 1992, 249).

The spill was not immediately brought to the attention of the public, let alone the Navajo people caught in its wake. As an example of the expendability of the Navajo people under internal-colonialism practices, when the Church Rock community attempted to seek compensation, including emergency water and food supplies for members of the community who were directly and immediately affected, United Nuclear refused any compassion or redress. Through a multitude of evasions and obstacles, United Nuclear was able to avoid any form of redress for over a year. Finally, a minimal out-of-court settlement was agreed to when a class-action suit was filed on behalf of the town. By then, the immediate danger had passed, yet the long-term effects are still unknown. Between Kerr-McGee, United Nuclear, and several other energy corporations operating in the area, well over half the jobs and nearly 80 percent of the income at Church Rock came from uranium production. "Dependency, in its more virulent colonial manifestation, had effectively converted Church Rock into an 'economic hostage'—and an expendable hostage at that—of the uranium industry (Churchill and LaDuke 1992, 249).

Government Response

In 1979 Senate hearings began as part of a proposal to compensate the miners for what investigators called deliberate negligence. Bills for miners' compensation were introduced, discussed, and died in Congress for twelve years. By 1990, the death toll among former miners had risen to 450 (Baker cited in Grinde and Johanson 1995, 217). Relatives of the deceased miners gave testimony about how the miners ate their lunches in the mines and drank contaminated water, all the while believing they were safe. No one from the mining corporations or the government had informed them that their lives were in danger (Grinde and Johansen 1995, 217). Even if they had, many of the men did not speak English, and the Navajo language does not have a word for radioactivity, so the corporations and the government were able to get away with a slow, agonizing form of murder.

After years of failed attempts, the U.S. Congress passed compensation for Navajo miners in 1990. Grinde and Johansen (1995) write that by the early 1990s, about 1,100 Navajo miners or members of their families had applied for compensation related to uranium exposure. Only 328 cases were approved, 121 were denied, and action was withheld on another 663 cases, significantly lower than in other cases of radiation compensation (Grinde and Johansen 1995, 217).

Can We Slay the Yellow Monster?

In one of the stories the Navajos tell about their origin, the Diné (the people) emerged from the third world into the fourth and present world and were given a choice. They were told to choose between two yellow powders. One was yellow dust from the rocks, and the other was corn pollen. The Diné chose corn pollen, and the gods nodded in assent. They also issued a warning. Having chosen the corn pollen, the Navajos were to leave the yellow dust in the ground. If it was ever removed, it would bring evil (Rondon cited in Eichstaedt 1992, 47).

Leetso, or "yellow monster," is the Navajo name for low-grade uranium ore, which is known as "yellowcake" in the mining industry for its yellow, powdered consistency. Uranium mining has left in its wake serious illnesses, environmental, and economic devastation, as foretold by the elders.

In an article published in *Space Daily* (2006, 1), staff writers discuss research being conducted at Northern Arizona University, Flagstaff, Arizona, by biochemist Diane Stearns and her Navajo students. The Navajos believe you must gain knowledge of a monster to slay it and restore nature's balance, and these researchers are adding to that knowledge with new discoveries about uranium.

Stearns and her collaborators have found that, in addition to damaging DNA by its radioactivity, uranium can also damage DNA as a heavy metal, independent of its radioactive properties. Stearns and her team are the first to show that when cells are exposed to uranium, it binds to DNA and causes cell mutations. When uranium attaches to DNA, the genetic code in the cells of living organisms can be altered. As a result, the DNA can make the wrong protein or wrong amounts of protein, which affects how the cells grow. Some of these cells can grow to become cancerous (*Space Daily* 2006, 1).

In the article, Stearns explains that, "if you get a heavy metal stuck on DNA, you can get a mutation." Other heavy metals are known to bind to DNA, but Stearns and her colleagues are the first to identify this trait with uranium. This groundbreaking research has far-reaching implications for people living near abandoned mine tailings in the Four Corners area of the Southwest, as questions continue to be asked about environmental exposure to uranium from mine tailings that can still be found across the Navajo Nation (*Space Daily* 2006, 2).

Speaking to the differences of traditional thinking in a linear world, the article describes another Navajo word, *hozho*, which relates to harmony, balance, and beauty. NAU senior Hertha Woody explains that the yellow monster disrupts hozho and that uranium should remain in the ground to ensure balance. Navajo Nation president Joe Shirley Jr. signed the Diné Natural Resources Protection Act in the spring of 2005, which bans further uranium mining and processing on the Navajo Nation.

Funding for Stearns's work is tied to improving health among Native American communities through a grant jointly awarded to Northern Arizona University and the Arizona Cancer Center by the National Cancer Institute. Through Stearns's and her students' important, groundbreaking research, we can gain valuable insight into why Navajo and Hopi may get cancer to a greater extent; why their survival rate is lower; why Navajo teens exposed to radiation from uranium mine tailings have seventeen times the national average of reproductive organ cancer; and a host of other questions (Russell cited in Westra and Lawson 2001 22–32, 24).

As late as 1979, Kerr-McGee, in whose mines many Navajo men worked, stated that uranium-related deaths among miners were mere allegations. Research being conducted today proves otherwise. When mining companies began operations on the Navajo Nation, they were not subject to taxes, labor was cheap, safety measures were ignored, warnings of the dangers of uranium mining were ignored, yet another economically depressed indigenous people were exploited, miners began developing cancer and dying by the hundreds, there was untold environmental devastation, and as we have seen from the research, scores of other people and children are now reaping the fallout of radiation decades later. As we have seen, the collusion between mining companies and the government resulted in state-corporate crime that produced a deadly pattern of disregard for indigenous life. Mine workers and their homelands were sacrificed in pursuit of profit; yet those responsible suffer no consequences.

One wonders how different things would be on the Navajo Nation today if circular thinking, and natural law of the cycles of the earth, had been taken into account, and *Leetso*, the yellow powder, had been left in the ground.

References

Baer, S. 1991. *Warrior: The life of Leonard Peltier* [film]. Produced by Shenandoah Productions, Eureka, CA.

Beirne, P., and J. Messerschmidt. 1995. *Criminology.* Philadelphia: Harcourt Brace.

———. 2006. *Criminology.* Los Angeles: Roxbury.

Churchill, Ward, and Winona LaDuke. 1992. Native North America: The political economy of radioactive colonialism. In *The state of Native America: Genocide, colonization, and resistance,* ed. Annette Jaimes, 243–49. Boston: South End Press.

Cole, Cyndy. 2006. The forgotten homeland. *Arizona Daily Sun,* August 6.

Eichstaedt, Peter H. 1994. *If you poison us: Uranium and Native Americans.* Santa Fe: Red Crane Books.

Fixico, Donald. 2003. *The American Indian mind in a linear world.* New York: Routledge.

Friedrichs, David O. 2007. *Trusted criminals: White collar crime in contemporary society.* 3rd ed. Belmont, CA: Thomson Higher Education.

Gedicks, Al. 1993. *The new resource wars: Native and environmental struggles against multinational corporations.* Boston: South End Press.

Grenier, Louise. 1998. *Working with indigenous knowledge*. Ottawa: International Development Research Centre.

Grinde, Donald, and Johansen, Bruce. 1995. *Ecocide of Native America: Environmental destruction of Indian lands and peoples*. Santa Fe, NM: Clear Light.

LaDuke, Winona. 1993. A society based on conquest cannot be sustained. In *The new resource wars: Native and environmental struggles against multinational corporations*, ed. Al Gedicks, ix–xv. Boston: South End Press.

Michalowski, Raymond, and Ronald Kramer, eds. 2006. *State-corporate crime: Wrongdoing at the intersection of business and government*. New Brunswick, NJ: Rutgers University Press.

Robyn, Linda. 2002a. A critical model for the study of resource colonialism and Native resistance. In *Controversies in white-collar crime*, ed. Gary Potter, 85–108. Cincinnati: Anderson.

———. 2002b. Indigenous knowledge and technology: Creating environmental justice in the twenty-first century. *American Indian Quarterly* 26:198–220.

———. 2006. Violations of treaty rights. In *State-corporate crime: Wrongdoing at the intersection of business and government*, ed. Raymond Michalowski and Ronald Kramer, 194–98. New Brunswick, NJ: Rutgers University Press.

Space Daily (Staff Writers). 2006. Can we slay the yellow monster? *Space Daily*, April 11.

U.S. Department of Energy and U.S. Department of the Interior. 2005. *Energy Policy Act of 2005, Title V, Sect. 1813, Indian Land Rights-of-Way Study*. http://www.oe.energy.gov (accessed August 7, 2007).

Westra, Laura, and Bill Lawson, eds. 2001. *Faces of environmental racism: Confronting issues of global justice*. 2nd ed. Oxford: Rowman & Littlefield.

Wolff, Robert P. 2007. In defense of anarchism. In *Trusted criminals: White collar crime in contemporary society*, 3rd ed., ed. David O. Friedrichs, 57–87. Belmont, CA: Thomson Higher Education.

8

The Jurisdictional Jungle

NAVIGATING THE PATH

John F. Cardani

MANY YEARS AGO, while working as a deputy sheriff, I was called to meet a Havasupai tribal officer, who had arrested a non-Native man for cultivating marijuana. The individual had been growing his crops near Havasupai Creek, down in the Grand Canyon. Much to his surprise, there were police officers who worked in the depths of the Grand Canyon, and his farming operation received attention from the tribal officer. It was not uncommon for Havasupai officers to call upon the sheriff's department, when they made arrests of non-Natives, so I drove to Hualapai Hill Top to meet the Havasupai officer. When I arrived, I was met by the tribal officer, whom I had known for years, and seated in his patrol vehicle was the arrestee whom I had been dispatched to transport. As the tribal officer and I visited, he explained how he had recovered a large number of the plants and had planned on pursuing felony charges against his unwilling passenger. I moved the arrestee's property to my patrol car and began looking at the booking sheet that outlined the felony charges. I then noticed a small sheet of paper that looked like a traffic ticket, a short-form criminal complaint, a criminal citation! I noticed the charge of cultivating marijuana, which had been written by the tribal officer. A felony, I thought, required much more than a traffic ticket! I turned to my friend the tribal officer and suggested that he "go long-form" with this complaint, as the crime was a felony. Long-form would include having a prosecutor draft a criminal complaint and taking the criminal complaint before a judge. Without missing a beat, he told me that the citation was the longest form he had in his clipboard. Although this scenario was somewhat amusing at the time, years later I wondered if he was serious. Legal and jurisdictional uncertainties have plagued both Native and non-Native law enforcement agencies for years. Ultimately, those who suffer from the lack of knowledge are both the victims and those accused of crimes in Indian country.

Recently, I was contacted by a good friend of mine who is employed as a tribal officer. He was extremely upset and frustrated, as he had just completed an investigation wherein a non-Native had confessed to sexually assaulting a Native juvenile. The investigative work was a lengthy process, and now he had identified a suspect to charge with the crime. An immediate telephone call to the Federal Bureau of Investigation, he thought, would close his investigation and place the alleged perpetrator in jail. No such luck, as the Native officer was told that an agent would not be responding to take disposition of the arrestee, nor was he given any instructions or direction to proceed. As of the writing of this chapter, the suspect is still residing in Indian country, the victim is still living in the same community, and no criminal justice action has occurred. Justice in this case has not been served, as lack of knowledge, apathy, or maybe a combination of both led to inaction.

This chapter discusses determination of jurisdiction in Indian country, and outlines some guidelines used by Native tribes, the U.S. government, and local agencies in effectively dealing with jurisdictional issues. It also briefly discusses Supreme Court cases that have impacted jurisdiction, sovereignty, and the application of criminal law in Indian Country. The chapter outlines the historical significance of events, including treaties; congressional actions, including the creation of Public Law 280; and statutory changes, which have occurred through time, continually changing the definition of jurisdiction. It compares the application of tribal law with the U.S. criminal code and state statutes. Finally, the chapter identifies ongoing challenges facing tribal, state, and federal criminal justice agencies, relating to jurisdiction.

Jurisdictional History

The study of jurisdiction requires a solid foundation to make it understandable, and the foundation for the study of criminal jurisdiction and legal issues begins with history. Although there are six identified periods in history that have shaped American Indian law and policy, the changes and legal challenges continue today. During each of the six historical periods, a common denominator of federal involvement is present (Myers 2002). The evidence of federal action or federal response can be easily recognized.

Many treaties and statutes enacted prior to 1890 control American Indian law and policy today. Treaties that were signed well over one hundred years ago are *still* pending litigation. Several very important concepts that have shaped federal Indian law and policy can be found in early legislation and three leading U.S. Supreme Court decisions, known as the Marshall Trilogy. These cases are discussed later in this chapter. The basic elements as outlined in these cases, laws, and early treaties are as follows.

There is a special trust relationship between the U.S. government and tribes. Indian tribes are not foreign nations but constitute "distinct political" communities that are referred to as "domestic, dependent nations" whose "relation to the United States resembles that of a ward to his guardian" (Marshall 1831). Tribal nations are sovereigns, "governments," and state law does not apply within reservation boundaries without congressional approval (Marshal 1832). Tribal rights, including rights to land and to self-government, are not granted to the tribe by the U.S. government. Under the Reserved Rights Doctrine, tribes reserved such rights as part of their status as prior and continuing sovereigns.

Courts have adopted fundamental rules and principles that give guidelines and rules pertaining to the interpretation of written documents such as treaties. These rules and principles are known as "canons of construction." In consideration of any treaty or case, a court must take into consideration and decide in favor of Indian rights, when reviewing a treaty, case, or law.

Congress has plenary power; that is, Congress has given itself absolute power. Pursuant to this plenary power, Congress can enact, amend, dissolve, or abrogate rights established by treaty or other documents. In a very basic sense, Congress can do anything it chooses because of this plenary power (U.S. Const., art. 1, sec. 8, clause 3).

1532–1828: *Treaty-making, Discovery, and Conquest*

During the seventeenth century, European explorers traditionally applied the laws of discovery and conquest when finding new lands. In simple terms, this meant that if you planted your flag in foreign soil or won a battle and then planted the flag, you claimed the land for your government. Because these new lands located in the Western Hemisphere were already occupied by Native Americans, and a war could not be rationalized, theologians such as Francisco de Victoria asserted that tribes had sovereign status equal to colonial governments; thus, tribes could own and occupy land (Doctrine of Discovery). Treaties would be needed to resolve boundary disputes and acquire land from tribes (Wheaton 1855).

The first treaty signed between the U.S. government and a Native American tribe was in 1778. Since then, well over six hundred treaties have been made and signed between the U.S. government and tribes. It's interesting to think about the treaty process. In the art of treaty making, the government would send the military to "negotiate" with the tribes (Myers 2002). Both sides came from totally different cultures, spoke different languages, and had a completely different system of government. Today, it could be compared to having an army, complete with tanks and other heavy armament in tow, show up on your doorstep. Rather intimidating? Even though the language was not understood, tribal leaders signed where requested on the dotted line, in most cases not knowing what they were signing or the significance of the agreement. Fortunately, governmental intimidation was not constant across all treaty making between tribes, as some early treaties were entered into by the United States from a position of some weakness and perceived need, and others were made without military intimidation. A lack of consistency by the U.S. government was evident in most treaty making throughout history.

1828–1887: Removal and Relocation

During this time period, the U.S. government and states determined that they needed more land as people moved west to settle. Removal of Native people from their aboriginal land was seen as a viable option, and many tribes were removed to the "Indian Territory," now known to us as Oklahoma (Tsosie 2001). People from different tribes would be moved by the federal government to one location or reservation, where they were then regarded by the government as one tribe, even though they had distinct differences. The Five Civilized Tribes, comprised of the Cherokee, Choctaw, Chickasaw, Seminole, and Cree, are an example of this mass removal, also known as the "Trail of Tears" (Hill 2005). Many people were forced to walk hundreds of miles to the "Indian Territory," and thousands died along the trip. The Navajo people in Arizona were forced to walk to the New Mexico Territory, known as the "Long Walk." By the time tribes were allowed to return to their aboriginal land, some had been reduced considerably in size, due to illness and death resulting from the removal process. Congress did not recognize some groups as tribes and used its plenary, or absolute, power to create new tribes, when in fact these groups of people were composed of individuals from many tribes. In 1871, Congress ended treaty making and provided that the U.S. government would protect all rights outlined under existing treaties; however, the federal government has continued to negotiate with tribes in much the same manner through intergovernmental agreements, executive orders, and statutes.

1887–1928: Allotment and Assimilation

In 1887, Congress determined that tribes owned way too much land, because this land ownership was impeding growth and settlement in the western states and territories. Therefore, the General Allotment Act, also known as the Dawes Act, was passed. Tribal land was significantly reduced, from approximately 138 million acres to 48 million acres. The U.S. government would allot parcels of land to individual tribal members or families. Each family head would be allotted 160 acres, and each single person over eighteen years of age would be allotted 80 acres. Most of this land was dry and unsuitable for farming. A result of allotment was the creation of a checkerboard of tribal, private, and government land, thus increasing confusion relating to jurisdiction. Some of this checkerboard land pattern exists today.

In 1907, those tribes in the "Indian Territory" were required to move again, as Oklahoma was to become a state. The land that was allotted during this period was to be held in trust, exempt from state tax and laws for a period of twenty-five years. Congress could extend or shorten this time period. Allotment of land was the first step in assimilating Indians into the larger, dominant society. Other steps included the suppression of Native religious activities and construction of boarding schools, built by the federal government. Native children were sent away to these schools, their hair was cut, and they were taught the ways of the dominant society. By using the authority granted to them by Congress, the Bureau of Indian

Affairs appointed a local superintendent to govern most reservations, and tribal government authority was discouraged. Native people were required to abandon their languages, traditional customs, and dress.

Following the passage of the Major Crimes Act of 1885, the federal government took jurisdiction from the tribes, as it pertained to certain crimes. In 1924, all Indians were made U.S. citizens, in an effort to further assimilate tribal people. This can be found in the Indian Citizenship Act of 1924. In 1928, the Meriam Report began significant changes in Indian affairs. The report, prepared by the Brookings Institution, illustrated the horrible living conditions on most reservations and outlined the need for additional funding and an end to the allotment policy. The Meriam Report encouraged tribal self-government.

1928–1945: Indian Reorganization Act and Self-Government

In 1934, the Indian Reorganization Act (IRA), also known as the Wheeler-Howard Act, was passed by Congress. It encouraged tribes to adopt a government structure, elect officials, adopt constitutions, form federally chartered corporations, and negotiate with federal, state, and local governments. Many tribes rejected the act, as it was viewed as another assimilation tactic (Myers 2002). Traditional tribal leaders, for example, were excluded from this process on some reservations. One positive outcome of the IRA was that it provided a framework for tribes to exercise political authority. The act was the first step in the creation of tribal courts, law enforcement, and tribal legislative bodies. Even today, this act is seen as both benefiting tribes and challenging tribal sovereignty, as the federal government outlined how tribes will govern themselves. To this point in the chapter, we have clearly seen that federal intervention in Indian affairs has had many shortcomings, all of which have had a direct effect on Native people.

1945–1961: Termination

Prior to 1946, tribes had no forum in which to sue the federal government when they believed that actions or lack of action on the part of the federal government was detrimental to their welfare. In 1946 Congress created the Indian Claims Commission to hear and decide causes of action originating prior to its creation. It was a very time-consuming process; tribes had to have the permission from the Secretary of the Interior, and only money damages were available. The Indian Claims Commission Act did not provide for recovery of land lost by tribes, and awards were paid to individual tribal members. In 1978, cases not completed by the Indian Claims Commission were transferred to the U.S. Court of Claims, which became the U.S. Court of Federal Claims in 1993. Many of the 617 original claims have still not been resolved (Myers 2002).

In 1953 House Concurrent Resolution 108, also known as HCR108, ended Congress's special relationship with Indian tribes. Termination was seen as an "experiment" by the federal government and completely changed the special relationship between the federal government and a select number of tribes. Some tribes were no longer recognized by the federal government as tribes and therefore lost federal funding and support. Those tribes included in the "experiment" are:

Alabama and Coushatta Tribes of Texas
Catawba Indian Tribe of South Carolina
Klamath, Modoc, and Yahooskin Band of Snake Indians, Oregon
Ponca Tribe of Nebraska
Mixed Blood Ute Indians of Unitah and Ouray-Utah
40 California Indian Rancherias
Western Oregon Indians, including Confederated Tribes of Siletz Indians, Confederated Tribes of the Grand Ronde Community, and Cow Creek Band of Umpqua
Menominee Tribe of Wisconsin
Ottawa Tribe of Oklahoma
Peoria Tribe of Oklahoma
Wyandotte Tribe of Oklahoma
Paiute Indian Tribe of Utah

Ten of the above tribes have since been restored to federal status. During the termination period, tribal land was sold to third parties, special federal programs were discontinued, state legislative jurisdiction was imposed, exemption from state taxing authority was ended, and state judicial authority was imposed except in the area of hunting and fishing rights. The tribal governments of the listed tribes were abolished, because the tribes were no longer recognized as government entities. This ended tribal sovereignty for the tribes in the "experiment."

In 1953, Public Law 280 permitted the state governments to assume both civil and criminal jurisdiction over Indians. This included the following states: California, Minnesota, Nebraska, Oregon, Wisconsin, and Alaska. The federal government did not provide for funding to the states that adopted PL 280. This meant that the entire cost of providing those services previously supplied by the federal government was now the responsibility of the states. The states did not have the fiscal resources to increase services; therefore, services to tribes were less than adequate. The impact of termination on the affected tribes was overwhelming. It was a huge setback, because tribes lost their identities, governments, and federal funding. States took control of tribal lands, whether by taxation or through seizure and sale.

Termination was seen by some as "emancipation," because it would "free" Indians from the control of the Bureau of Indian Affairs. Termination, however, extinguished status and rights of tribes without their consent or input. Today, many Public Law 280 states are attempting to return jurisdiction to the tribes. The main reason for this change in policy is money. States don't want the economic burden of providing services to tribes.

1961–Present: Self-Determination

During the civil rights movement of the 1960s, federal Indian law saw reform. The Indian Civil Rights Act (ICRA) of 1968 (25 U.S.C. 1301–1303) is an outstanding example of this reform. This act afforded protections found in the U.S. Bill of Rights to tribal members from tribal government actions. The Constitution does not impose the Bill of Rights on tribes. The ICRA is similar to the Bill of Rights with two exceptions: the right to counsel for the defense is "at his/her own expense," due to the varied fiscal resources available to each tribe, and there is no separation of church and state from tribal government. This is due to traditional religious beliefs being an important part of all proceedings. The ICRA also allowed states that had assumed Public Law 280 jurisdiction to transfer jurisdiction back to the tribes and federal government.

In 1970, President Richard Nixon officially rejected termination as a national policy and stated to Congress that the policy of termination was "morally and legally unacceptable."

In 1975, the Indian Self-Determination and Education Assistance Act (25 U.S.C. 450 et seq.) directed the secretary of the interior to contract with the tribes to "plan, conduct and administer programs." One example would be Public Law 638, which allows tribes to contract with outside vendors for services normally provided by the federal government. Some tribes used these funds to establish and develop their own law enforcement agencies instead of relying upon the Bureau of Indian Affairs to provide law enforcement services. During his term in office, President Clinton reinforced this concept in a memorandum for the heads of executive departments and agencies, dated May 3, 1994, and it has continued with President George W. Bush, in a press release (dated November 19, 2001) concerning the National American Heritage Month proclamation.

U.S. Supreme Court Decisions

When engaged in the study of jurisdiction, it is important to review the significance of landmark U.S. Supreme Court decisions. A number of these decisions have altered the way laws are applied in Indian country. Law enforcement, prosecutors, and courts within Indian country, and those bordering Indian country, must have a good working knowledge of these decisions and how they apply to the law in given situations. The Marshall Trilogy set the stage for federal Indian law. Chief Justice John Marshall in 1823, 1831, and 1832 delivered opinions from the U.S. Supreme Court that ultimately changed the focus of federal policy as it relates to Indian law. The following are brief summaries of each case:

Johnson v. M'Intosh, *21 U.S. (8 Wheat) 543 (1823)*

Chief Justice Marshall held that as the successor to England, the original discoverer of the area in question, the United States had acquired the preemptive right to procure Indian land by purchase or conquest according to the Doctrine of Discovery; thus, title obtained through a direct grant by an Indian tribe to a private individual could not prevail against title obtained by means of a patent of land acquired by the government from the same tribe. The government must be involved in all land exchanges involving Indians.

Cherokee Nation v. Georgia, *30 U.S. (5 Pet.) 1 (1831)*

The Cherokee Tribe is a state in the sense that it is a "distinct political society," but it is not a foreign state within the meaning of Article III of the Constitution. It is more like a "domestic dependent nation," with the relation of the tribe to the federal government like that of a "ward to a guardian."

Worcester v. Georgia, *30 U.S. (6 Pet.) 515 (1832)*

State law could not interfere with the relations established between the federal government and the tribes, and attempts to do so were "repugnant." Tribes, as nations, were "claiming and receiving the protections of a more powerful nation."

A summary of other major cases that have had a significant impact on justice issues involving Indian country follows.

Ex parte Crow Dog (1883)

Prior to the Crow Dog case, Indian tribes had exclusive jurisdiction over all crimes involving Indians in Indian country. Details of the Crow Dog case involve the murder of one Sioux tribal member by another Sioux tribal member. In the application of traditional Indian justice, the tribe involved the families of both the victim and the offender. Restitution, not revenge, was the goal of the tribe. All parties agreed to a payment of six hundred dollars, eight horses, and a blanket as restitution for the murder. The Bureau of Indian Affairs became involved, following political pressure from non-Natives, who claimed the punishment did not fit the crime.

Subsequently, Crow Dog was tried in a non-Native court, convicted, and sentenced to death. As a result of public outcry, the Major Crimes Act (18 U.S.C. 1153) was passed by Congress in 1885. This act took jurisdiction from the tribes in selected major crimes, including murder, and placed jurisdiction with the federal government.

Major Crimes Act (18 U.S.C. 1153, 1885): Offenses Committed within Indian Country

The most important part of this piece of legislation reads:

(a) Any Indian who commits against the person or property of another Indian or other person any of the following offenses, namely, murder, manslaughter, kidnapping, maiming, a felony under chapter 109A (U.S.C. 224 et seq.) (sexual abuse), incest, assault with intent to commit murder, assault with a dangerous weapon, assault resulting in serious bodily injury, arson, burglary, robbery, and a felony under Section 661 of this title within the Indian country, shall be subject to the same law and penalties as all other persons committing any of the above offenses, within the exclusive jurisdiction of the United States.

(b) Any offense referred to in subsection (a) of this section that is not defined and punished by Federal law in force within the exclusive jurisdiction of the United States shall be defined and punished in accordance with the laws of the State in which such offense was committed as are in force at the time of such offense.

Other crimes were added later, including assault against an individual under sixteen years of age, kidnapping, and felony theft.

United States v. Wheeler, *435 U.S. 313 (1978)*

This U.S. Supreme Court decision addresses the constitutionality of double jeopardy when both the federal government and tribes prosecute a tribal member for the same crime. The Supreme Court ruled that the tribes and federal government are separate sovereigns and have concurrent criminal jurisdiction. The double jeopardy protections afforded by the U.S. Constitution do not apply.

Oliphant v. Suquamish Indian Tribe, *435 U.S. 191 (1978)*

In the Oliphant case, the U.S. Supreme Court held that tribes do not have jurisdiction to prosecute non-Indians in tribal court. Mark Oliphant had been arrested by Port Madison tribal police for resisting arrest and assaulting a police officer, and was subsequently brought to trial in tribal court on these charges. The Oliphant conviction was overturned, as he was not an Indian. This decision, therefore, challenges sovereignty and tribal jurisdiction. Following the Oliphant case, many tribes decriminalized some offenses to fill the void in dealing with the conduct of non-Indians in Indian country. An example of this would be game violations, involving the illegal taking of wildlife in Indian country. The tribe's interests may be served best by the tribe filing a lawsuit against the offender, when the offender is a non-Native. This would explain why at times, criminal law and civil law seem to blend in tribal court situations.

Duro v. Reina, *495 U.S. 676 (1990)*

Following the restrictions placed on tribal courts as a result of the Oliphant case in 1978, the U.S. Supreme Court further limited tribal court jurisdiction in 1990 when ruling on a case involving a nontribal-member Indian offender. Albert Duro, an enrolled member of the Torres-Martinez Band of Cahuilla Mission Indians from California, and a fourteen-year-old Gila River Indian tribal member were both visiting the Salt River Pima-Maricopa Community, located in southern Arizona. Albert Duro shot and killed the fourteen-year-old boy. Salt River tribal police arrested Duro on a tribal violation of discharging a firearm. The Supreme Court ruled that the Salt River tribe had no authority to hold Duro, as he was not a tribal member. The court ruled that the definition of "Indian" was for use in federal jurisdiction and did not apply to the tribes. The Supreme Court held that tribal courts had no criminal jurisdiction over Indians who are members of other tribes. Later in 1990, Congress overturned the Duro decision through an amendment to the Indian Civil Rights Act. This is known as the "Duro Fix." Congress recognized the inherent authority of tribes to exercise criminal jurisdiction over all Indians who commit crimes within their borders.

Nevada, et al. v. Hicks, et al. *No. 99–1994 533 U.S. 353 (2001)*

The *Nevada v. Hicks* case is probably one of the most conflicting rulings by the Supreme Court to date. The case involves Floyd Hicks, who is a member of the Fallon Paiute-Shoshone of western Nevada. A Nevada

State Game Officer suspected Hicks of illegally killing and possessing a California bighorn sheep, a protected species. The sheep had allegedly been killed off the reservation. A Paiute-Shoshone tribal officer had seen a sheep's head at Hicks's residence, located on the reservation. The information was given to the state officer, and a search warrant was obtained through a tribal court. The state officer, accompanied by the tribal officer, went to Hicks's home and conducted a search. No contraband was located. The state officer obtained a second warrant at a later date, and a subsequent tribal search warrant was obtained by the state officer through the tribal officer and tribal court. A search of the home was conducted, with negative results. Floyd Hicks filed a civil rights claim in federal court against the state of Nevada, the Fallon Paiute-Shoshone Tribe, and each officer involved. The resulting court ruling involving the circumstances in this case allowed for both a broad and a narrow interpretation. The court found that tribal authority to regulate state officers in executing processes related to the off-reservation violation of state laws is not essential to tribal self-government. The court further ruled that Congress has not stripped the states of their inherent jurisdiction on reservations with regard to off-reservation violations of the law. The ruling in this case is in direct conflict with the concept of tribal sovereignty, whereas it suggests that a warrant from a state court may be served in Indian country against a tribal member, without tribal permission.

United States v. Patch, *cert. 118 S.CT. 445 (1997)*

State, county, or municipal officers may stop a moving vehicle in Indian country when a violation has occurred, whether or not the officer has jurisdiction, to ascertain the race of the alleged violator. If the officer lacks jurisdiction, he may detain the person and turn the person over to tribal authorities. Many state, county, and municipal law enforcement officers travel through Indian country or work along state highways, county roads, or city streets that border or pass through Indian country.

Although many other cases involving crimes in Indian country have gone before the U.S. Supreme Court, these cases give the basic framework for the study of criminal jurisdiction. The lack of consistency in court rulings involving the application of criminal law in Indian country may never be fully understood; however, it is recommended that each case summarized above be read in its entirety. Each seated U.S. Supreme Court has had its own political personality over the years, and each has viewed Indian policy in a very different fashion, redefining previous court rulings.

Indian Country as defined in 18 U.S.C. 1151

Congress set forth its definition of Indian country in 18 U.S.C. 1151 as follows:

(a) all land within the limits of any Indian reservation under the jurisdiction of the United States Government, notwithstanding the issuance of any patent, and, including rights-of-way running through the reservation,

(b) all dependent Indian communities within the borders of the United States, whether within the original or subsequently acquired territory thereof, and whether within or without the limits of a state, and

(c) all Indian allotments, the Indian titles to which have not been extinguished, including rights-of-way running through the same.

To be considered Indian country, the land must have been set aside by the federal government for use by the tribes, and the lands must be under federal superintendence.

Determining Criminal Jurisdiction

The first question we must ask when determining jurisdiction is, Where did the crime occur? Did the crime occur in Indian country? If the crime was committed outside Indian country, the state court has jurisdiction. If the crime was committed in Indian country, we must ask, What is the race of the victim and that of the offender? If both victim and offender are non-Indians, the state court has jurisdiction (*United States v. McBratney* [1881]). If both the victim and offender are Indians, tribal court has jurisdiction, except in the case of crimes enumerated in the Major Crimes Act, whereby the tribe and federal government share jurisdiction, or as Public Law 280 states, where the state would have exclusive jurisdiction. We must ask, What is the crime? (Tribal codes are limited to misdemeanors and fines of not more than $5,000, and not more than one year in jail [18 U.S.C. 1153]). If either the victim or the offender is an Indian and the other party is a non-Indian, the federal government has jurisdiction. The U.S. Attorney's Office will sometimes decline criminal prosecution against non-Indian offenders in Indian country. This may be attributed to lack of knowledge relating to specific jurisdiction at the time of the initial investigation, apathy, time involved in case preparation, remote location of tribal lands, prosecutorial costs, or the inability to locate and interview witnesses. This lack of criminal prosecution even involves major crimes. Victims and their families may never see justice served, and violators may be allowed to reoffend. An example of this result is outlined earlier in this chapter.

The key to effectively addressing jurisdictional issues is cooperation. Tribal and nontribal agencies are developing strong working relationships in conducting investigations and prosecutions in Indian country, as described in the chapter by Eileen Luna-Firebaugh. Many tribal governments have entered into intergovernmental agreements, memorandums of understanding, memorandums of agreement, or mutual aid agreements, with state, county, and municipal agencies. State agencies are familiarizing their officers with the law as it relates to tribal nations, and many tribal officers are familiar with state law. Some Native tribes require that their officers hold police certification from the tribe, state, and federal government, so that they can take enforcement action regardless of jurisdiction. State, county, and municipal officers are receiving cross-tribal certification as well, allowing them to legally assist tribal authorities. While great strides have been made in recent years to improve the understanding of criminal jurisdiction in Indian country, much work is left unfinished.

Residents, law enforcement authorities, and political leaders, both Native and non-Native, are learning that crime has no boundaries. They continue to work together to find innovative solutions to address jurisdictional issues. Cross-deputization of Native and non-Native officers has proven effective in some locations. Prosecutors have begun to communicate, and joint advisory committees with representation from tribal nations, state, local, and federal organizations are sharing information relating to crime trends, crime prevention, victims services, and mutual obligations. One area that remains a challenge is the sharing of information between Native nations and states, as it relates to sexual offenders, domestic violence, criminal histories, and motor vehicle violations. Although the state crime information is available via the National Crime Information Center computer, most states do not allow for the entry of information pertaining to tribal offenses.

TABLE 8.1 Criminal Jurisdiction in Indian Country

Offender	Victim	Jurisdiction
Indian	Indian	Federal jurisdiction for felonies listed in the Major Crimes Act (18 U.S.C. 1153); tribal jurisdiction for misdemeanors; no jurisdiction for felonies not listed in 1153.
Indian	Non-Indian	Federal jurisdiction for felonies listed in 18 U.S.C. 1153 and for other felonies and misdemeanors not listed in 1153, including assimilative crimes, unless the tribe has already punished the offender; tribal jurisdiction for misdemeanors.
Non-Indian	Indian	Federal jurisdiction for both felonies and misdemeanors, including assimilative crimes.
Non-Indian	Non-Indian	State jurisdiction for both felonies and misdemeanors.
Indian	Victimless Crime	Primary jurisdiction to the tribe; some cases may also have federal jurisdiction.
Non-Indian	Victimless Crime	Primary jurisdiction to the state; federal jurisdiction in some cases.

Tribal courts have criminal jurisdiction over any Indian who commits any offense prohibited by tribal code, law, or ordinance. Federal courts have jurisdiction over serious offenses committed within Indian country, including all of the offenses listed in the Major Crimes Act, along with other felonies included in provisions within the U.S. Code. A crime committed in Indian country must have Indian involvement to be eligible for prosecution by the federal government. State courts have jurisdiction over crimes committed within Indian country where there is no Indian involvement. It is important to remember that federal crimes such as bank robbery, no matter who the offender is, or the location, will be prosecuted by the federal government. Table 8.1 will assist in determining criminal jurisdiction in Indian country.

While I did not go into specific detail, it is important to know that the Assimilative Crimes Act (1948) gives federal and tribal agencies the authority to use state statutes when needed (18 U.S.C. 13). In simple terms, tribal or state authorities can use state law when tribal or federal law does not exist as it relates to criminal conduct. This incorporates (assimilates or changes) state law into federal law. It should also be noted that Public Law 280 states, the state has criminal jurisdiction in Indian country.

Although these guidelines are in use by criminal justice agencies today, there are still many gray areas regarding jurisdiction in Indian country. Invariably, jurisdiction and the constitutionality of legal application will continue to be challenged in courts throughout the United States. The unique relationship between the federal government and tribal governments is continually challenged, and redefinition is attempted by those wishing to gain.

The 1994 Crime Act, also known as the Violent Crime Control and Law Enforcement Act of 1994, expanded federal criminal jurisdiction in Indian country in such areas as guns, violent juveniles, drugs, and domestic violence. Under the Indian Gaming Regulatory Act, the Federal Bureau of Investigation has jurisdiction over any criminal act directly related to casino gaming. The FBI also investigates civil rights violations, environmental crimes, public corruption, and government fraud occurring in "Indian country" (Federal Bureau of Investigation 2006).

Jurisdiction in Indian country will continue to be a challenge to those charged with the responsibility of enforcing laws, prosecuting criminal offenses, and protecting the lives of those residing within tribal boundaries. Education, cooperation, and determination throughout the criminal justice community are essential ingredients to success. The courts must protect tribal sovereignty.

Indian Gaming Issues

While criminal jurisdiction is the focus of this chapter, it would be incomplete without the discussion of Indian gaming issues. Many Native tribes throughout the United States operate gaming facilities as a direct result of the Indian Gaming Regulatory Act (IGRA) of 1988. In some cases, gaming is the sole source of economic development for the tribes and is relied upon to provide much-needed improvement in tribal services. The IGRA is a direct result of the following U.S. Supreme Court case.

California v. Cabazon Band of Mission Indians, 480 U.S. 202 (1987)

The Cabazon Band of Mission Indians ran a bingo operation on tribal land in California. It should be noted that California is a PL 280 state. The state did not want the Cabazon tribe to conduct gaming, probably because the state of California was not profiting from the operation. In an effort to stop the bingo operation, California attempted to use the authority from Public Law 280 to stop the operation based on state criminal law (California penal code). California generally permitted other gaming, including horseracing, so that gaming was not entirely prohibited in California but was regulated by the state. In the attempt to use criminal law to cease the bingo operation, the case ended up in the U.S. Supreme Court.

The U.S. Supreme Court explained that a state could enforce its criminal laws on reservations only if the state has Public Law 280 jurisdiction. For Public Law 280 to apply, the conduct must be criminally prohibited (criminal/prohibitory) in the state and against public policy, and not generally permitted but regulated (civil/regulatory). If an act is regulated by the state, then the state cannot use its criminal authority under PL 280. The "Cabazon test" was thus developed, and states must allow Indian gaming if gaming is generally allowed with regulation.

Indian Gaming Regulatory Act of 1988, 25 U.S.C. 2701 et seq.

One year after the *Cabazon* case, the IGRA was signed into law. The IGRA is considered a compromise between states and tribes, as it created a framework for regulation by states of Indian gaming. The IGRA classified gaming into three areas.

Class I gaming is classified as social games, traditional Indian games, or ceremonial gaming, and is subject to tribal regulatory jurisdiction.

Class II gaming includes games such as bingo, lotto, pull tabs, punch boards and non-banking games as long as they are not prohibited by the state. Class II gaming falls under tribal regulation with extensive oversight by the National Indian Gaming Commission.

Class III gaming includes all other games, including full casinos and banking games. Class III gaming is legal on Indian lands only if such activities are conducted pursuant to a tribal ordinance that permits such gaming; is located in a state that permits such gaming for purpose by any person, organization, or entity; and is conducted in conformance with a tribal-state compact.

There has been much litigation over whether the states have negotiated these compacts in good faith. There have been recent U.S. Supreme Court decisions, such as in *Seminole Tribe of Florida v. Florida*, 513 U.S. (1995), that have attempted to address the compacting procedures; however, many issues are yet unresolved. Indian gaming is vulnerable, as various interests will continue to debate legalities. Tribes need to work together to protect gaming, as it is a very viable economic resource.

References

Federal Bureau of Investigation. 2006. Statement regarding Indian Country jurisdiction. http://www.fbi.gov.

Hill, Sarah. 2005. *Cherokee removal: Forts along the Georgia Trail of Tears.* Washington, DC: U.S. Department of the Interior.

Marshall, John, Chief Justice for the U.S. Supreme Court. U.S. Supreme Court opinions: *Johnson v. M'Intosh*, 21 U.S. (8 Wheat) 543 (1832); *Cherokee Nation v. Georgia*, 30 U.S. (5Pet.) 1 (1831); *Worcester v. Georgia*, 31 U.S. (6Pet.) 515 (1832).

Myers, Joseph. 2002. *Critical issues in federal Indian law.* Washington, DC: National Indian Justice Center.

Tsosie, Rebecca. 2001. Indian Country law enforcement: Issues and answers. Sixteenth Annual Crime in Arizona Conference, Phoenix.

Wheaton, Henry. 1855. *Elements of international law.* 6th ed. Boston: Little Brown.

Legislation

Assimilative Crimes Act, 18 U.S.C. 13 (1948).
California Penal Code (California State Criminal Law).

Crime Act (1994) (see *Violent Crime and Law Enforcement Act* of 1994, Public Law 103–322, 108 Stat. 1796, codified as amended in sections of U.S. Code, Titles 18, 21, 28, 42).

Doctrine of Discovery, 21 U.S. (8 Wheat) 543, 5 L.Ed. (1823).

General Allotment Act, 24 Stat. 388, ch. 119, 25 U.S.C.A. 331 (1887) (*Dawes Act*).

House Concurrent Resolution 108 (Termination) 1953.

Indian Citizenship Act of 1924, 43 Stat. 253, ante, 420.

Indian Reorganization Act of 1934 (*Wheeler Howard Act*).

Indian Claims Commission Act of 1946, 60 Stat. 1049, 23 U.S.C. 70.

Indian Civil Rights Act of 1968, 25 U.S.C. 1301–03.

Indian Gaming Regulatory Act of 1988, 25 U.S.C. 2701 et seq.

Indian Self-Determination and Education Assistance Act of 1975, 25 U.S.C. 450 et seq.

Major Crimes Act, 18 U.S.C. 1153 (1885).

Public Law 83–280, (1953).

Public Law 93–638, (see the *Indian Self-Determination and Education Assistance Act* of 1975).

United States Code, Title 18.

United States Constitution.

Supreme Court Cases

California v. Cabazon Band of Mission Indians, 480 U.S. 202 (1987).

Duro v. Reina, 495 U.S. 676 (1990).

Ex parte Crow Dog, 109 U.S. 556, 3 S. Ct. 396, 27 L.Ed., 1030 (1883).

Nevada v. Hicks, 533 U.S. 353 (2001).

Oliphant v. Suquamish Indian Tribe, 435 U.S. 191 (1978).

Seminole Tribe of Florida v. Florida, 513 U.S. (1995).

United States v. McBratney, 104 U.S. 621, 14 Otto 621, 26 L.Ed., 869 (1881).

United States v. Patch, 114 fed. 3rd 131, 9th circuit, Arizona (1997).

United States v. Wheeler, 435 U.S. 313 (1978).

More than Just a Red Light in Your Rearview Mirror

Eileen Luna-Firebaugh

WHAT DOES it mean to you and to Indian country when you are stopped by a tribal police officer on Indian land? Is it going to mean simply a different kind of ticket? Or rather, is it a bold assertion of sovereignty, of the right of an Indian nation to make and enforce its own laws? In the field of law enforcement services, there is nothing that holds more promise than tribal policing. But the role of tribal police, and the rights of Indian nations to establish tribal police, is also confusing to many. This chapter addresses this confusion.

Tribal police agencies assert tribal sovereignty in very real ways. They implement laws and rules promulgated by Indian nations, hold wrongdoers accountable, and assert tribal jurisdiction over Indian land. One fundamental premise is advanced: that through the creation of empowered and accountable tribal justice systems, tribes can seize the opportunity to advance their sovereignty, their right to self-government, and improve the lives of tribal members. So let's look at the approaches tribal governments are taking to expand sovereignty through the development and implementation of tribal police departments.

Tribal Sovereignty as It Relates to Tribal Policing

At its most basic level, tribal sovereignty is simply the right of an Indian nation to govern itself, to make and enforce its own laws. Through the negotiation of treaties with American Indian nations, and through subsequent legal rulings and legislation, the United States very early on in its history recognized the inherent sovereignty and right to self-rule of tribal governments.[1] Other rulings firmly asserted that the sovereignty and powers of self-government that American Indian tribal governments possess were not granted to the tribes by the Constitution, but rather were retained powers that pre-dated the U.S. Constitution.[2]

Through this power of internal self-government, Indian nations have the legal authority to create and enforce civil and criminal codes,[3] and to regulate conduct on their lands. Tribal territorial jurisdiction encompasses what is known as "Indian country," as defined in 18 U.S.C.A. sec. 1151. Indian country includes: (1) all land within the limits of any federal Indian reservation, (2) all dependent Indian communities, and (3) all Indian allotments.

Rarely do states have enforcement authority in Indian country. In most states this tribal power over Indian lands is shared only with the federal government. Tribal police departments are an essential component of this concept of tribal sovereignty. Tribal police departments stand for the premise that the rule of law prevails on tribal land, and that tribes have the right and responsibility to enforce their laws for their citizens.

A tribal police department serves as a declaration that the tribe intends to render justice in a manner understandable to and supported by the tribal community. Through the development and adherence to rules and procedures and codes of conduct that are understandable to non-Indian law enforcement, tribal police engender the support of non-Indian justice organizations and communities as well. This helps to create an environment where tribal and non-Indian communities can work together harmoniously, and together achieve more than either could do alone.

The expansion of sovereignty is based in part on *Wheeler v. United States*.[4] In *Wheeler* the court held that tribes remain a separate people, with the power of regulating their internal and social relations. The court held that the Navajo tribe had never given up the sovereign power to punish tribal offenders and that therefore the tribal exercise of that power is the continued exercise of retained tribal sovereignty.

While the definition of tribal sovereignty and self-determination has evolved over the years, there has been one overriding construct that tribal governments have a recognized authority to make their own laws, and to enforce them against all Indians and, in some instances, against non-Indians who reside or work upon tribal lands.

This self-governance authority is essentially a police power, which empowers and enables tribal police officials to control misdeeds on tribal lands. This has the immediate effect of focusing tribal attention on the reduction of crime, while also expanding tribal sovereignty.

There is a difference between "de jure" sovereignty, that which comes from the courts and legislation, and "de facto" sovereignty, that which arises from the assertion of rights through the actions of tribal governments (Cornell and Kalt 1992).[5] Tribal police owe their development to both of these concepts.

The recent growth in tribal police departments is a result of the need of tribal governments to provide services to tribal citizens and reservation residents in the face of serious cutbacks in the provision of BIA services. The tribes have developed and implemented tribal police departments through the allocation of federal funding, predominantly through the Indian Self-Determination and Education Assistance Act of 1975 (Public Law 93–638)[6] and the Tribal Self-Governance Act of 1994 (Public Law 103–413).[7] Federal funding to tribal police departments has also been made available through Community Oriented Policing Services (COPS) grants (Reno 1995).

These federal funding sources have been invaluable in assisting tribes to develop, implement, and sustain tribal police departments. They have also served as federal recognition that the tribes can responsibly and accountably conduct law enforcement for themselves.

Policing in Indian Country

Prior to colonization of the North American continent and even until the late 1700s, the keeping of order in Indian country was the duty of clans or specially designated societies. Often clans were responsible for the conduct of their members. In other instances, military or warrior societies were entrusted with this responsibility for the good of the whole tribe. The clan or society was not only responsible for law enforcement but also for the form that such law enforcement would take. Subsequent to colonization, and with the expansion of the frontier, the federal government took more and more of a role, and traditional modes of tribal policing largely disappeared.

Policing during the Reservation Period

By 1880, two-thirds of the reservations in the United States had Indian police forces under the auspices of the federal government (Tate 1977).

By 1890, federal Indian police forces were to be found at virtually all reservation agencies (Hagan 1966). These police forces varied in size from two members to forty-three (Hagan 1966). Over time, the federal government centralized Indian policing, requiring that all Indian police become assimilated and follow procedures developed in Washington, rather than in the local areas. Members of the federal Indian police forces were generally identified as "progressives" rather than "traditionals." They were expected to set an example for their tribes by wearing modern clothing, cutting their hair, and practicing monogamy. They were to be hardworking, to refrain from the use of alcohol, and to report on members of the tribe who were identified as falling below this standard (Etheridge 1975).

This ensured a degree of "civilization" as perceived by the federal government, and created the idea of the Indian police force as an "agent of civilization" (Hagan 1966).

With the official establishment of the Indian police, their duties were formalized. The police were charged with the curtailment of tribal chief prerogatives. They advanced the primacy of non-Indian law as the mode of operation, a function that provoked violent opposition from traditional Indian leaders. Indian police generally served as reservation handymen and assistants to the reservation agent. They cleaned irrigation ditches, killed beef cattle for the meat ration, took the census, built roads, and performed other duties as assigned by the agent (Hagan 1966).

They also acted as truant officers and thus took a lead role in seizing children and taking or returning them to government boarding schools, often against the wishes of their parents (Etheridge 1975).

The centralization of Indian police within the federal government had both good and bad results. Pay was standardized and, even though low initially, was raised incrementally. Uniforms were standardized and issued to police. Horses were made available, as was feed, although supplies were often scarce, and requisitions often denied.[8] While rifles were originally issued to Indian police, by 1882 rifles were no longer allowed.[9] This change was due to express fears of arming Indians with rifles. Revolvers were then issued to Indian police, leaving them significantly underarmed, in comparison with miscreants. It was not until the late 1890s that this policy was changed.

Non-Indians welcomed the use of Indian police to pacify and "civilize" Indian communities. However, these changes created an adversarial relationship between tribal citizens and Indian police that had not existed traditionally.

Indian police often drew the line at use of force against their communities. There are many examples of this unwillingness to act against clan and community. In 1879, when the entire Jicarilla Apache police force resigned rather than act against renegades of another band, it was a shock felt throughout the federal government (Hagan 1966).

The Dawes Act of 1887 (24 Stat. 388 et seq.), and the Curtis Act of 1898 (30 Stat. 497 et seq.) were hallmark pieces of legislation during the reservation period of the late 1800s and early 1900s. They were intended to ensure the demise of reservations in the United States. Through allotments and the extension of state authority over Indian country, most tribal courts and reservation-based law enforcement were disbanded. Courts of Indian Offenses and federal law enforcement advanced the jurisdiction of the Bureau of Indian Affairs over Indian life. However, while the reservation period saw the rapid decline of self-governance in Indian country, tribal sovereignty did not wholly disappear.

Federalization of Indian Police (1920–50)

As the nation's attention turned away from advancing the frontier, so did the concern regarding the state of Indian country. The numbers of Indian police dropped from 900 in 1880 to 660 in 1912. By 1925 this number had been reduced to 217. Throughout the 1930s and 1940s, the numbers of Indian police continued to slide, with the federal budget of 1948 allowing for only 45 Indian police officers nationwide (Etheridge 1975). With the massive reduction of law enforcement services in Indian country, incidents of crime began to rise.

Self-Determination (1960–present)

Finally, in the 1960s there was a reawakening of Indian self-determination. In 1963, more than 100 Indian police officers were added to the Bureau of Indian Affairs (BIA) payroll, and in 1969 the Indian Police Academy (IPA) was established (Luna 1998).

Through the exercise of the Indian Self-Determination and Education Assistance Act of 1975 (25 U.S.C.A. Sec. 450 et seq.) and the Indian

Self-Governance Act of 1994 (H.R. 4842), tribes began to take over certain law enforcement functions from the Bureau of Indian Affairs. Tribal police departments, accountable to the tribe rather than to the federal government, were created and expanded throughout Indian country. The role of the Bureau of Indian Affairs, Law Enforcement Services became one of support, rather than control.

During the final decade of the twentieth century, the number of tribal police departments grew. National studies determined that, since 1995, there had been a very rapid growth in tribally funded police departments. In 1995 there were 114 tribal police departments. In 2000 the Bureau of Justice Statistics reported that American Indian tribes operated 171 law enforcement agencies. A total of 2,303 full-time sworn officers were employed.

However, the July 2003 U.S. Civil Rights Commission report entitled *A Quiet Crisis*, found that spending still lagged. The commission found that per capita spending on law enforcement and justice systems in American Indian communities was roughly 60 percent of the national average. This remains true today, even though crime rates over the last ten years, particularly for violent crime, are significantly higher in Indian country than in the non-Indian community.

So who are these tribal police? According to a 2004 survey I conducted at the Indian Police Academy, approximately 70 percent of the IPA trainees have a high school diploma. About 2 percent have some college education, and some have vocational training. Approximately 18 percent are ex-military. Over 25 percent have family members with law enforcement service, and 10 percent have a family history of firefighting.

The incorporation of women into the ranks of tribal police has been of particular note (Luna 2002). In 2000, 14.8 percent of tribal police officers were women, which compared favorably with 13.5 percent in large non-Indian police departments (more than 100 sworn officers),[10] and 8.1 percent in small non-Indian police departments (under 100 sworn officers). In tribal law enforcement 15.2 percent of women officers held the rank of sergeant and above, a rate that exceeded their representation in tribal police departments overall. This percentage was markedly higher than the 9.6 percent of female supervisors and 7.3 percent of female command-level personnel in large non-Indian departments, and the 4.6 percent female supervisors and 3.4 female command-level personnel found in small non-Indian police departments. The advanced rank of women tribal police is a direct reflection of their qualifications for advanced training, and the openness of tribal police agencies and tribal communities to the role of women generally.

My survey also revealed that tribal police personnel see themselves as "the community" (Luna 1999). Tribal police tend to be very involved with their tribal communities and are often religious and cultural leaders. They view their job in law enforcement as a relationship with the tribe, as an extension of the community. They are responsive to the needs of the community and feel a level of responsibility to that community. In short, they see themselves and their departments in relationship to each other, not as separate. This is in stark contrast with mainstream justice, where most police tend to view themselves as crime fighters rather than as community problem solvers.

Obstacles to Effective Tribal Law Enforcement

Tribal police departments generally fit within the community-policing model but face unique problems. The provision of adequate services is complicated by a high attrition rate for personnel, fragmentation of jurisdiction and police service, and a widespread lack of training or up-to-date technology (Wakeling et al. 2001).

Tribal police face heightened crime rates and a lack of those resources that most mainstream police officers take for granted, that is, working patrol vehicles, functioning 911 systems, access to police radios, and unlimited phone service. They are often responsible for vast geographic distances. Pay rates and benefits are generally very low, which can result in a significant turnover of personnel. These problems create major obstacles for adequate tribal police service.

Many tribal police departments have difficulty receiving assistance from other law enforcement agencies when they need it. Most tribal police departments are small and very challenged. Often there is but one officer on shift at a time, and the area for which they may be responsible can be enormous. The ability to call on state or local law enforcement to assist in an emergency situation can literally mean the difference between life and death. In fact, tribal police officers die on duty at a rate that is four times that of mainstream law enforcement (Johnson 2000).

Mutual aid between types of police forces is conditioned upon state certification of officers, and state certification is conditioned upon federal- or state-approved training of officers. Unfortunately many tribal officers may not be eligible for state-sponsored Police Officer Standards and Training (POST) programs, due to a lack of a high school degree or a past criminal history, even if it was a misdemeanor. Thus many tribal police departments do not have mutual aid or cross-deputization agreements with other departments. For state certification to advance, training of tribal police officers is crucial.

Jurisdictional Issues

Issues of jurisdiction also complicate tribal justice. Personal jurisdiction requires that the tribe have jurisdiction over the perpetrator and/or the victim. Seventy percent of the violent crime experienced by American Indians is interracial, with the criminal perpetrator being white in 60 percent of the cases (Greenfeld and Smith 1999; Perry 2004).

This alone is a serious problem for tribal police and tribal courts, given that the ruling case in the field, *Oliphant v. Suquamish*, limits tribal personal jurisdiction over non-Indians.[11] Thus, a critical issue of personal jurisdiction for tribal governments is the extent to which they may enforce tribal laws against non-Indians living or working on their reservation.

In general, in the absence of federal statutes limiting it, tribal criminal jurisdiction over the Indian in Indian country is complete, inherent, and exclusive (Luna 2007). Most states have no criminal jurisdiction over Indians in Indian country, even if the Indian is not a tribal member of the prosecuting tribe. However, states have the jurisdiction to arrest and prosecute non-Indians for crimes committed in Indian country, just as they would on state land. The federal government, pursuant to the Major Crimes Act,[12] has the sole jurisdiction to prosecute fourteen enumerated felonies. Tribes may arrest and prosecute any misdemeanor and some major crimes, so long as the punishment for the individual crime does not exceed a fine of $5,000 or more than a year in jail. Some tribes are "stacking charges," so that they may incarcerate an Indian individual for more than a year. Other tribes, particularly those without tribal police or tribal courts, do not assert criminal jurisdiction over Indian wrongdoers, leaving this instead to federal agencies.

Tribal police are empowered to enforce all tribal laws against Indians, including both civil and regulatory laws, and may enforce banishment against non-Indians. Tribal police also have authority to investigate crimes committed by non-Indians, and to detain non-Indians until they can be transferred to state authorities.

Inside Indian country, tribal law enforcement has full authority to act, subject to the exercise of federal law. Outside Indian country, the right of tribal law enforcement to act is subject to state certification and/or the existence of mutual aid and cross-deputization agreements.

Tribal governments may act only in those areas dictated by their constitutions. Thus, if a tribe's constitution restricts criminal jurisdiction, the tribal police may not act, even if allowable under federal law.

The primary question for tribal law enforcement is how to address the critical need for law enforcement services while also developing the appropriate format and style of policing for Indian country. The decisions that must be made, the policies and protocols that must be developed, and the staff that must be recruited and trained are challenges that must be overcome if crime and criminality is to be reduced in Indian country.

Tribal Codes

Tribal sovereignty, or power of self-government, is generally exercised pursuant to tribal constitutions and law and order codes. Indian nations, given their power to make laws and regulations, have the authority to enforce those laws and codes. The establishment and implementation of a tribal justice system is an exemplary expression of this power of enforcement.

A code is a series of laws or statutes arranged by subject. Tribal police apply those laws or codes that have been adopted by the tribal government. However, given the challenges faced by many tribal governments, some have not adopted both criminal and civil codes. Often, tribal codes are simply adopted from surrounding tribes or from state codes. Tribal codes are often outdated, Anglo-oriented, and/or poorly reflective of tribal philosophy and culture. In addition, even where tribal government codes may be in place, many tribal police departments operate without written rules or protocols, thus leaving officers to guess about appropriate behavior in a given situation. Most tribal codes pertain only to actions committed on the reservation, although Hopi law, for example, makes it a crime to conduct religious services off-reservation for profit.

The Training of Tribal Police

Training is essential if tribal police are to be recognized by federal and state agencies as effective and competent, while also meeting the needs of tribal communities. The question is how best to accomplish training in a manner that does not bankrupt the tribe.

Training law enforcement personnel is a challenge that faces all police agencies. It is difficult to keep up with changes in technology and laws while also coping with the recruitment, hiring, and development of new personnel, and with the training of existing personnel for present assignments and for promotional opportunities. When these challenges are combined with other problems inherent in tribal policing, it is truly amazing that tribal police departments have grown and prospered. Tribal police departments have found ways to undertake the challenge to protect and serve, while retaining their cultural compatibility.

Training of tribal law enforcement is of different types. Some training is aimed at becoming state- or federal-certified. As I mentioned before, state-certified officers may be cross-deputized with surrounding agencies or with federal law enforcement, thus allowing them to act off-reservation or with non-Indian perpetrators. Other training is aimed at continuing education, necessary to retain certification, and/or to enhance an officer's professional knowledge and abilities.

Both state certification and continuing education can be done at a training site, at a training conference, or through video or Internet. Tribal-specific training is also done on site. This training develops knowledge and competency in tribal rules, regulations, protocols, codes, and ordinances. Finally, some tribes are encouraging tribal police officers to obtain formal education, at the university or community college level. Often, as with the Navajo Nation, formal education and promotional opportunities are intentionally linked.

Training new officers and maintaining and enhancing the training of existing officers are constant challenges. Because of high attrition, training of police personnel must be done in a manner that ensures that an officer does not leave the department without passing on the knowledge obtained. Thus, the development of written procedures and protocols, and an infrastructure of training personnel, is necessary to protect the body of essential knowledge.

If an officer is to be state-certified, he or she must complete a course of training at a state-certified academy or obtain a number of POST-certified mandatory continuing education credits. Some tribes take the shortcut of hiring officers who are already state-certified. Others require that all tribal officers attend state law enforcement academies. However, this raises a cultural/professional issue for some tribes, as they want their officers to adhere to tribal cultural values and modes of behavior, rather than being trained in the ways and values of law enforcement generally.

Some tribes deal with this issue by sending their officers to the sixteen-week Indian Police Academy (IPA), which awards federal certification. The IPA is the gold standard for tribal law enforcement. However, this course of study requires the officers to complete their training at the Federal Law Enforcement Training Center (FLETC) in Artesia, New Mexico. This is difficult for many tribes and officers, as the necessary time and resources can be barriers to training in many instances. An officer is in on-the-job status at full pay while in training at the IPA. A significant tribal financial expenditure is required, although the officer is not available for reservation police duties. Also, tribes often cannot spare the personnel for the time necessary to attend a law enforcement academy. Therefore, tribes will often conduct training in-house or will send officers to local training seminars on specific issues.

The training conducted by the IPA is different from that conducted by state and local police academies. Officers participating in this program reported that the differences included:

- An emphasis on wisdom, and the exercise of discretion in a manner that focused on Indian communities.
- An emphasis on information needed for day-to-day work, and a "hands-on" approach.
- A less stressful environment, resulting from tribal officers being trained together and the emphasis on Indian country issues.
- The fact that the trainers are Indian themselves, and are involved and knowledgeable about Indian country, made the training easier to understand and support.

Internal training can be excellent; however, neither the Indian Police Academy nor internal training is recognized by the states as meeting the requirements for state certification of police.

While culturally specific training is essential for Indian country, training differences have ramifications. Often tribal officers are not viewed as "regular police" by mainstream police officers. They may not be seen as having the level of skill or knowledge that a state-trained officer might have. They may be viewed as similar to security guards, rather than as "real" police. These attitudes can be overcome with the involvement of POST training personnel in the training of tribal police.

Conclusion

The provision of effective and responsible services to citizens is the job of any government. This is particularly the case where services may not be routinely or uniformly provided by other governmental structures. The concept of de facto sovereignty both allows for and encourages the development of tribal police.

The decision to develop and implement a tribal police department is an assertion of tribal sovereignty. But it isn't easy. Little research has been done on the effectiveness of tribal police in reducing crime in Indian country, so for many tribal governments this is a leap of faith. Tribal councils must be convinced of the necessity for such a system, in the face of competing priorities. The development of a tribal police department can be expensive. Tribal codes and rules of procedure must be written and passed through the political process. Tribal personnel must be hired and trained, and their pay and benefits should be enhanced.

So, what is the future of tribal justice? Research needs to be conducted to ascertain the effectiveness of tribally based criminal justice systems. However, even without this empirical information, it is clear that tribal justice systems, including tribal police departments, advance tribal sovereignty.

What, then, does it mean when you see that red light in your rearview mirror? It means the tribe is stronger, more cohesive, more self-aware, and more focused on the common good. That tribal police car gives a sense of security to all, to tribal members and to those who reside or who would consider investing in Indian country. Regardless of the financial cost of developing tribal police departments, and the investment of personnel in ensuring that culturally compatible ordinances, codes, and protocols are promulgated, the value is clear. Everyone benefits.

References

Cornell, Stephen, and Joseph P. Kalt. 1992. Reloading the dice. In *What can tribes do? Reloading the dice*, ed. Stephen Cornell and Joseph P. Kalt, 2–51. Los Angeles: American Indian Studies Center, University of California.

Etheridge, David. 1975. *Indian law enforcement history.* Washington, DC: Bureau of Indian Affairs, Division of Law Enforcement Services.

Greenfeld, Lawrence A., and Steven K. Smith. 1999. *American Indians and crime.* Washington, DC: U.S. Bureau of Justice Statistics.

Hagan, William T. 1966. *Indian police and judges.* Lincoln and London: University of Nebraska Press.

Johnson, Kevin. 2000. Tribal police isolated in darkness, distance. *USA Today*, March, A19.

Luna, Eileen M. 1998. The growth and development of tribal police. *Journal of Contemporary Criminal Justice* 14:5–86.

———. 1999. Police oversight in the American Indian community. *Georgetown Public Policy Review* 4:149–64.

———. 2002. Women in tribal policing. *Social Science Journal* 39:583–92.

———. 2007. *Tribal policing: Asserting sovereignty, seeking justice.* Tucson: University of Arizona Press.

Perry, Stephen. 2004. *American Indians and crime.* Washington, DC: U.S. Bureau of Justice Statistics.

Reno, Janet. 1995. U.S. Department of Justice commitment to American Indian tribal justice systems. *Judicature* 79:113–17.

Tate, Michael L. 1977. John P. Clum and the origins of an Apache constabulary, 1874–1877. *American Indian Quarterly* 3:99–120.

Wakeling, Stewart, Miriam Jorgensen, Susan Michaelson, and Manley Begay. 2001. *Policing on American Indian reservations: A report to the National Institute of Justice.* Washington, DC: U.S. Department of Justice, Office of Justice Programs.

Policing On and Off the Reservation

SOURCES OF INDIVIDUAL STRESS

Larry A. Gould

DISCUSSED IN THIS chapter are issues specific to the struggles of Native American police officers as they attempt to work both within two cultures and outside of their own cultural base. While the focus of the chapter is on those officers working on reservations, some attention is paid to Native American officers working in communities off reservations.

The premise of this chapter is based on two bodies of research. The first involves the work of Boldt and Long (1987, 537–47); the second, of Gould (1999, 2002). Boldt and Long identified concepts and values intrinsic to European-based means of social control such as authority, hierarchy, punishment, and ruling entity. They found these concepts to be in conflict with Native American means of social control, which value spiritual compact, tribal will, and a customary/traditional worldview that relies more on repairing wrongs than on punishment. For illustrative purposes, these concepts will be discussed in their more ideal type in this chapter. In reality, neither Native American nor European concepts of justice can be reduced to monolithic and/or mirror images of each other. Generally speaking, Native American concepts of justice would tend toward the end of a continuum that supports healing or making whole as a first response to transgressions of cultural norms. In fact, repeated offenses could result in severe actions, up to and including the death of the offender (see the chapter by Luna-Firebaugh). On the other hand, European concepts relative to the treatment of offenders tend more often to fall toward the end of the continuum that promotes punishment of the individual as the first, and many times the only, response to transgressions of cultural norms.

Gould's research on Native American police officers suggests that many are impacted by cultural dissonance while trying to perform their duties. Cultural dissonance, according to Gould (2002, 1999), signifies an anomic state (Hilbert 1996) in which individuals are faced with having to operate within the confines of two or more competing cultures. The anomic state results from situations in which following the rules of one culture places the individual at risk of violating the rules of the other culture(s) or from when the individual does not have a clear concept of what is and what is not proper and acceptable behavior (Gould 1999). Gould suggests that while many officers can successfully navigate the conflicts involved in having to pay heed to the collective conscience of two competing cultures, there are those who have difficulty. Those who have difficulty are faced with a situation or series of situations in which to some extent they feel lost or continually in conflict. Often, the results are loss of self-identity; increased conflicts with family friends, associates, and the community; and/or a feeling of being ostracized by one or both of the communities. In sum, cultural dissonance (2002, 1999) can result when acting in accord with one set of cultural rules places the officer at risk of punishment for violating the rules of the other culture. Any impact of cultural dissonance comes on top of the general stress of being a police officer.

Policing on Reservations

Stress Related to Policing

There are approximately four decades of research on non-Native American police officers concerning the sources of stress and their negative impact on police officers (Gould and Funk 1998; Gould 1996).

Gould (2002, 1999) found similar levels of stress-related problems in Native American officers, including but not limited to high blood pressure, cardiovascular disease, chronic headaches, and digestive tract disorders (Gould 2002, 1999; Stratton 1978; Kroes, Margolis, and Hurrell 1974). In aggravated cases, stress can lead to severe depression, substance abuse, and dysfunctional behavior, including high levels of cynicism and possibly suicide (Gould 2002, 1999, 1998; Carpenter and Raza 1987; Langworthy 1987; Regoli and Poole 1979).

Gould (2002, 1999) found—as is the case for departments off the reservation—that unrelieved stress can also have consequences for the reservation police department, such as excessive absenteeism, high disability and retirement compensation, and high replacement costs for disabled or disenchanted officers (National Institute of Justice 1986). Gould (2002) also found that retention of Native American officers was a problem for reservation police departments. Illness, excessive absenteeism, high disability and retirement compensation, and lower retention rates have a high cost for departments, because they have to pay overtime to ensure that shifts are fully covered and have to train officers to replace those who stay on the job for only a short period of time (Gould 1999). Another, sometimes hidden, cost of unrelieved stress can result from aberrant behavior on the part of police officers, which could lead to an increased risk of liability for the department. Stress can lead to poor decision making, over- or underreaction to potential threats, and an increased likelihood of conflict with the public (Gould 1999, 1998; Carpenter and Raza 1987; Langworthy 1987; Regoli and Poole 1979).

Sources of Stress

It is not uncommon for police officers, including Native police officers, to face both internal and external stress while performing the duties with which they have been charged. Police officers are required to operate within the organizational culture of their department while working within the culture of the communities they serve (Gould 1999). Generally, the police subculture is based on the time-honored notion of "professionalism" (discussed more later) that emphasizes crime control over crime prevention, thus isolating the officers from the communities and the people they serve (Christopher Commission 1991). The resurgence in the Native American communities of the traditional models, which emphasize healing over punishment, places the Native police officers, particularly those officers steeped in the European-based system of social control, at odds with much of the community.

An analysis of existing research (Dantzker 1997; Kurke and Scrivner 1995; Kroes 1985; Roberg and Kuykendall 1993) suggests that the sources of stress normally expected in policing fall into four categories: (1) stressors inherent in police work; (2) stressors internal to the law enforcement organization; (3) stressors external to the law enforcement organization; and (4) internal stressors confronting individual officers. In addition to these stressors, Native American police officers are faced with the possibility of an additional stressor, such as cultural dissonance, which is not normally found in other groups of police officers (Gould 1999).

Stressors inherent in police work. These stressors include such things as irregular or rotating days off, holiday work, unexpected or excessive overtime, court appearances on regular days off and on-call requirements (Kurke and Scrivner 1995). Poor eating patterns, poor sleep patterns and poor domestic patterns (Blau 1994; Hurrell and Kliesmet 1984); role conflicts and role ambiguities, and decision-making responsibilities (National Institute of Justice 1986; Kroes 1985) also fall into this category. Finally, inherent stressors include danger, fear of serious injury and disability (Brown and Campbell 1994; Eisenberg 1975); and transitory post-traumatic stress (Neidig, Russell, and Seng 1992).

Stressors internal to the law enforcement organization. These include such things as inadequate resources, excessive paperwork, poor training, inadequate pay, inadequate rewards and recognition, inadequate career development opportunities, poor supervision and lack of administrative support (Roberg and Kuykendall 1993; Brown and Campbell 1994). Insufficient or inadequate equipment, insufficient backup; not enough time to do quality work (Kurke and Scrivner 1995; Kroes, Margolis, and Hurrell 1974); poor training and support (Kurke and Scrivner 1995; Kroes 1985); and significant lack of promotion or advancement opportunities (Brown and Campbell 1994) are additional stresses in this category.

Stressors external to the law enforcement organization. Such stressors include changes in or challenges to status quo legislation, court actions, lawsuits, executive decisions, demands on the police made by the community, and social, political, economic, and structural changes (Kurke and Scrivner 1995; Kroes, Margolis, and Hurrell 1974; Roberg and Kuykendall 1993; Brown and Campbell 1994). In particular, Nielsen and Gould (2003) and Gould (2002) found a great deal of tension between the views of Native police officers and tribal courts. It seemed to be more often the case that tribal police officers found tribal courts to be far too liberal in their decisions.

Internal stressors confronting individual officers. These include such issues as inadequate training or inadequate application of training, role conflict, inappropriate behavioral issues, lack of psychological aptitude, and personal pressures from family and friends (Kurke and Scrivner 1995; Brown and Campbell 1994).

Cultural Dissonance as a Source of Stress

Skoog (1996) has identified three models of policing that may exist in the Native American community: (1) the crime control model, (2) the community policing model, and (3) the political sovereignty model. Conceptually, these are three distinct models; however, in reality there is generally some overlap between some of their features, and contrary to Skoog's categorization of these models as being somewhat separate, it is entirely possible that the political sovereignty model could be superimposed on either of the other two models. Luna-Firebaugh (2007) found that of the 171 reservations that have their own law enforcement departments, 164 have received Community Oriented Policing Service (COPS) grants, thus most adhere in some form to the community policing model. For the purposes of this discussion, these models are discussed separately, with the understanding that the best manner in which to construct an overview would be to think of them in a two by two table in which variations of sovereignty would compose the columns while the crime control and community policing models would compose the rows of the table.

The *crime control model* emphasizes public order, and the absolute power of the law to ensure public safety, with minimal input from citizens and the demand for respect for police priorities, policies and procedures (Trojanowicz and Carter 1988, 8). Skoog (1996) notes that, should such a model be adopted by a Native American community, it would appear to be indistinguishable from any small-town police department in which administrative control is in the hands of a few local political leaders, who may or may not reflect the grassroots concerns of the community. There tends to be both internal pressure from nontraditional members of the Native American community and external pressure from federal and state agencies to adopt this model of policing in Native American communities. This is also the model most often found on reservations, but the trend is changing toward a community policing model.

Community policing models are currently receiving much attention in the mainstream police literature (Trojanowicz and Bucqueroux 1990; Goldstein 1987). It is significant that the Manitoba Aboriginal Justice Inquiry in Canada called for the adoption of "a community policing approach, particularly in Native communities" (Hamilton and Sinclair 1991, 600). The community-based model of policing seems to have great applicability to Native American communities because of its capacity to be far more culturally sensitive than the crime control model, due to its focus on local control, with an emphasis on conflict resolution (Gould 2002, 1999; Skoog 1996). The Navajo Nation received significant funding for the development of a community policing program; however, there was a disconnection between the promoters of the program and the rank-and-file police.

The *political sovereignty model* is the most politically radical model of the three. Under this model, Native American communities would have their own courts, which could adjudicate any and all issues occurring within their jurisdiction, and the police would form one part of an integrated criminal justice system based on Native American values (Skoog 1996). This model has its own drawbacks for Native American police officers. Gould (2002) found that both individuals and organizations view political sovereignty in different ways. For example, some Native police officers would like to see a return to traditional means of social control; however, a much larger percentage of the officers see political sovereignty as a means by which the professional model could be applied. This is at odds with the trend in the judiciary to view political sovereignty as a means to move more toward traditional means of social control, such as those found in peacemaking (Nielsen and Gould 2003).

Of the three systems illustrated by Skoog (1996), the one that is most in conflict with the values and traditional structure of Native communities, but not necessarily the view of Native American policing agencies, is the crime control model. As noted by Luna (1997), the concept of "professionalization" dominates policing in the United States. The development of standardized codes and protocols and the standardization of training and structures of administration are widely perceived as worthy goals; however, there are many problems with a "professionalized" policing approach as it is attempted in Indian country. Professionalized policing is based within an adversarial context, with the police officers holding the "thin blue line" against wrongdoers, for the benefit of an uninvolved community. This approach is based on quick response to calls for service and on a hierarchical system of management and decision making. This structure and these emphases, by their nature, are difficult to apply in most Native American communities (Luna 1997). The concept of "professionalized" policing, with its emphasis on technology, specialized police activities, and restricted use of police discretion, does not conform to the style of peacekeeping most commonly used in traditional or rural communities (Luna 1999). Gould (2002, 1999) found that while there are both traditionalists and nontraditionalists in the ranks of most Native police agencies, the agencies themselves tend more toward the crime control model. This can, of course, put the agencies at odds with some parts of the communities they serve, and it adds to the conflict experienced by the officers.

As previously noted, the questions explored in this chapter concern the ability of the Native American police officers to deal with the additional stress resulting from working in a system in which two very different approaches to social control are expected to be practiced. It is suggested here that the cultural cost to the police officers results, in part, from the conflict between the expectations of these two general types of legal system: the European-based adjudicatory (in this case the crime control model) system, with its emphasis on arrest and punishment (Skolnick and Fyfe 1993; Skolnick 1975), and the traditional restorative approach, with an emphasis on healing and making the people involved whole again (Bluehouse and Zion 1993; Dumont 1996, 20–33). Adjudication with an emphasis on punishment and crime control—the European system—is the primary system linked to the modern state. This system is most often based on the use of power and authority, involving adversarial methods of coercion and forces to control the behavior of individuals (Yazzie 1994; Dumont 1996, 20–33). It is often based on an adversarial approach to resolving issues, which puts the different parties in a conflictual position. This is the system, a crime control police model of justice, that was imposed upon the Indian nations toward the close of the nineteenth century.

Cultural cost can come in many forms, of which one of the most important is ostracism by family, friends, or colleagues, either for being "not Navajo enough" or for being "too Navajo" (Gould 2002, 1999). The terms "not Navajo enough" and "too Navajo" were first used by one of the respondents in the 1998 study. Other respondents used very similar terms. In this case being "not Navajo enough" would generally refer to an officer who tends to rely heavily on European-based forms of social control and is thus likely to be criticized by more traditional Navajo people, while being "too Navajo" refers to officers who tend more often to rely on traditional methods of social control, and thus are criticized by other law enforcement officers. It is interesting to note that it is possible for an officer to be viewed by different groups as being both too Navajo and not Navajo enough at the same time and in the same situation.

As previously mentioned, the specific points of conflict, according to Boldt and Long (1987), stem from the European concept of authority based on a belief in the inherent inequality of men. In the European-based societies, individual autonomy was regarded as the foundation for the successful acquisition of private property and achievement through competitive pursuits. Social control in terms of authority was deemed necessary to protect society against rampant individual self-interest; thus, authoritative power was believed essential for maintaining the integrity of a sovereign society. In modern societies based on the European model, the most visible source of the power and control of the state is the police. This also meant that hierarchical power structures were necessary to ensure the distribution of privileges and the maintenance of order, from the most authoritative to the most powerless (Dumont 1996, 20–33). The police are often viewed as the means by which the state ensures the hierarchical power structure—thus, the distribution of privileges and power.

The European-based concepts of authority, hierarchy, and power are fundamentally different from the Native American concept of sovereignty or responsible and egalitarian governance (social control). In traditional Native American societies, self-interest is inextricably intertwined with the tribal interest (Dumont 1996, 20–33; Boldt and Long 1987). One of the strongest tenets of European-based forms of social control is the social contract, a concept of how authorities should more humanely exercise the right to govern others and devise egalitarian methods of extending authoritative rule from the ruler to the ruled (Dumont 1996, 20–33). In most traditional Native American societies, it is believed that no human being rightfully controls the life of another (Boldt and Long

1987); however, this is exactly what police officers must at times do in order to carry out their duties. In Native American belief systems, social control is often viewed as a spiritual compact, while the European-based means of social control derive from personal authority, hierarchical relationships, and the concept of a separate ruling entity (Dumont 1996, 20–33; Boldt and Long 1987). Native American police officers are placed in the role of having personal authority and a hierarchical relationship, and in many ways they are a separate ruling entity (Gould 2002). This, of course, puts the police department and the police officers at odds with parts of the community that they serve.

Peacemaking and other forms of restorative justice are examples of traditional Native American forms of social control. Restorative justice is dissimilar from adjudication in that it views crime and offending as a conflict between individuals, a conflict out of which healing or making the individuals involved whole again is one of the major goals. Restorative justice, in particular peacemaking, is often confused with typical forms of European-based dispute resolution. The goals of restorative justice are to seek reconciliation between the parties and to repair the injury that occurred as a result of the dispute, through the active participation of victims, offenders, and the community (Nielsen and Gould 2003; Hudson and Galaway 1996).

Following more than a century of suppression of traditional Native American forms of social control, the resurgence of *hozhooji naat'aanii*, Navajo peacemaking, is a part of major changes taking place in Native American criminal justice systems in North America (Zion 1997; Belgrave 1995). The reinstitution of peacemaking began in 1982 as the result of a conscious effort on the part of the judges of the courts of the Navajo Nation (Bluehouse and Zion 1993). This process involves the judiciary and the tribal council; however, little apparent thought was given to involving the police.

Zion (1999) posits that restorative justice is, in part, a response both to the inadequacies of the federal, state, and local adjudication in handling Native American problems and to the effects of colonialism. Thus, indigenous peoples use restorative justice for both an immediate purpose (a case at hand) and as a method of healing the wounds of internal colonialism (Duran and Duran 1995), "going back to the future" through the use of traditional means of social control (Austin 1993). Nielsen and

Gould (2003) and Gould (2002, 1999) found that restorative justice is at odds with the general models of policing currently used by most Native American police departments.

As mentioned above, the values found in peacemaking and other forms of traditional Native American methods of social control are at odds with the core values composing the European-based means of social control, which is the type of social control most apparent as part of the policing function on most reservations. For example, in traditional Native American thought, one doesn't correct the actor: that would be a violation of the "it's up to him" value; one corrects the action. This is certainly one of the main points of the cultural dissonance faced by the Native American police officer (Nielsen and Gould 2003). Another point at which dissonance occurs involves the issue of judgment. In Native American culture it is generally accepted that passing judgment (arrest) on somebody else is a behavior for which there are always consequences (Gould 2002, 1999). This means that making an arrest creates a cultural dissonance, which leads to some of the cultural costs previously mentioned. It is also important to note that for some officers, *not* making an arrest also leads to cultural dissonance, with its own set of subcultural costs, such as loss of respect from some of the less traditional officers, other law enforcement agencies, and non-Native American courts.

Native Officers in Non–Native American Departments

There is very little research available on Native American officers working in non–Native American departments. Gould (1998, 1996) found that it is often the case that the first person of color, member of a minority group, or female to enter a police department suffers from a lack of a support group, has trouble fitting into the cadre of white male officers of which most departments are composed, and has difficulties in navigating the mostly white male police subculture. Anecdotal information suggests that Native American officers, particularly those raised on a reservation, tend to have a greater potential for having the same problems as did women and blacks entering the police force. This is an additional stress to all the other stresses common among police officers.

Some additional stress appears to come from the failure of white police officers to recognize differences in tribal affiliation among Native police officers. For example, in a recent incident a Native American officer was called to the scene of an investigation to act as an interpreter (personal communication 1998). The problem was that the officer was Navajo and the victim of the crime was Pima. This was problem enough, but then the white officer who called for the help stated, "But, I thought all Indians spoke the same language?"

It has also been reported that white officers often feel that Native American officers will be soft on their own people. This is not dissimilar from the feeling that white officers had or have about black officers. Those reporting this attitude often feel that if they don't take a rigid stand in the enforcement of the law when they encounter other Native Americans, white officers will not respect them. This, of course, is yet one more form of stress.

Police officers often share the stresses and strains of the job with one another, but they generally do it off-duty in an informal way, through social processes such as social gatherings. Native American officers report that they are often not invited to such functions or that when invited, they are usually the only Native person present. In other words, the informal means by which police officers let off a little steam or the means by which they often seek reinforcement from peers are not generally available to Native American officers.

In sum, anecdotal information suggests that Native American officers working in a non-Native setting suffer the same types of stress as do other officers but tend to lack the informal support systems that are a part of the policing subculture.

Conclusions

The body of research on which this chapter is based suggests four overall findings. First, for most situations in which enforcement actions become necessary, the officers who expressed a stronger connectedness to traditional ways still tended to rely more on the European-based law than on the tribal common law; however, these officers expressed interest in an increased relationship with peacemakers and other traditional methods of social control for many types of minor and juvenile offenses. For these officers the likelihood of increased stress comes from two sources. They tend to feel more comfortable with the European-based forms of social control; however, they recognize the value of more traditional methods. This has the likelihood of placing these officers at odds with other law enforcement agencies, thus being categorized as being too Native American in their behavior. They are also faced with increased internal conflict as a result of having to balance their law enforcement efforts with their own traditional values without guidelines on how to do so.

Second, those officers expressing stronger ties to traditional ways tend more often to believe that peacemaking and other traditional methods of social control could be useful; these same officers more often suffered from a sense of dissonance as a result of maintaining social control through the use of European-based methods. These officers more often expressed a sense of loss of their spirituality, thus increasing the likelihood of stress, as a result of the internal conflict that results from the dissonance. It was noted that the reliance on European-based legal structures (the formal court system) rather than on more traditionally based programs such as the peacemakers has not, for many officers, come without some personal cost in terms of a feeling of cultural loss. Those officers expressing a stronger attachment to traditional ways more often noted that their decisions to rely on European-based systems rather than on the traditional systems tended to violate their sense of the community healing process. Most of the officers reporting a violation of their own sense of the healing process were able to rationalize their decision to rely upon European-based approaches by relying very heavily on their academy training and by modeling their efforts on other law enforcement agencies. Rationalizing does not relieve stress but only serves to redirect its impact for short periods. If the source of the stress, in this case cultural dissonance, is not relieved, it is expected that the outward signs of stress will not be alleviated.

Third, those officers who tend to practice the European-based professional model of policing and the crime control model of enforcement often felt that they did not have the respect of other Native Americans. While this was a problem for most of the officers at this end of the continuum, some of these officers felt that the only way to achieve self-determination was to abandon the traditional methods of social control or to restrict those methods to very narrow categories of use. These officers faced considerable stress, because they often felt rejected by their own people (not being Native American enough), but felt that they were, in their own way, fighting for cultural and political independence.

Fourth, the feeling of being too Native American or not being Native American enough was moderated to some extent by some specific situations, such as the type of investigation, the seriousness of the crime (with the exception of drunken behavior), and the individuals involved.

In sum, the literature (Skolnick and Fyfe 1993; Skolnick 1975) suggests that simply being a police officer puts a lot of strain on the individual. While Skoog (1996) and Gould (1999) support the findings of Skolnick, they also suggest that there is a significant added burden of stress for Native American police officers. In addition to having to deal with the normal conflicts and stressors that are part of a police officer's duties, the Native American police officer, either on or off the reservation, must attempt to walk the fine line between two cultures that have conflicting and competing value systems; and in some cases they do so without the support network common to the policing subculture.

References

Austin, Raymond D. 1993. ADR and the Navajo peacemakers court. *Judges Journal* 32:9–49.

Belgrave, J. 1995. Restorative justice: A discussion paper. Wellington: New Zealand Ministry of Justice.

Blau, Theodore. 1994. *Psychological services for law enforcement*. New York: Wiley.

Bluehouse, Phil, and James W. Zion. 1993. *Hozhooji naat'aanii*: The Navajo justice and harmony ceremony. *Mediation Quarterly* 10:327–37.

Boldt, Menno, and J. Anthony Long. 1987. Tribal traditions and European-Western political ideologies: The dilemma of Canada's Native Indians. *Canadian Journal of Political Science* 17:537–47.

Brown, Jennifer, and Elizabeth Campbell. 1994. *Stress and policing: Sources and strategies*. New York: Wiley.

Carpenter, Bruce N., and Susan M. Raza. 1987. Personality characteristics of police applicants: Comparisons across subgroups and with other populations. *Journal of Police Science and Administration* 15:10–17.

Christopher Commission. 1991. *Report of the Independent Commission on the Los Angeles Police Department*. Washington, DC: Department of Justice.

Dantzker, Mark. 1997. *Contemporary policing: Personnel issues and trends*. New York: Butterworth.

Dumont, James. 1996. Justice and Native peoples. In *Native Americans, crime, and justice*, ed. Marianne O. Nielsen and Robert A. Silverman, 20–33. Boulder, CO: Westview.

Duran, Eduardo, and Bonnie Duran. 1995. *Native American postcolonial psychology*. Albany: SUNY Press.

Eisenberg, Thomas. 1975. Labor-management relations and psychological stress. *Police Chief* 42:54–58.

Goldstein, Herman. 1987. Toward community-oriented policing: Potential, basic requirements and threshold questions. *Crime and Delinquency* 33:1–16.

Gould, Larry A. 1996. Can old dogs be taught new tricks? Teaching cultural diversity to police officers. *Police Studies* 19:43–59.

———. 1998. The dilemma of the Navajo police officer: Traditional versus European-based means of social control. *The Refereed Proceeding of the 11th International Congress, Commission on Folk Law and Legal Pluralism*, Moscow.

———. 1999. The impact of working in two worlds and its effect on Navajo police officers. *Journal of Legal Pluralism* 44:53–71.

———. 2002. Indigenous people policing Indigenous people: The potential psychological and cultural costs. *Social Science Journal* 41:1–19.

Gould, Larry A., and Steve Funk. 1998. Does the stereotypical personality reported for the male police officer fit that of the female police officer? *Journal of Police and Criminal Psychology* 13:25–39.

Hamilton, A. C., and C. M. Sinclair. 1991. *The justice system and Aboriginal people*. Vol. 1 of *Report of the Aboriginal Justice Inquiry of Manitoba*. Winnipeg: Queen's Printer.

Hilbert, Ray. 1996. Anomie and moral regulation of reality: The Durkheimian tradition in modern relief. *Sociological Theory* 4:1–19.

Hudson, Joe, and Burt Galaway. 1996. *Restorative justice: International perspectives*. Monsey, NY: Criminal Justice Press.

Hurrell, Joseph, and Raymond Kliesmet. 1984. *Stress among police officers*. Cincinnati: National Institute of Occupational Safety and Health.

Kroes, William H. 1985. *Society's victims, the police: An analysis of job stress in policing*. 2nd ed. New York: Butterworth.

Kroes, William, Brian L. Margolis, and Joseph Hurrell. 1974. Job stress in policemen. *Journal of Police Science and Administration* 2:145–55.

Kurke, Martin, and Ellen M. Scrivner. 1995. *Police psychology into the 21st century*. Hillside, NJ: Erlbaum.

Langworthy, Robert H. 1987. Police cynicism: What we know from the Niederhoffer scale. *Journal of Criminal Justice* 15:17–35.

Luna, Eileen. 1997. Community policing in Indian country. *Church and Society Magazine*, March/April, 7–14.

———. 1999. Law enforcement oversight in the American Indian community. *Georgetown Public Policy Review* 4:149–64.

Luna-Firebaugh, Eileen. 2007. *Tribal policing: Asserting sovereignty, seeking justice.* Tucson: University of Arizona Press.

National Institute of Justice. 1986. *Coping with police stress.* Washington, DC: Government Printing Office.

Neidig, Peter, Harold Russell, and Albert Seng. 1992. Interspousal aggression in law enforcement families: A preliminary investigation. *Police Studies* 15:30–38.

Nielsen, Marianne, and Larry A. Gould. 2003. Developing the interface between the Navajo Nation police and Navajo Nation peacemaking. *Police Practice and Research* 4:429–43.

Regoli, Robert M., and Edward D. Poole. 1979. Measurement of police cynicism: A factor scaling approach. *Journal of Criminal Justice* 7:37–51.

Roberg, Roy R., and John Kuykendall. 1993. *Police and society.* Belmont, CA: Wadsworth.

Skolnick, James. 1975. *Justice without trial: Law enforcement in democratic society.* New York: Wiley.

Skolnick, James, and James Fyfe. 1993. *Above the law: Police and the excessive use of force.* New York: Free Press.

Skoog, Douglas M. 1996. Taking control: Native self-government and Native policing. In *Native Americans, crime and justice,* ed. Marianne O. Nielsen and Robert A. Silverman, 118–31. Boulder, CO: Westview.

Stratton, John G. 1978. Police stress: An overview. *Police Chief* 45:3–5.

Trojanowicz, Robert, and Bonnie Bucqueroux. 1990. *Community policing: A contemporary perspective.* Cincinnati: Anderson.

Trojanowicz, Robert, and Donald Carter. 1988. *The philosophy and role of community policing.* Detroit: National Neighborhood Foot Patrol Center.

Yazzie, Robert. 1994. Life comes from it: Navajo justice concepts. *New Mexico Law Review* 67:177–80.

Zion, James W. 1999. Monster Slayer and Born for Water: The intersection of restorative justice and Indigenous justice. *Contemporary Justice Review* 2:359–82.

———. 2005. The dynamics of Navajo peacemaking: Social psychology of an American Indian method of dispute resolution. In *Navajo peacemaking: Living traditional justice,* ed. Marianne O. Nielsen and James W. Zion, 85–99. Tucson: University of Arizona Press.

Beyond Colonialism

INDIAN COURTS IN THE PRESENT AND FUTURE

James W. Zion

AMERICAN INDIAN nation courts (popularly called "tribal courts") are an anomaly. They were created as instruments for non-Indian control of Indian populations, but twentieth-century reforms attempted to make them responsive to the needs of self-governing tribes, their members, and the general public. There is nothing new about the idea of judicial bodies as instruments of control when law is viewed as a product of conquest and external and internal colonialism (where "external" evolves into "internal" colonialism with the rise of the modern state).

There is no firm figure of how many tribal courts there presently are in the United States, but a round figure of three hundred is adequate, not counting traditional justice systems in Pueblo government and informal customary arrangements in traditional communities. The concern here is formal judicial systems. Tribal courts are sometimes controversial, with varying views of federal and state judges (some of whom consider tribal courts to be something other than a "court" and question their legitimacy), practitioners (some of whom attack tribal courts), and even dissatisfaction from the public that tribal courts are to serve. Indian judges, academics, and some Indian nation political figures defend tribal courts as legitimate and effective instruments of justice—despite their colonial origins.

There is a context that must be understood to better appreciate the nature and role of tribal courts in their modern settings. They are a product of a consistent historical line of thinking, from Roman law to the present, that balances the reality of the continued existence of customary law and indigenous (i.e., existing) judicial institutions with internal colonialism and outside control of Native populations (MacLachlan 1994, 343). This chapter traces the origins of tribal courts in Roman, Spanish, British, and American law to show their evolution and current standing. This historical review also focuses on a particular kind of court, the English "justice" or "justice of the peace" court as the model for tribal courts. Part of the negative perception of Indian courts comes from modern attitudes about "courts of limited jurisdiction" (the formal classification of justice, magistrate, and city courts), many of which have judges without formal law training. The chapter will then discuss how tribal courts operate, delineate criticism of their staffing and functions, and describe trends in court reform that combine traditional and modern expectations to predict and advocate in favor of tribal courts of the future.

Roman, Islamic, Spanish, and English Precedents

Rome was the first empire built on conquest, and as it was with later empires and conquests, the dilemma that conquering policy makers had was how to control indigenous populations without a large infrastructure or the commitment of many sandals on the ground. There were three questions. First, can peoples who are conquered keep their own laws? Second, can they have their own judicial institutions? Third, when does the law of the conqueror override the law of the conquered? The Romans approached those questions, and "it was a general principle which marked the early Roman policy in Italy to allow a subject community to retain its own municipal laws, and to administer justice between its own citizens, so far as this was consistent with a state of subjection to Rome" (Morey 1900, 64). Romans also had to respond to the legal needs of foreigners who lived in Rome, and that led to a body of supplementary law that applied solely to them (Morey 1900, 66–68). It eventually became *jus gentium*, or "the law in common to all nations," as its utility was accepted (Morey 1900, 68–69). One of the leading examples of the application of the Roman principle of recognition of indigenous law and judicial institutions was the trial of Christ, where Christ was tried by the Jewish Sanhedrin but executed by the Roman governor Pilate, who recognized the "tribal court" judgment (Kaye 1909).

The next wave of conquest began the century after the death of Muhammad in 632, and a third began with Christian efforts to retake Spain from the Moors, culminating in the fall of Granada in 1492 (Seed 1995, 73), shortly before Columbus sailed for a fourth wave of conquest.

Both Islamic and Christian rulers recognized rights of self-government and the law of conquered peoples (Seed 1995, 87; Borah 1983, 94–95). The principle was purely a pragmatic one. Without the means to control subjected populations by force, there must be some accommodation of indigenous law and dispute resolution or judicial systems.

The Spanish faced the same dilemma in the New World and turned to their medieval institutions and principles to deal with Indians. One of the applicable principles was the legacy of Roman recognition of preexisting law and institutions. Another was a canon law judicial procedure for certain kinds of civil cases that was "simple and equitable" and used in situations "involving poor or oppressed persons and those for which an ordinary legal remedy was not available" (Berman 1983, 250–51). The summary procedure involved an examining judge who used inquisitorial procedure to question the parties to give prompt judgments and remedies for vulnerable individuals who could not afford a lawyer.

The principle of Spanish recognition of Indian law was formalized in a decree of Holy Roman Emperor Charles V, and his mother (Queen Juana or Jane), on August 6, 1555, that gave an "order and command" that "the laws and good customs" of Indians, and their "customs and usages" "which are not incompatible with our holy religion" or Spanish law, must be "kept and executed" (Juneau 1983, 13). That assured that Indian customs and legislative enactments would be enforced as applicable substantive law.

That law was applied in two kinds of fora. The first, patterned after the canon law summary procedure and forum for poor and "miserable" people, was the Juzgado General de Indios or General Court of Indians (Borah 1983). It was an administrative body under the viceroy in Mexico City, and it functioned well as a forum to resolve disputes between Indians and Spaniards. Its process extended into the far reaches of New Spain, even Nuevo Mexico, and Pueblo leaders of the Rio Grande Valley used it (Cutter 1986).

The Spanish also evolved a court for Indians that Europeans could "see," in place of Indigenous procedures. The basic body of Spanish municipal government was the *cabecera*, and its jurisdiction included judicial functions. There were Indian cabeceras, called a *governadoryotl*, with a "presiding native figure," who, like his Spanish counterparts, was a *gobernador* or *juez gobernador* ("governor" or "judge-governor")

(Gibson 1964, 167). Although the Mexican government that followed colonial Spain largely rejected those principles of recognition and implementation, Indigenous justice systems do persist in municipal government in Mexico today (Nader 1990).

When England, and later Britain (a colonial construct), initiated processes of exploration, conquest, and colonialism following Henry VIII's break with Rome, it too faced problems of indigenous law and institutions. Common law principles were used to recognize existing customary and pre-conquest law, and British colonizers established various kinds of judicial bodies to "find" and apply indigenous customary law, including courts with lay assessors or assistants, native or village courts, and other bodies that were either part of the westernized colonial government or independent of it (in principle, at least) (St. J. Hannigan 1961; Green 1977a, 99–132, 1977b, 61–98).

One of the most important institutions of English courts was the justice of the peace. A primary problem of the Norman Conquest of 1066 and later was maintenance of the peace, called "the king's peace" in law; and the primary official responsible to keep the peace on the local county level (other than the sheriff as a law enforcement officer) was the justice of the peace (Blackstone 1884). That sort of judge was responsible for the maintenance of local order (including road maintenance), and the justice of the peace was one of the essential English institutions that was transported to America (Notestein 1962, 211–27). The "J.P." was a model for social control in local government in the United States, ultimately the model for tribal courts, and a source of common identity for Indian and state judges in modern times (Zion and Cloud 1996, 7–11).

American Indian Courts

It is difficult to know, from the literature on tribal courts, the extent to which the British village or native court was a specific model for Indian courts in the United States. The Cherokee Nation adopted its own American-styled court system early on, but it is in a separate line of development (Strickland 1975). Otherwise, the first example of the imposition of a native or village court system is found in an experiment on Navajos who were interned in a concentration camp–reservation on the Pecos River of eastern New Mexico from 1863 through 1868 (Bailey 1998).

Following initial attempts to settle Navajo captives in villages (Bailey 1998, 115, map of proposed villages), a board of army officers convened at Fort Sumner adopted a plan of settlement and legal and political organization on April 26, 1865 (Bailey 1998, 117). It provided for twelve villages, to be governed by "twelve principal men among the Navajos," with a kind of judicial power within the village, under the supervision of the fort commanding officer, and a tribunal for the trial of more serious offenses by the commander, with a jury composed of the twelve "chiefs" (Bailey 1998, 117–18). The board also adopted a code of law to define and punish offenses, and the officers attempted to adapt the code to the condition of the Navajo captives (Bailey 1998, 118–19). (We do not know how well the code and "courts" functioned, because later reports did not report their work.)

The Navajo Wars of the mid-1860s were part of a process that began before the Civil War, and culminated after it, to conclude a series of treaties with Indian nations west of the Mississippi to limit Indian country (the legal definition of lands reserved by or to Indian nations) and redefine it for reservations under treaties. The remaining land would then be open to settlers. Once that was done, the dilemma was what to do with Indians once they had been confined to the reservations created by the treaties.

There was a public policy debate about that from approximately 1880 through 1900 that involved public officials and an ad hoc association of individuals who saw themselves as reformers, called the Friends of the Indian (Prucha 1973). The "Friends" felt that "law for the Indians" was a means of civilization and eventual assimilation, and they debated how law could be such an instrument (Prucha 1973, 147–90, collection of essays and reports). That was the background for the first Indian courts (Hagan 1966). A new Secretary of the Interior, who was formerly a U.S. senator, instructed the commissioner of Indian Offenses to devise a code and court for Indians (Teller 1973, 295–99), and Commissioner Thomas J. Morgan responded by promulgating "Rules for Indian Courts" in 1883 (Morgan 1973, 300–305 [rules as reissued in 1892]). The justice of the peace model is apparent from the qualifications to be a judge (set in an Indian context of not having more than one wife and wearing "citizen's dress"), and the offenses and procedures set out in the code (Morgan 1973, 300–305).

The new court was the Courts of Indian Offenses, an administrative body of the Bureau of Indian Affairs under the control of a local Indian agent, which had only congressional appropriations as a statutory foundation for the judicial system (Morse 1980). Its judges were Indians, as were the police who brought offenders before the court (Hagan 1966), and they functioned under the eye of the (usually non-Indian) reservation superintendent or agent. Their function to control the Indian population and maintain order as expected by the federal government was apparent in code provisions and operation.

That government's direct administration and control of Indian reservations was questioned in the 1928 "Meriam Report," or *The Problem of Indian Administration* (Meriam 1928). The survey results of the report were extensive, including a lengthy review of the legal aspects of the "Indian problem" and the Indian courts. While noting that the Indian judges were applying customary law and operating outside the justice of the peace model, the report concluded that they were effective, in their own way, and recommended that the Indian court system continue until there had been further education and "civilizing" work to prepare Indians for assimilation and the use of state justice systems.

Tribal Courts

The Meriam Report was a baseline for the Roosevelt administration's Indian policies, and the reform president who entered office in 1933 recruited John Collier to develop them. The key was a "reorganization" of Indian governments on reservations in the Indian Reorganization Act of 1934 (Indian Reorganization Act 1934). In section 16 it recognized the existing power of Indian tribes. Shortly after Congress adopted the act, Collier had his Interior Department lawyer (the Solicitor) define what those "powers of Indian Tribes" were "by existing law" (Mangold 1934). They included powers for "the Administration of Justice" (Mangold 1934, 56–64), and that is the source of authority for tribal courts.

Another Collier reform was a revision of the rules or code for the Courts of Indian Offenses, and they were promulgated in "law and order" regulations that would apply until tribes adopted their own constitution and by-laws and they became effective (*Law and Order Regulations 1938*, 952, 953–59).

The historical development of the Indian Reorganization Act and Collier reforms was such that many Indian nations adopted constitutions and by-laws within a few years after 1934. Some did not (with Navajos as the most notable example). Many tribes did not provide for court systems in constitutions. Others adopted a separate court code, whether or not a court system was set out in a constitution. Most Indian nations adopted the 1938 Courts of Indian Offenses "Law and Order Code" word-for-word (including jurisdiction over Bureau of Indian Affairs officials). Despite John Collier's intention that constitutions and codes should reflect local concerns, bureaucracy drove the imposition of both, without regard to local conditions or desires.

The Law and Order Regulations are an example of a "police model" of law, where the primary function of the law is to criminalize various activities and give law enforcement officers authority to arrest and prosecute individual Indian offenders (Barsh and Henderson 1976, 25–60). As it was with the 1883 code and its revisions, the 1938 Law and Order Code was largely a criminal code. It had probate and civil jurisdiction provisions, but they were largely ignored in favor of a system of Indian police and judges whose focus was criminal punishment. There were few amendments to the word-for-word code, with the exception of children's codes to deal with abuse, neglected or delinquent children, and some traffic codes.

The Indian Civil Rights Act of 1968 caused major changes in how tribal courts were perceived. It imposed most (but not all) limitations and protections of the U.S. Bill of Rights on Indian nation governments, and while not specifically mentioned, tribal courts became the enforcer of last resort under the new ICRA. That is, the act did not say that tribal courts would enforce and protect individual civil and political rights under the ICRA, but that was implicit in tribal court provisions. That led to decades of internal turmoil over the powers of tribal courts in tribal government, and the act provided a lingering and still-persisting source of confusion and resulting instability in Indian nation government.

The federal government soon began to ask why tribal courts were not effectively enforcing the Indian Civil Rights Act, and that question was examined in reports issued in 1977 (American Indian Policy Review Commission 1977), 1989 (Select Committee on Indian Affairs 1989), and 1991 (U.S. Commission on Civil Rights 1991). All three concluded that Indian courts could be effective bodies to protect and enforce civil rights, *if* there were sufficient federal financial support for their operations. Congress made no appropriations to implement those conclusions.

Following additional debate on the subject, and a 1991 U.S. Civil Rights Commission Report that summed up the history of Indian courts under the ICRA, Congress adopted the Indian Tribal Justice Act of 1991. It is a law that *authorizes* the appropriation of funding for tribal courts, and there are time limits on the periods of authorization. It has been reenacted, but at no time has the U.S. House of Representatives initiated funding that is authorized by the act and its reenactments.

How Tribal Courts Operate

It is difficult to accurately describe a "typical" tribal court, because of the numerous variations, but its composition and functions have not changed much since a 1978 National American Indian Court Judges Association review of how tribal courts function, largely under the 1938 code that became a "model" code (National American Indian Court Judges Association 1978). Many Indian reservations are small in terms of land base and population, so many have a court that consists of a chief judge and two associate judges. Most often, the three judges constitute an appellate court that hears appeals from one of the three. Depending upon the size of the court budget, usually federal funds under the Indian Self-Determination and Education Assistance Act, there may be a chief judge and two associate judges and one or more clerks of court. Some courts have pro tem and ad hoc judges to make up a three-judge court or to assist judges with a larger caseload. A "typical" court will have at least some judges and a clerk, and often a probation officer or officers. Other courts have administrative staffers such as a court administrator, accountant, deputy clerks, secretaries, and other support staff.

Tribal courts vary in the identity of their judges. Some constitutions or judicial codes provide that only a member of the given tribe is qualified to be a judge. Possession of a law degree is seldom required, and that is also true of many state justices of the peace, magistrates, or city court judges. Some tribes require judges to have a law degree, and some require that the judge be "Indian," whether or not that person is a member of the given tribe. Most courts function using a law code that is largely a modern adaptation of the 1938 Law and Order Code. The core of that code—with criminal provisions, a short probate code, and a few bare provisions on civil jurisdiction—remains largely in place, supplemented by a children's code (abuse, neglect, and delinquency) and codes on special subjects that have been of importance to the given tribe over the years. Some codes are a collection of various codes, amendments, or resolutions enacted over the years, while others are comprehensive revisions or adopted "model" codes. Few codes are formally published (the leading exceptions are the Navajo Nation and the Cherokee Tribe of Oklahoma). Many are "published" in a photocopy format, and some courts have codes on an electronic disk that can be distributed to users.

Some courts rely almost exclusively on their codes for an almost European form of civil law procedure. Others follow the general American procedure of blending statutes with case decisions and principles of laws such as a tribal bill of rights or the Indian Civil Rights Act of 1968. That distinction is not generally appreciated, but it has important court planning implications in terms of "lay" judging using a code model, or the more sophisticated case law and "constitutional" approach that requires greater sophistication.

Some courts publish their decisions, at least in a loose-leaf format, but most do not. Some courts have made arrangements with a commercial electronic publisher for publication of case decisions in an electronic format. Several courts have their own Internet sites to publish case decisions, rules, tribal statutes, or information for the public to use the court system.

Criticism and Controversy

The most comprehensive survey of tribal courts was done by Samuel J. Brakel, supported by an American Bar Foundation grant (Brakel 1978). Brakel, a Dutch lawyer, toured several tribal courts throughout the United States; his conclusions are summed up in the title of a short piece he wrote for the *American Bar Association Journal*: "American Indian Tribal Courts: Separate? 'Yes.' Equal? 'Probably Not'" (Brakel 1976). He did not understand what he "saw" when he visited tribal courts, read their codes and rules, and concluded that most Indian judges were ignorant of the law or unduly influenced by political forces. The National American Court Judges Association 1978 report was the product of an effort to make tribal courts effective institutions and partly a response to controversy fueled by Brakel's ABA piece.

At the reservation level, practitioners quietly criticize courts and judges among peers, and some lawyers refuse to practice in tribal court. More recently, there is a growing "tribal bar" of lawyers who see the value of Indian courts because they have discovered they can make money practicing there. The author has evaluated six tribal courts, in Montana (two courts), Washington, California, Arizona, and South Dakota, where a major component of fieldwork was interviews with practicing attorneys, and they did not voice undue criticism of the given court. (That may be out of fear of retaliation, although each was given assurances of confidentiality.)

There is also controversy at the national level, with at least one U.S. Supreme Court justice praising traditional Indian justice while warning against political influences on Indian courts (O'Connor 2005, 171) and a concurring decision by a justice in a major Indian jurisdiction case who doubts that tribal courts should ever have jurisdiction over any non-member (Souter 2001). His concern was that given the independence of Indian courts (including the coverage of the U.S. Bill of Rights), their use of customary law, and a lack of federal judicial review of decisions, the dangers of the denial of the rights of non-Indians override the policy merits of jurisdiction over non-Indians.

The Future of Tribal Courts?

A question mark follows this heading because we do not know how the early Brakel–National American Indian Court Judges Association and later O'Connor-Souter debate points will be resolved. There is currently a presumption that tribal courts do not have jurisdiction over non-Indians, and that may be extended to "nonmember Indians" (Indians residing on a reservation who belong to another tribe). Despite that, most of the work of tribal courts involves criminal and civil adjudications involving members, with most of it falling under the "police model" of judicial systems.

There are at least three visible trends that tell us something about the future of Indian courts. First, developments in the use of customary law (Cooter and Fikentscher 1998a, 1998b); second, developments in the revival of traditional dispute-resolution procedures and interaction with mediation and restorative justice movements (LeResche 1993; Nielsen and Zion 2005); and third, possibilities that arise from a combination of traditional Indian law and procedure and modern judicial practice.

Many Indian courts and judges, now assisted and supported by academics who are doing work in traditional Indian law, utilize customary and traditional law in modern opinions written in English, and some tribal courts are developing a corpus of "Indian common law." Some tribal courts (see particularly the chapter on peacemaking by Meyer in this volume) are making innovative use of traditional procedure for processes that are much like mediation and restorative justice.

The third possibility for the future will come from a combination of work that has already been done in the development of bodies of Indian common law in written decisions and modern legal trends. One of the modern trends in American judicial systems in general is the adoption of standards to measure the performance of trial courts (Commission on Trial Court Performance Standards 1990). They state five "performance areas" that sum up expectations on what trial courts need to do to be seen as "just" (i.e., access to justice; expedition and timeliness; equality, fairness, and integrity; independence and accountability; and public trust and confidence), and twenty-two concrete standards to achieve those performance areas or goals. The standards have been used by the author and others to evaluate tribal court operations (including a short self-evaluation "inventory") (Bureau of Justice Assistance 1998). Despite objections that tribal courts are so uniquely Indian or use customary law, traditions, and values so that the standards do not apply, the author and others have found them to be useful to evaluate court systems and recommend reforms. The standards address competence and legitimacy issues in the use of an understandable western evaluation instrument that can be adapted to Indian country use.

A lot of work is being done in "visionary law," a general term used to describe various efforts to rethink what it is that courts actually do or should do and to initiate reforms (Zion 2002, 563–64). Many initiatives, such as restorative justice, access to courts without lawyers, or judges acting as mediators, have been anticipated by Indian judges who have done those kinds of things for years.

Conclusion

A great deal of the debate over the existence, utility, or possibilities of tribal courts has been about absolutes. Should they exist at all, given the availability of state courts? Should they have jurisdiction over non-Indians or nonmember Indians? Are Indian judges competent? Are Indian judges overly influenced by politicians (without asking the same questions about federal and state judges)?

· We return to the original dilemma the Romans had: is it practical, as a matter of policy, to impose the law of the conqueror as law on "alien" peoples? The answer, simply put, is no. That answer is reinforced by the recent interest in the use of Indian customary law in modern tribal courts, and by the emergence of traditional dispute-resolution methods.

There has never been an effective public dialogue with Indian judges about what it is they do and how they approach the resolution of problems posed to them by litigants. American courts generally have the same problem of having to apply a "police model" of law, and American judges ask the same questions about whether the police model really works or is possibly counterproductive.

It is possible that answers lie in innovative discussions of "visionary law" or the like, and even in a re-examination of the role of the English justice of the peace, as discussed by Zion and Cloud (1996). In any event, tribal courts will continue to function for the foreseeable future, and they will continue to administer their own brand of "justice." There are issues about the use and abandonment of the police model, and whether or not tribal courts are indeed popular fora, but application of the 1990 Trial Court Performance Standards to state courts shows that such is an issue to be addressed by all courts.

References

American Indian Policy Review Commission. 1977. *Final report*. Washington, DC: Government Printing Office.

Bailey, Lynn R. 1998. *Bosque Redondo: The Navajo internment at Fort Sumner, New Mexico, 1863–68*. Tucson: Westernlore Press.

Barsh, Russel Lawrence, and J. Youngblood Henderson. 1976. Tribal courts, the model code, and the police idea in American Indian policy. In *American Indians and the law*, ed. Lawrence Rosen, 25–60. New Brunswick, NJ: Transaction Books.

Berman, Harold J. 1983. *Law and revolution: The formation of the Western legal tradition*. Cambridge: Harvard University Press.

Blackstone, William. 1884. Cooley edition. *Commentaries on the laws of England*. Chicago: Callaghan.

Borah, Woodrow. 1983. *Justice by insurance: The General Indian Court of Colonial Mexico and the legal aides of the half-real.* Berkeley: University of California Press.

Brakel, Samuel J. 1976. American Indian tribal courts: Separate? "Yes." Equal? "Probably not." *American Bar Association Journal* 62:1002.

———. 1978. *American Indian tribal courts: The costs of separate justice.* Chicago: American Bar Foundation.

Brookings Institution. Institute for Government Research. 1928. *The problem of Indian administration.* Baltimore: Johns Hopkins Press.

Bureau of Justice Assistance. Court Performance Inventory. 1998 *Court Review* 35(4): 31–33 (form).

Commission on Trial Court Performance Standards. 1990. *Trial court performance standards with commentary.* Williamsburg: National Center for State Courts.

Cooter, Robert, and Wolfgang Fikentscher. 1998a. The role of custom in American Indian tribal courts (part I). *American Journal of Comparative Law* 46:207–330.

———. 1998b. The role of custom in American Indian tribal courts (part II). *American Journal of Comparative Law* 46:509–80.

Cutter, Charles R. 1986. *The Protector de Indios in colonial New Mexico 1659–1821.* Albuquerque: University of New Mexico Press.

Gibson, Charles. 1964. *The Aztecs under Spanish rule: A history of the Indians of the valley of Mexico, 1519–1810.* Stanford, CA: Stanford University Press.

Green, L. C. 1977a. "Civilized" law and "primitive" peoples. In *Law and Society,* ed. L. C. Green, 99–132. Leyden: A. W. Sijthoff.

———. 1977b. Native Law and the Common Law: Conflict or harmony. In *Law and Society,* ed. L. C. Green, 61–98. Leyden: A. W. Sijthoff.

Hagan, William T. 1966. *Indian police and judges.* New Haven: Yale University Press.

Indian Civil Rights Act, 1968. 1990. *Documents of United States Indian Policy.* 2nd ed., ed. Francis Paul Prucha, 249–52. Lincoln: University of Nebraska Press.

Indian Reorganization Act. 1934. 1990. *Documents of United States Indian Policy,* 2nd ed., ed. Francis Paul Prucha, 222–25. Lincoln: University of Nebraska Press.

Indian Tribal Justice Act. 1991. Public Law 103–176, December 3, 1993 (as reenacted).

Juneau, Donald. 1983. The light of dead stars. *American Indian Law Review* 11:1–55.

Kaye, John Brayshaw. 1909. *The trial of Christ in seven stages.* Boston: Sherman, French.

Law and Order Regulations and Application of Law and Order Regulations to Tribes Organized under Act of June 18, 1934. 1938. *Federal Register, Wednesday, May 18, 1938, 952–959.* Washington, DC: Government Printing Office.

LeResche, Diane, ed. 1993. Special issue: Native American perspectives on peacemaking. *Mediation Quarterly* 10.

MacLachlan, Bruce B. 1994. Indian law and Puebloan tribal law. *North American Indian anthropology: Essays on society and culture,* ed. Alfonso Ortiz, 340–54. Norman: University of Oklahoma Press.

Mangold, Nathan. 1934. Powers of Indian tribes. *Decisions of the Department of the Interior* 55:14–67.

Morey, William C. 1900. *Outlines of Roman law: Comprising its historical growth and general principles.* New York: Knickerbocker Press.

Morgan, Thomas J. [1892] 1973. Rules for Indian courts. In *Americanizing the American Indians: Writings by the "Friends of the Indian," 1880–1900,* ed. Francis Paul Prucha, 300–305. Lincoln: University of Nebraska Press.

Morse, Bradford W. 1980. *Indian tribal courts in the United States: A model for Canada?* Saskatoon: University of Saskatchewan Native Law Centre.

Nader, Laura. 1990. *Harmony ideology: Justice and control in a Zapotec mountain village.* Stanford, CA: Stanford University Press.

National American Indian Court Judges Association. 1978. *Indian courts and the future.* Washington, DC: National American Indian Court Judges Association.

Nielsen, Marianne O., and James W. Zion. 2005. *Navajo Nation peacemaking: Living traditional justice.* Tucson: University of Arizona Press.

Notestein, Wallace. 1962. *The English people on the eve of colonization, 1603–1630.* New York: Harper & Row.

O'Connor, Sandra Day. 2005. Lessons from the third sovereign: Indian tribal courts. In *Navajo Nation peacemaking: Living traditional justice,* ed. Marianne O. Nielsen and James W. Zion, 171–76. Tucson: University of Arizona Press.

Prucha, Francis Paul, ed. 1973. *Americanizing the American Indians: Writings by the "Friends of the Indian," 1880–1900.* Lincoln: University of Nebraska Press.

St. J. Hannigan, A. 1961. The imposition of western law forms upon primitive societies. *Comparative Studies in Society and History: An International Quarterly* 4:1–9.

Seed, Patricia. 1995. *Ceremonies of possession in Europe's conquest of the New World, 1492–1640.* New York: Cambridge University Press.

Select Committee on Indian Affairs, U.S. Senate. 1989. *Final report and legislative recommendations: A report of the Special Committee on Investigations of the Select Committee on Indian Affairs, United States Senate.* Washington, DC: Government Printing Office.

Souter, David H. 2001. *Concurring Opinion, Nevada v. Floyd Hicks. 533 U.S.* Washington, DC: Government Printing Office.

Strickland, Rennard. 1975. *Fire and the spirits: Cherokee law from clan to court.* Norman: University of Oklahoma Press.

Teller, Henry M. [1883] 1973. Courts of Indian Offenses. In *Americanizing the American Indians: Writings by the "Friends of the Indian," 1880–1900,* ed. Francis Paul Prucha, 295–99. Lincoln: University of Nebraska Press.

U.S. Commission on Civil Rights. 1991. *The Indian Civil Rights Act: A report of the United States Commission on Civil Rights.* Washington, DC: The Commission.

Zion, James W. 2002. Navajo therapeutic jurisprudence. *Touro Law Review* 18:563–640.

Zion, James W., and Charles R. Cloud. 1996. Indian judges in America. *Court Review* 33:7–11.

"How Do We Get Rid of Crime? Restore It to Harmony"

TRIBAL PEACEMAKING AS AN ALTERNATIVE TO MODERN COURTS

Jon'a Meyer

LONG BEFORE they received the "gift" of a court system mod-
eled on the Anglo-Saxon justice system, Native Americans had their own
justice systems, which were effective in addressing and containing mis-
conduct within their communities. Many Native American tribes utilized
a process now called peacemaking, in which a respected member of the
tribe brought disputing individuals together and assisted in restoring harmony between them and working out a suitable remedy to victimization,
often restorative in nature (e.g., Meyer 1998). This chapter discusses the
history of peacemaking approaches, as well as modern peacemaking programs. The Navajo Nation's peacemaking program is reviewed in detail,
as it is the country's largest and has served as a model and reference point
for indigenous peoples around the world who wish to revive their own
traditional forms of justice. The role of peacemaking and tribal identity
is also briefly addressed.

Peacemaking as a Process: What Is It?

Now used to collectively describe tribal restorative-justice approaches
that involve elders or others assisting disputing parties to work out a
mutually acceptable solution, the coining of the term *peacemaking* to
describe a mediation-like process to restore harmony must be attributed
to Anglos. One of the earliest uses of the term appears in the 1683 Pennsylvania legal codes, which describe a system of "common peace-makers"
who heard and settled minor disputes; by 1692, however, their use was
eliminated (Howard 1889, 373–74). Of course, the term is somewhat

misleading; peacemakers don't actually make peace; they instead restore harmony where it once existed. This is an essential component of peacemaking, one that both limits and expands the applicability of peacemaking as a problem-solving process.

Coinciding in part with the explosive growth of restorative and other victim-centered justice procedures in mainstream America, Native Americans began seeing the value in revitalizing their own "original" justice approaches that rely on restorative justice. While peacemaking systems vary somewhat from tribe to tribe, the fundamental core elements include the bringing together of two or more disputants under the guidance of a facilitator, discussion of the real or perceived injustices and potential remedies to those injustices, deliberation of suitable reparations, and the attempted restoration of harmony between the disputants and among their fellow community members. During the peacemaking process, discussions of blame are typically eschewed, allowing the focus to be on restoring the parties to their pre-injustice status (Arsenault 2000, 822; Yazzie 1994, 179).

Peacemaking has been compared to mediation and shares many similarities with that process. That peacemaking takes place outside the typical courtroom setting and that the goal is to work out a mutually agreeable solution are two major similarities to mediation. Where peacemaking diverges from mediation, however, is in the function of the facilitator, the roles assigned to the disputants, the types of cases for which the process is suitable, and the emphasis placed on prevention.

A mediator often guides the mediation process using relatively strict legal guidelines, is valued for the fairness of the solutions he or she suggests, and sometimes renders quasi-judicial decisions. A peacemaker, on the other hand, uses traditional knowledge in an attempt to teach and empower the disputants to communicate with one another and design a solution with minimal input from the peacemaker, can quickly tailor to the process depending on the needs of the situation or disputants, and rarely makes quasi-judicial decisions. Peacemakers are often valued for both their traditional knowledge and their ability to bring disputants together to solve their own problems (e.g., Zion and McCabe 1982, 20).

The roles assigned to the disputants also differ between mediation and peacemaking. In mediation, the disputants are often asked early in the session to suggest workable compromises, so that through their concessions, an at least partially palatable solution can be worked out (e.g., Dye 1983, 145). No side fully loses in mediation, but neither does one always win, because the outcome is seldom what both initially sought. Much like haggling with a merchant over a price at a bazaar, the two sides may dicker until they find a tolerable outcome, but it is infrequently the end result they had desired. Both parties may feel they got a bargain; they may also feel they could have gotten a better deal had they negotiated harder or had a different starting position. In peacemaking, however, the goal is for both sides to move toward each other through hearing each other out and valuing the other party's situation and input. By the end of a peacemaking session, all of the disputants should see the outcome as a good one, rather than as a compromise into which they were forced by the realities of negotiation.

Another difference in the roles assigned to the disputants is what the parties are expected to do during the session. In mediation, the disputants must come prepared to work out a give-and-take solution in a value-neutral, courtlike setting. In peacemaking, however, the disputants must come prepared to discuss root issues to conflict, sometimes described as peeling away the layers of an onion to find the real cause of a dispute, in an often emotion-laden setting, and be willing to make true changes if necessary to resolve conflict and better themselves.

Still another difference in the roles assigned to the disputants concerns who is able to participate in the session. While mediation sessions are often limited to those directly involved in the dispute, peacemaking encourages the disputants to bring family members and others who are sometimes only peripherally associated with the conflict, to learn what insight those individuals can share on the root cause of a dispute and potential solutions to it (LeResche 1993, 2).

A third major difference between mediation and peacemaking concerns the types of cases for which the process is suitable. Mediation is typically best suited for businesslike decisions (e.g., resolving how to address the wrongs perceived by a business client), disputes between parties who do not know one another (e.g., routine auto accidents), and other issues that do not have strong emotional undertones (e.g., loud music played by neighbors at night). Peacemaking, on the other hand, was designed to address conflicts between parties from the same community whose relationship to one another is important to rebuild and maintain. Peacemaking attempts to reconcile disputants and restore peace and harmony where it once existed, while mediation attempts to create agreeable situations. Peacemaking is suitable for all types of conflicts, ranging from the petty to the very serious, as long as some prior relationship exists between the disputants. Family disputes and child custody cases have been identified as particularly appropriate for peacemaking (Arsenault 2000, 819–22). Mediation, on the other hand, is best suited for cases in which the parties are not previously connected somehow and the cause of the dispute is not emotion-laden and/or complex. Contract disputes between Native Americans and non-Native business owners, for example, have been identified as less appropriate for peacemaking (Lieder 1993, 36), though such cases may be ideal for mediation.

The fourth major difference between mediation and peacemaking is the time-oriented goal of the two processes. While the goal in mediation is to address a past or ongoing wrong, there is little focus on preventing future injustices to other victims or even the same victim; a focus on the future is a central goal in many peacemaking programs, however. This emphasis on prevention means that root causes versus surface causes for disputes must be resolved and that both parties must be willing to change the way they interact, think, or act in order to prevent future conflict. In a typical peacemaking session, this means the individual causing the harm must agree to seek help for his or her psychological or dependency issues, while an injured party must sometimes agree to separate temporarily from his or her abuser (e.g., in domestic violence cases such as those observed by Coker 1999, 73) or to seek counseling for the harms they have endured (e.g., in sexual or chronic abuse cases, personal interview with peacemaker #63). Individuals in peacemaking are often surprised to learn how their own actions have enabled harm to take place, even when they are the victims (e.g., parents who have denied that their alcoholic adult children have a problem, spouses who have hidden their abuse from others rather than seek help, etc.). Unlike mediation, which is simply another form of court process, albeit an alternative one, peacemaking is typically considered to be a sacred or religious ceremony (e.g., Bluehouse and Zion 1993). In modern schemes, peacemaking typically serves as a sort of small claims court, family counseling program, and criminal diversion program all rolled into one.

History of Peacemaking

When talking about the history of peacemaking, one must separate the "original" tribal peacemaking systems from the ones currently in use. We know that most, if not all, tribes had some sort of restorative justice process that was used in at least some cases. This should not be surprising, given the widespread proliferation of restorative routines before adversarial justice systems were formalized in the twelfth century as a way for King Henry I to collect funds for breaches of what he said was the king's peace (e.g., Stubbs 1906, 121; Umbreit 1994, 1).

Even homicides were dealt with through restorative justice. The Karok, Iroquois, Ponca, and Omaha, for example, are documented as allowing the family of a killer to make reparations to the victim's family or clan as a sanction (Kroeber and Gifford 1980, 99–100; Macleod 1937, 197; Morgan 1851, 332). One goal of these reparative systems was to provide for the victim's family, especially when a breadwinner was killed. If a Kiowa murderer was able to get himself near a medicine bundle (a package of items used in rituals), he was protected while nearby, and the owner of the medicine bundle could serve as a peacemaker to help him work out reparations with his victim's family (Hagan 1966, 17). One of the most famous peacemaking cases followed the 1881 killing of Spotted Tail by a fellow Brule Sioux, Crow Dog; though peacemakers who met with both families worked out a mutually agreeable sanction, local whites were infuriated because Spotted Tail had been sympathetic to their cause. Fallout from this case led Congress to pass the Major Crimes Act, which removed from tribes the ability to prosecute serious offenses (Bradford 2000, 568; Deloria and Lytle 1983, 169–70).

Offenses less serious than homicide were routinely subject to restorative justice approaches on this continent. Typically, the process was overseen by one or more respected individuals (sometimes a full panel) who guided the process or discussion. Among the Sauk-Suiattle, for example, marital disputes and other cases of misbehavior were heard by a council of elders who all gave advice on how to settle the problem (Mansfield 1993, 344). Tribal leaders among the Métis had disputants smoke a peace pipe after which attention was turned to working out reparations (Bark-well 1993, 31).

In some tribes, specific individuals were asked to serve as peacemak-ers when their skills were needed. The Oglala Lakota hunt police, for example, were called in to arbitrate in disputes over division of the pro-ceeds from a successful hunt (MacLeod 1937, 187). Jicarilla Apaches chose band leaders whose many responsibilities included arbitrating disputes within the tribe and with outsiders; these men "governed by persua-sion, and their powers were only as great as their abilities to act in the capacity as advocate and to achieve a consensus and promote peaceful coexistence" (Tiller 1983, 14). Restitution was common for insults, thefts, damage to property, and injuries among the Apache; if the affected par-ties could not work out a suitable settlement on their own, a subchief or another respected person could step in to help them do so (Baldwin 1978, 149–50).

From the above examples, it is clear that tribes across North Amer-ica had some form of restorative justice process that could be employed when necessary to resolve disputes and address crime or other injuries. Some tribes were able to successfully retain and utilize their traditional justice processes for at least some cases even after they were ordered, around the end of the nineteenth century, by the federal government to adopt an adversarial approach that was closer to the Anglo-Saxon ideals of justice (e.g., Meyer 1998). During the 1920s, for example, Navajos continued to rely on head men to settle disputes in peacemaking "rather than call in Government authority" (Coolidge and Coolidge 1930, 72). Indian agents assigned to the reservation may have ignored the wide-spread use of peacemaking because it indirectly made them look good by keeping cases out of the mainstream courts and legal system statis-tics. Observers in the early 1940s continued to note that very few cases were processed through the Navajo tribal civil courts because "many civil troubles [were] solved by arbitration with head men" (Boyden and Miller 1942, 16). Twenty years later, the Navajo Agency report (1961, 284) and other reports noted that many cases appropriate for the civil courts were instead resolved by family and clan members. Due to the value they assigned to peacemaking, Navajos continued to utilize their original dis-pute resolution system into modern times and still retain knowledge of their traditional restorative justice processes.

Unfortunately, not all tribes were as successful as the Navajo in retaining remnants of their original justice systems, so they have had to refashion restorative approaches based on what contemporary tribal members feel the systems may have been like. In a few societies, at least partial knowledge of their original justice system has survived through documents written by anthropologists or tribal historians, through the tribe's oral history, or through traditional stories, songs, or ceremonies. Other societies, however, have all but lost contact with their original justice system and are now forced to borrow elements from other tribes' approaches and tailor them to their own needs. Tribes from every level of the cultural retention spectrum are in the process of incorporating peacemaking into their legal codes. For example, the Cherokee, whose original peacemaking system was later "abandoned" (Strickland 1975; Porter 1997, 259), are now attempting to recreate a peacemaking program that is compatible with both their traditions and their current needs.

Peacemaking programs are quite popular in modern Native America (Haberfeld and Townsend 1993, 418; Porter 1997, 251), with hundreds of tribal court systems employing them (Bradford 2000, 578). Some tribes, such as the Ojibway of the northern plains and the Inuit of Alaska and Canada, involve large numbers of people in their peacemaking sessions (Ross 1989, 5–6). Others have long traditions of peacemaking; the Seneca, for example, have utilized peacemaking for centuries to settle marital and other disputes between tribal members (Porter 1997, 240). A few indigenous nations' peacemaking programs involve intensive personal self-searching, such as the method utilized by Navajos (e.g., Yazzie 1994) and Hawaiians (Meyer 1995). Regardless of the form peacemaking took in historical times, the process has been adopted far and wide in Native America due to its effectiveness in reducing conflict and crime, reduced cost when compared with using the mainstream courts, and appeal to both traditional individuals and those who romanticize tradition.

The Navajo Model

As the nation's largest and best-known program, much has been written about Navajo peacemaking. Authors rarely discuss the traditional Navajo form of peacemaking, however, as many individuals either erroneously assume that peacemaking began in 1982 with the launching of the court-annexed program based on the original form of peacemaking or they simply dodge discussion of the program's early roots. Essentially, it is not known precisely when peacemaking "began," though some traditional Navajos have described the approach as given by the deities to keep people in harmony with one another. Given that peacemaking is the original form of dispute resolution for the Navajos, assuming that peacemaking was contemporaneous with the settling of Navajos into social units seems quite acceptable.

The original form of Navajo peacemaking has been described as *achiyati*, or "a talking to" (e.g., personal interview with peacemaker #63 and peacemaker liaison #64 1997), and "family meeting" has been used to describe peacemaking that takes place within families to resolve familial conflicts or utilizes consensus-based decision making for important issues (e.g., personal interview with disputant #2 1998). The reader of anthropological or historical writings, autobiographies, interviews, and other documents about Navajos will often find mentions of what is easily recognized as peacemaking by even the non-savvy reader. A book of oral histories, for example, includes one interviewee's recounting of a late 1920s event that clearly describes a peacemaking session:

> At home at Gray Mountain my parents must have had problems, and they were not living together any more. There was a conflict, and I was confused as to whom to go with that summer. My grandparents insisted that I should go with them, and a small group of people gathered around to help settle the argument. A local noted Navajo leader was asked to intervene between them for a decision. Finally, it was decided that I should go with my father. (Johnson 1977, 86)

Peacemaking was employed by elders, community leaders, and the occasional judge with some regularity, but their use of the process did not attract any academic or governmental attention in a real sense. It was almost as though researchers did not recognize the process when they witnessed it or assumed it was so universal that it did not deserve comment. All that changed in the early 1980s when traditional peacemaker Albert Ross was having trouble getting some individuals to attend a peacemaking session he had arranged. Recognizing that peacemaking cannot take place without participation of the affected parties, Mr. Ross went to a local judge and asked if he could compel the parties to attend the session and could provide a police guard at the session (personal interview with peacemaker Albert Ross, 1998).[1] Everyone showed up and the session went on as planned. Mr. Ross describes that pivotal session as the first time he "used the judiciary," and from that experience the modern program was designed. Mr. Ross went to talk with Nelson McCabe, then chief justice of the Navajo Nation Supreme Court, who felt the program had some merit.

In 1982, the court-annexed "Peacemaker Court" was launched, giving individuals another way to seek peacemaking for their problems. The court-annexed program "is a modern version of the traditional Navajo forum for dispute resolution" (Austin 1992, 5). In the court-annexed version, individuals who want to seek peacemaking can see the peacemaker liaison stationed at their local courthouse and fill out some simple forms, with help from the liaison if needed. The liaison then arranges for a peacemaker to hold a session and summons the parties to the meeting. If possible, peacemakers are matched to the dispute or the parties as appropriate. In addition to matching on language use (Navajo or English) and religion, some peacemakers are assigned because they specialize in certain types of cases (e.g., domestic violence, marital issues, land disputes, etc.). Though traditional peacemakers were not paid for their services (they were usually fed a meal or sometimes given a gift such as a sheep after a session), the peacemakers in the court-annexed program are paid a nominal fee for their services by the parties who seek the session.

Though peacemakers with the court-annexed program undergo training in the basic principles of peacemaking, they are chosen by their communities because they already know what needs to be known. The training is helpful, however, because the candidates are also shown how to complete the paperwork that the program requires, such as how to document the agreements that are fashioned in their sessions.

The modern process differs from its traditional roots but is considered an improvement by some, due to the ease in obtaining a session (by simply contacting the peacemaking liaison at each district's courthouse), because each outcome must be signed off by a judge to ensure fairness, and because the final decisions become binding court rulings once they are signed by a judge (Navajo Nation Judicial Branch 1993, 26; Wallingford 1994, 147). Of interest, Mr. Ross went on to become a peacemaker with the court-annexed program and served in that capacity until his death in 2006.

Unfortunately, there has not been an abundance of research on the effectiveness, per se, of peacemaking. In the only quasi-experimental comparison of Navajo Nation family conflict cases, Gross (2005, 121) found that abusers whose cases were processed through peacemaking rather than the family court were 60 percent less likely to reoffend (and the participants also felt that they had been treated fairly). An evaluation of a youth peacemaking program (Yaa Da'Ya) found that youth who participated in the process were much more likely to make positive changes in their lives beyond simply discontinuing any criminal activities they had previously engaged in, concluding "it is clear that the peacemaking portion of the program had beneficial results for the youth who took advantage of it" (Meyer 2005, 136–38). Some scholars writing about peacemaking have asked about recidivism and report low rates of re-offending among peacemaking participants: Wallingford (1994, 148), for example, reported a recidivism rate of 5 percent based on interviews with the peacemaking coordinator, while Yazzie and Zion (1996, 170) reported a general recidivism rate of 20 percent and widespread satisfaction with the process, based on reports from peacemaking staffers. Yazzie and Zion (1996, 172) also noted that drunk drivers processed through a pilot program designed to use peacemaking to help them recognize their drinking problems were less likely than their counterparts processed through the courts to continue in that behavior. Overall, peacemaking appears to have good results and to be rated highly by participants.

Due to the abundance of documentation about the process, the Navajo program has served as a model for other tribes and non-Native American jurisdictions, too. Representatives from tribes across the United States and overseas have considered adopting portions of Navajo peacemaking (e.g., Bielski 1995, 39; Navajo Nation Judicial Branch 1993, 21). The Mashantucket Pequots, for example, adapted the Navajo system to fit their own traditions. Instead of choosing their peacemakers from the general population, as the Navajos do, the Mashantucket Pequots asked each of the "eight traditional families, from which all tribal members trace their roots," to select representatives to serve on the Peacemakers Grievance Council, which hears disputes (Waldman 1994, A1). Representatives from the Eastern Band of Cherokee recently traveled to the

Southwest to observe the process and conduct research on how they could incorporate peacemaking into their own tribal justice system. In a curious role switch, dominant white society is now attempting to borrow justice ideals from the Navajos rather than impose their own beliefs on the tribe; the Virginia Peacemaker Court is patterned on the Navajo process. That program differs from the Navajo model in that the peacemakers are all volunteers and that prayers, an integral part of the Navajo peacemaking ceremony, are absent in the Norfolk, Virginia, program due to the wide diversity of clients served by that program (Navajo Nation Judicial Branch 1994, 4).

Peacemaking and Tribal Identity

Some tribal scholars point to another benefit of tribal peacemaking. In addition to being an effective way to resolve conflicts and appealing to tribal members who seek a return to traditional ways, peacemaking may actually help restore or maintain tribal identity. Robert Porter, a scholar among the Seneca (who have used peacemaking for centuries), is one of the most vocal supporters of the process. Porter notes that one of the neglected values of peacemaking is that it differentiates tribal justice systems from their state and federal counterparts, which may be important in stemming a possible future attempt to terminate tribal sovereignty (Porter 1997, 276).

Porter also lauds the ability of peacemaking programs to alert tribal members about the necessity of using culturally acceptable methods of dispute resolution rather than depending on mainstream litigation to solve their problems (Porter 1997, 276). It is this tendency, however, that has attracted some criticism when overzealous tribal supporters push peacemaking into avenues where it is not helpful or welcome. Some Native American victims, for example, have reported being "pressured" by program staff not to choose the adversarial processes to which they are entitled (e.g., Griffiths and Hamilton 1996, 186). Coker (1999, 82) notes that victims of domestic violence may feel "a subtle form of coercion," because peacemaking is viewed as a traditional approach that should be supported by tribal members. In rare cases, victims may find their cases involuntarily sent into peacemaking if prosecutors feel the case doesn't warrant prosecution (e.g., Manolescu 1999, A8). Some individuals may "feel more secure in the formal legal system," (LeResche 1993, 5), and those individuals should not be shuttled into peacemaking as a way for the justice system to save money or dispose of what may be termed a "junk case." To retain the respect they have carefully earned over centuries, peacemaking programs should never be forced onto people, lest they risk being classified as antivictim programs that cannot create real results for disputants.

It is also important to recognize that peacemaking is no panacea, according to scholars and those who work within the criminal justice field. Even those who work with the Navajo justice system worry about peacemaking being applied to the wrong cases; while prosecutors tend to fret over transferring inappropriate cases (e.g., those involving physical harm), peacemakers are troubled by the potential for inappropriate individuals (e.g., those who are not ready to actively engage in the process) in their caseload (Meyer 2006). Mainstream courts are necessary for disputes in which parties are not ready to sit down and engage in real discussion of the harms they have perpetrated or suffered and for cases in which there is no preexisting peace to restore. It is important not to overuse peacemaking in situations for which it is unsuitable, as doing so may detract from the beauty of the effective and worthwhile process. In the end, however, it is imperative that we acknowledge the many benefits peacemaking can bring to individual disputants and to society as a whole when it is used to its full potential. It is a simple gift through which we might achieve the lofty solution suggested by a Navajo judge when asked how society can eliminate crime: "Restore it to harmony."

References

Arsenault, Laurie A. 2000. The great excavation: "Discovering" Navajo tribal peacemaking within the Anglo-American family system. *Ohio State Journal on Dispute Resolution* 15:795–823.

Austin, Raymond D. 1992. Incorporating tribal customs and traditions into tribal court decisions. Paper presented at the Federal Bar Association Indian Law Conference, April, Albuquerque.

Baldwin, Gordon C. 1978. *The Apache Indians: Raiders of the Southwest.* New York: Four Winds Press.

Barkwell, Lawrence J. 1993. Early law and social control among the Métis. In *The struggle for recognition: Canadian justice and the Métis Nation,* ed. Samuel W. Corrigan and Lawrence J. Barkwell, 7–37. Winnipeg, MA: Pemmican Publications.

Bielski, Vince. 1995. In search of tribal justice. *California Lawyer,* November: 36–45.

Bluehouse, Philmer, and James W. Zion. 1993. *Hozhooji naat'aanii*: The Navajo justice and harmony ceremony. *Mediation Quarterly* 10:327–37.

Boyden, John S., and William E. Miller. 1942 (March 23). Report of Survey of Law and Order Conditions of the Navajo Indian Reservation. Unpublished material reproduced at the National Archives and Records Administration, Washington, DC.

Bradford, William C. 2000. Reclaiming indigenous legal autonomy on the path to peaceful coexistence: The theory, practice, and limitations of tribal peacemaking in Indian dispute resolution. *North Dakota Law Review* 76:551–604.

Coker, Donna. 1999. Enhancing autonomy for battered women: Lessons from Navajo peacemaking. *UCLA Law Review* 47:1–111.

Coolidge, Dane, and Mary R. Coolidge. 1930. *The Navajo Indians.* Boston: Houghton Mifflin.

Deloria, Vine, and Clifford M. Lytle. 1983. *American Indians, American justice.* Austin: University of Texas Press.

Dye, Jessie. 1983. What is mediation? *Contest* 1983:145–48.

Griffiths, Curt T., and Ron Hamilton. 1996. Sanctioning and healing: Restorative justice in Canadian Aboriginal communities. In *Restorative justice: International perspectives*, ed. Burt Galaway and Joe Hudson, 175–91. Monsey, NY: Criminal Justice Press.

Gross, Eric K. 2005. Perceptions of justice: The effect of procedural justice in Navajo peacemaking. In *Navajo Nation peacemaking: Living traditional justice*, ed. Marianne O. Nielsen and James W. Zion, 115–24. Tucson: University of Arizona Press.

Haberfeld, Steven, and Jon Townsend. 1993. Power and dispute resolution in Indian Country. *Mediation Quarterly* 10:405–22.

Hagan, William T. 1966. Indian police and judges: Experiments in acculturation and control. New Haven: Yale University Press.

Howard, George E. 1889. *An introduction to the legal constitutional history of the United States.* Baltimore: Johns Hopkins University Press.

Johnson, Broderick H., ed. 1977. *Atk'idą́ą́' yéek'ehgo Diné Kéédahat'inéę́ Baa Nahane'* (*Stories of traditional Navajo life and culture by twenty-two Navajo men and women*). Tsaile, Navajo Nation, AZ: Navajo Community College Press.

Kroeber, Alfred L., and E. W. Gifford. 1980. *Karok myths.* Berkeley: University of California Press.

LeResche, Diane. 1993. There are at least four reasons for revitalizing tribal peacemaking. *Indian Law Support Center Reporter* 16:1–6.

Lieder, Michael D. 1993. Navajo dispute resolution and promissory obligations: Continuity and change in the largest Native American nation. *American Indian Law Review* 18:1–71.

MacLeod, William C. 1937. Police and punishment among Native Americans of the Plains. *Journal of Criminal Law and Criminology* 28:181–201.

Manolescu, Kathleen. 1999. "Common law" means what is only Navajo in peacemaking process. *Navajo Times*, June 10.

Mansfield, Emily. 1993. Balance and harmony: Peacemaking in Coast Salish tribes of the Pacific Northwest. *Mediation Quarterly* 10:339–53.

Meyer, Jon'a F. 1998. History repeats itself: Restorative justice in Native American communities. *Journal of Contemporary Criminal Justice* 14:42–57.

———. 2005. *Bił Háí'áázh* ("I am his brother"): Can peacemaking work with juveniles? In *Navajo Nation peacemaking: Living traditional justice*, ed. Marianne O. Nielsen and James W. Zion, 125–42. Tucson: University of Arizona Press.

———. 2006. Peacemaking as viewed by criminal justice professionals. Paper presented at the annual meetings of the Western Social Science Association, April, Phoenix.

Meyer, Manu. 1995. To set right—*Ho'oponopono*: A Native Hawaiian way of peacemaking. *Compleat Lawyer*, Fall: 30–35.

Morgan, L. H. 1851. *League of the Ho-De-No-Sau-Nee, or Iroquois. Vol. 2*. Rochester, NY: Sage and Brothers.

Navajo Agency. 1961. *Navajo yearbook*. Report no. 8. Window Rock, AZ: Navajo Agency.

Navajo Nation Judicial Branch. 1993. *The Navajo Nation judicial branch*. Window Rock, AZ: Navajo Nation Judicial Branch.

Navajo Nation Judicial Branch. 1994. *Newsletter*, February/March/April. Window Rock, AZ: Navajo Nation Judicial Branch.

Porter, Robert B. 1997. Strengthening tribal sovereignty through peacemaking: How the Anglo-American legal tradition destroys indigenous societies. *Columbia Human Rights Law Review* 28:235–305.

Ross, Rupert. 1989. Leaving our white eyes behind: The sentencing of Native accused. *Canadian Native Law Reporter* 3:1–15.

Strickland, Rennard. 1975. *Fire and the spirits: Cherokee law from clan to court*. Norman: University of Oklahoma Press.

Stubbs, William. 1906. *Lectures on early English history*. Edited by Arthur Hassall. New York: Longmans, Green.

Tiller, Veronica E. V. 1983. *The Jicarilla Apache tribe: A history, 1846–1970*. Lincoln: University of Nebraska Press.

Umbreit, Mark S. 1994. *Victim meets offender: The impact of restorative justice and mediation*. Monsey, NY: Criminal Justice Press.

Waldman, Hilary. 1994. Tribal justice system continues to grow; a justice system develops, based on tribal law; Mashantucket Pequots establish own police, courts. *Hartford Courant*, Feb. 13.

Wallingford, Jayne. 1994. The role of tradition in Navajo judiciary. *Oklahoma City University Law Review* 19:141–59.

Yazzie, Robert. 1994. "Life comes from it": Navajo justice concepts. *New Mexico Law Review* 24:175–90.

Yazzie, Robert, and James W. Zion. 1995. "Slay the monsters": Peacemaker court and violence control plans for the Navajo Nation. In *Popular justice and community regeneration*, ed. Kayleen M. Hazlehurst, 67–87. Westport, CT: Praeger.

Yazzie, Robert, and James W. Zion. 1996. Navajo restorative justice: The law of equality and justice. In *Restorative justice: International perspectives*, ed. Burt Galaway and Joe Hudson, 157–73. Monsey, NY: Criminal Justice Press.

Zion, James W., and Nelson J. McCabe. 1982. *Navajo peacemaker court manual.* Window Rock, AZ: Navajo Nation Judicial Branch.

The Search for the Silver Arrow

ASSESSING TRIBAL-BASED HEALING TRADITIONS
AND CEREMONIES IN INDIAN COUNTRY
CORRECTIONS

William G. Archambeault

AMERICAN INDIANS are subject to the same American justice system—federal, state, and local—as any other American citizen. In addition, they are also subject to other layers of justice and regulatory bureaucracy to which no other groups of Americans are subject, creating a complex labyrinth of components, processes, and laws not understood by many, even by the bureaucrats charged with administering them. (See Cardani in this volume.) One justice labyrinth faced disproportionately by Indian people is the focus of this chapter; it is called "corrections."

Corrections is that component of the American and tribal justice systems that is compelled to control offenders committed or sentenced to it by the courts, while at the same time providing a modicum of programs and services that aid offenders in habilitating and reintegrating back into society. The central thread running through all correctional programs, facilities, organizations and services is that the offender is sentenced by the authority of the courts to be controlled by others. In general, American corrections operate on three levels that correspond to legally defined political government jurisdictions: federal, state, and local. In addition to these, Native peoples who are enrolled in or living on federally recognized tribal reservations are subject to tribal corrections.

Native peoples account for about 1 to 1.5 percent of the total number of offenders under correctional control nationwide. Between 70 and 90 percent are on probation or parole or are confined in local (county, parish or municipal) jails or in tribal facilities. The national numbers and percentages are deceptively low, creating an inaccurate and distorted understanding about the number of Indians in corrections. These inaccuracies are used by some researchers and government policies to ignore

American Indians in the reporting of corrections data because they seem to be a minority group of no significance (Archambeault 2003b, 16–19).[1] A more exact measurement of the numbers of Indians caught in the web of steel that is American corrections starts with the realization that government policies of the nineteenth century forced Native people onto reservations. Consequently, American Indian populations are concentrated in certain regions and states where these reservations are still located. Contrary to the assertion that Native peoples are too insignificant in terms of numbers to be of research interest, American Indians are disproportionately overrepresented in the correctional offender data in these areas. Prisons, jails, and probation/parole services in states with large Indian populations or reservations report Indian correctional populations from seven to fifteen times the national average. Since all major felony crimes on Indian reservations fall under federal jurisdiction, American Indians account for approximately 16 percent of all offenders who annually enter federal corrections (new intakes) and approximately 15 percent of all federal prisoners currently confined in federal facilities (Perry 2004). However, as discussed in detail elsewhere (Archambeault 2003a, 293), the exact numbers of American Indians under some form of correctional control cannot be precisely determined.

Tribal Justice Systems

Tribal justice philosophy, practices, characteristics, and the configuration of a tribal justice system are unique to each federal reservation. Some factors that shape a tribal justice system include treaty conditions and obligations recognized (or ignored) by the U.S. government; tribal agreements with BIA regarding law enforcement jurisdiction; and tribal agreements with local, state, and federal law enforcement and Park Services. The Federal Bureau of Investigation exercises primary enforcement jurisdiction regarding the investigation of serious felony crimes on all Indian reservations. However, enforcement jurisdictions became more complicated after 1968 and subsequent federal court rulings on the enactment of Public Law 280 (Perry 2005).[2] To date, eight states have chosen to enforce criminal laws of the state under this law on Indian reservations. These are Arizona, Utah, Nevada, North Dakota, Iowa, Washington, South Dakota, and Montana. In states where Public Law 280 does not apply, the federal government (FBI) retains exclusive criminal jurisdiction for serious crimes.

Furthermore, on some reservations, such as Red Lake Chippewa Reservation in Minnesota, treaty agreements give total autonomy, including law enforcement authority, exclusively to the tribes themselves. By contrast, on other reservations, such as the Chitimacha Tribe in Louisiana, people are dependent on outside law enforcement provided by the St. Mary's Parish sheriff. Both Red Lake and the Chitimacha have their own court systems, however. While Red Lake has its own jail and corrections department, the Chitimacha do not. Such contrasts in reservation justice systems add to the complexity of understanding Indian justice systems.

A 2005 study of tribal justice agencies (Perry 2005) yields a general profile of reservation tribal justice systems in the United States. Among the findings were the following. Nearly all tribes had some form of judicial system, although their structure and operations vary from one to another. Most enacted their own written laws and enforced BIA as well as some federal laws. Most had formalized courts that included trial and appellate courts, juvenile court, civil, or domestic family courts, while a few operated only informally. Some reservations, such as the Navajo, also made use of traditional tribal processes such as peacemaking. Most tribal systems handled misdemeanor and some minor felony matters, although tribal authority to sentence offenders in Indian country is limited to a maximum of one year imprisonment and fines up to $5,000, or both. Most systems made and enforced child custody and support orders, handled divorces and divorce property settlements, and other reservation-related property issues. Most provided victims services.[3]

In terms of tribal corrections, the 2005 report found that fewer than one-quarter of the reservations provided their own detention or jail facilities. Many provided residential and nonresidential programs for substance abuse treatment of offenders. About two-thirds relied on local or county agencies to provide correctional services beyond what is provided on the reservation. In terms of correctional services, some reservations have sophisticated treatment and correctional programs for offenders sentenced under tribal law, while other reservations rely on facilities and services outside the reservation. At any given time, almost all the reservations have a significantly large number of enrolled tribal members on probation or parole but under different jurisdictions. Probationers may be serving either tribal court or federal court sentences. Parolees may be serving either state or federal sentences. Treatment programs on any reservation may have a combination of different offenders under different types of sentences.

Some, but not all, tribes integrate traditional customs and healing traditions into the operations of reservation jails and security institutions. Luna-Firebaugh's recent article provides insight into some of the ways that this integration is possible (Luna-Firebaugh 2003).

While only a small portion of any reservation's enrolled population is under any form of correctional control at any time, *all tribal members* are subject to certain tribal civil laws and jurisdictions. These civil matters include such issues as reservation property, inheritance, child care and living conditions, child support, marriages and divorces, property settlements, and related domestic subjects. Regardless of where a tribal member lives, an enrolled American Indian is subject to tribal law and authority on most civil matters. Failure to comply with tribal court orders for such matters as child or spousal support, or other domestic court orders, could result in the individual being sentenced to reservation correctional control. Justice, then, in Indian country is highly complex, because there are so many legal jurisdictions and different agencies involved.

Healing Traditions in Indian Corrections

Assessing Utility for Correctional Intervention

American Indian healing traditions and ceremonies are many and as diverse as there are practitioners. Unfortunately, many other ceremonies and traditions have been lost or forgotten because of European and American oppression of Indian peoples over the last five centuries. This oppression took many forms, including murder, torture, slavery, stealing of Indian babies, reservation systems, the cultural genocide of boarding schools, and imprisonment. Despite these efforts, some of the ancient knowledge and practices survive today. Among some Indian cultures all members of a tribe, band, clan, or hereditary family have knowledge of the "sacred" and the "healing ways." By contrast, among other Indian people such knowledge is held by only a few people or members of a special society of practitioners. By convention, spiritual leaders among many Indian people are called *medicine men/women*, and those with unusually high levels of knowledge and skills are called *shamans*. Some traditional healers focus on the use of herbal plants, roots, and bark from certain trees. Others use spirit power to diagnose and treat various illnesses, and still others combine both.

In general, the healing traditions of most Indian medicine ways are *holistic*. The human is viewed as having a body, mind, and spirit. Furthermore, the human lives in continuous interaction with his or her environment, which has physical and spiritual dimensions to it. Health and peace of mind depend on being in balance or harmony with that environment, which includes people, animals, and the physical environment itself. When disharmony develops between a person's mind and spirit, it manifests itself through physical illnesses or mental illness. Likewise, when a person becomes unbalanced in dealing with other people or when the environment itself becomes sick (such as through pollution), physical or psychological manifestations of illness or disease result.

Healing traditions, regardless of culture, are crafted to restore balance, to heal the spirit as well as the body. Long before modern medicine, Indian peoples recognized that many illnesses and patterns of self-destructive behavior are also linked to damaged spirits and minds. Thus, the approach taken in most healing traditions is a *holistic* one: mind, body, and spirit must be treated at the same time. Modern treatment would label this approach as "multiple diagnosis," at least in terms of treating mental health problems and physiological problems at the same time, as illustrated by the treatment of substance abuse as a manifestation of other underlying psychological disorders. Traditional methods are sometimes incorporated into modern therapy for mentally ill patients (Coleman and Dufrene 1994).

Healing traditions are based on tribal culture and religious beliefs and are grounded in both things of the earth—such as plants, animals, roots, and tree bark—and things of the spirit world. Ceremonial objects, such as sweat lodges, in many cultures reflect this dualism. Domed or half-sphere-shaped sweat lodges are found in most of the better-known tribal traditions, but there are many other variations in construction. Lodge leaders generally explain that regardless of shape, what is seen is only half a lodge. The other half is connected to the spirit world, and the lodge draws healing energies from both the physical and the spirit worlds. Ceremonies conducted within the physical lodge, and its participants, are connected with the spirit as well as the tangible world. Ceremonial rituals allow the crossing over from the physical to the spirit plane as well as allowing healing spirits to cross in the opposite direction. Rituals also protect both the participants and the spirits from harm. While sweats are part of many First Nations cultures, the particulars of lodge construction, the source of its heat, the sacred language spoken, the prayers said, the songs sung, and other aspects of the "correct" ritual vary widely from one tribal-based culture to another. Yet each reflects the physical-world environment from which the particular culture emerged over the ages. Although different from one another, all seem to reflect what Gill labels a common worldview. Writes Gill (2002, 177): "Most Native Americans saw themselves as part of the fabric of nature and not the most important element. The Native American attitude toward the environment included the belief that the natural order is only one facet of the cosmic spiritual reality which encompasses and pervades both the heavens *and the earth*."

In terms of understanding the use of tribal-based healing traditions with offender populations, it may be useful to classify them into two general categories: (1) tribal/community restorative traditions, and (2) individual/small-group healing traditions.

Tribal Community Restorative Traditions

Ages before Euro-American academia started debating the utility of restorative-justice concepts, most Indian communities evolved ceremonies that restored balance and harmony among tribal community members. Navajo peacemaking, the council meetings of the Sioux and many other tribes, and other forms of traditional community problem-solving structures all had as their purposes the restoring of harmony, balance, and peace among tribal members, together with some forms of restitution to the victims or the victims' families. If disharmony continued and balance could not be restored, then the individuals or groups who caused the problems were banished or simply killed.

In general, the process involved four steps. First, an open meeting or council was held in which anyone who had been injured or affected by the actions of other tribal members was allowed to speak. Second, a skilled elder or council of elders would lead the discussion in the direction of resolving the issue, restoring balance and harmony, and preventing retaliation on the part of the victim or victim's family. In effect, they would broker a deal that would be acceptable to all parties. Third, the wrongdoer would be required to perform whatever actions were agreed to. Finally, when the restitution or other requirement was completed, the person was allowed to fully participate in the tribe's social and cultural life as if nothing had taken place. Consider two examples.

The famous conflict between Crow Dog and Spotted Tail and its tribal resolution illustrates this approach. As a result of a shootout between the two warriors, Crow Dog killed Spotted Tail. To prevent clan/family retaliation and an ongoing blood feud from erupting, a general council of elders was held. The objective was to restore balance and harmony among the tribe, and this was achieved by mutual agreement of all parties. Among the provisions was that Crow Dog would have to support Spotted Tail's family. Yet, as history records, this was not acceptable to the whites who took Crow Dog prisoner, dragged him to Rapid City, South Dakota, tried him and sentenced him to hang. He was reprieved at the last minute by an order of the U.S. Supreme Court, ruling that local and state law enforcement had no jurisdiction in Indian country, that only the federal government had such jurisdiction.

In another example, the now-revered Sioux leader Crazy Horse caused a married woman to leave her husband and move in with him. The former husband, who had other wives (whom he would beat), was afraid of Crazy Horse, so he appealed to a council of chiefs/elders. After hearing the complaint against him in a public meeting, an agreement was reached: Crazy Horse could keep the woman if he surrendered a wampum belt of honor given him by the tribe for his bravery, and if he provided the offended husband with twice the number of horses that the husband initially paid for his youngest wife. Crazy Horse agreed, and harmony and balance was once again restored to the tribe. History notes that the former husband was "supposed to receive" the wampum honor belt too as compensation, but oral accounts indicate that other chiefs held onto the wampum belt and never gave it to the former husband whose behavior they did not condone.

On some reservations, the formalized criminal justice process and mental health/substance-abuse treatment models of the dominant society have been adapted to handle conflicts and problems within the Indian community. These replaced traditional approaches. By contrast, tribal or community restorative traditions still are practiced on other reservations. These are generally used when a tribal member or members or tribal property have been stolen or harmed in some way. However, these may also be used when a substance abuser returns after completing treatment. Related healing ceremonies may also be used to "purify" soldiers returning from battle after killing enemies. Somewhat similar ceremonies are also used for offenders returning from long-term periods of incarceration.

Community restorative traditions and ceremonies can be helpful for offenders who are trying to readjust to reservation life. They are particularly useful in dealing with offenders who are on probation or parole, especially if the offense committed was against another tribal member or tribal property. To have a chance at being successful, at least the following elements must exist. First, the individual offender must desire to be restored to respected membership in his or her community. Second, elders and community leaders must believe that to do so is in the best interest of the community. Finally, a community leader knowledgeable and trained in the community restorative ceremony must lead the healing process. Restoring an offender back to the community successfully cannot be done by everyone, nor is it expected to succeed with everyone.

Community restorative programs are also employed with juveniles, although these approaches may be regarded as diversionary, rather than correctional. One example is the Ho-Chunk Nation Community Service Program (Ho-Chunk Youth Services Program 2001) in Wisconsin, which intervenes in the lives of Indian youth who have become involved in the justice systems of either a tribe or local government. The program utilizes "culturally relevant" approaches for "correcting" or "restoring" the youth by engaging them in appropriate community service. Furthermore, efforts on some reservations to prevent family violence and to support its victims utilize traditional approaches both individually and by integrating them into other service program designs. Finally, some traditional approaches are integrated into programs that target urban dwellers as well. Most of these efforts integrate three sets of program elements: (1) support for the victims, (2) involvement of the community in a healing process and increasing public awareness of the problem, and

(3) structured program support for the offender in acknowledging the harm caused to the victim and in learning behaviors aimed at preventing future abuse. For many American Indian families, this involves dealing with problems of substance abuse combined with multiple generations of abuse.

Individual and Small-Group Healing Traditions

Individual and small-group healing traditions take several different forms, depending upon the tribal culture, history, and sociopolitical context. Among some tribes, such as the Chashatta of Louisiana, medicine way traditions or ceremonies are family secrets, passed on from one generation to another. Among other tribes, healing knowledge and ceremonies are maintained in special societies, such as the Mide'wiwin or Grand Medicine societies of the Ojibwe/Chippewa Bands. Similar patterns are found among members of ceremonial kivas of the Southwest Pueblo cultures.

All of these forms of individual and small-group healing have several characteristics in common. Some of these groups date back dozens to hundreds of generations. All are mechanisms of survival and of quality control for the knowledge and traditions that were once deemed critical to the survival of a people. All take on their present characteristics because of the historical oppression by the dominant society.

Individual and small-group healing ceremonies and traditions are healing ceremonies that target individuals or a small group. Interestingly, some of these offer another form of community restoration. In many tribes, medicine people are organized into small groups or societies. Some of these date back many generations and were the keepers of medical knowledge and ceremony during times of oppression by the dominant society. Today, membership is selective, training is comprehensive, and commitment to core beliefs and standards is required for continued membership in some of these groups. A person is not admitted until he or she is ready and has proven personal commitment. Furthermore, continued membership is premised on compliance with certain standards of behavior.

When any medicine society member or apprentice falls prey to alcohol or another form of substance abuse or engages in other prohibited behaviors, the person is said to have "fallen from the red road." If the person returns to the "red road" and desires reinstatement in a medicine society, each tribal society has ceremonial mechanisms or traditions for restoring the individual to the status of a respected member in that medicine society, kiva, or other group. In addition, some treatment programs, substance-abuse research, and treatment approaches have integrated traditional values and beliefs into formalized techniques that are "culturally sensitive." The 2002 study of Indians and Alaskan Natives illustrates this approach (Walters, Simoni, and Evans-Campbell 2002).

Among individual and small-group healing or medicine traditions that are known to many whites are those listed below. Most, except for the Sun Dance (Hull 2000), are available to some U.S. federal prisoners in most federal correctional institutions, and in some state facilities.

- Praying within prayer circles made of rocks or simply drawn in the earth;
- Making tobacco, corn meal, or herbal/bark substance offerings to the four directions, Mother Earth and the Creator;
- Smudging ceremonies, using sage, sweetgrass, cedar, or other herbs to cleanse the air, are often used prior to other ceremonies;
- Use and smoking of pipes, reeds, or husks, together with tobacco, tree bark, or other herbs as a form of prayer in which the smoke carries the prayers to the Creator;
- Vision quest traditions in which individuals go to a remote place, fast, and meditate with a pipe for four to seven days, seeking a vision of one's place in the universe and one's life works;
- Use of feathers, sand paintings, wood or rock carvings, or crystals for healing or seeking understanding;
- Use of sweat lodges or houses, either above or in the ground; and
- The sun dance, rain dance, or other traditions that involve fasting, dancing, and, in many but not all cultures, piercing or blood offerings, lasting from two to six days. These are not approved by the Federal Bureau of Prisons but are widely and successfully used in Canadian corrections.

The specific medicine practices and traditions of different Indian Nations vary widely among the many tribes, bands, clans, and individual keepers of medicine knowledge. Many healing traditions and ceremonies are unknown except to a select group of medicine people within a specific tribal culture. They may specialize in certain forms, such as herbal/plant medicines, spirit healing, sand painting, or one of many other forms. Additionally, some ceremonies and traditional healing ways are known and practiced only by one gender or the other.

Each generation of medicine keepers and practitioners, regardless of tribal culture, has a two-edged responsibility. On one side, Native culture and traditions compel respected medicine men and women to find young people who are interested in and worthy of learning traditional medicines and ceremonies. These future medicine keepers must be trained in traditional ways dating back hundreds of generations. On the other hand, the medicine keepers have an even greater obligation to preserve the integrity and sacredness of the healing knowledge itself, because these are gifts given by the Creator. Consequently, if current medicine keepers of any generation are not able to find worthy and interested candidates to teach, then the medicine keeper is compelled to let the knowledge die with him or her.

During the centuries of Euro-American colonial oppression of American Indian culture (1630–1940s), historical accounts support the notion that there was a continuous stream of young candidates from every tribe who were eager to prove themselves worthy recipients of tribal medicine knowledge and traditions. For example, Black Elk and others record the experiences and the consequences of having to learn tribal traditions covertly in the back country. Detection by reservation authorities might cost participants in traditional ceremonies the loss of food subsidies for months, a consequence that could lead to starvation.

Ironically, however, where all other historical efforts failed to exterminate traditions, contemporary technology and social values are succeeding in undermining generational transmission of sacred knowledge to younger people. Commercialism, through satellite television advertising and programming, beam a worldview that values only money, materialism and an MTV desire for immediate gratification into even the most remote corners of reservations. Medicine knowledge is often seen by younger people as irrelevant to the world in which they must survive. The cumulative effect of these influences on traditional sacred values and knowledge led the late Vine Deloria Jr. to conclude (Deloria 2006, xvii) that "the overwhelming majority of Indian people today have little understanding or remembrance of the powers once possessed by the spiritual leaders of their communities." Deloria (2006, xviii–xix) condemns the blind acceptance of consumerism and modernism for eroding American Indian spirituality. He writes: "This uncritical acceptance of modernism has prevented us from seeing that higher spiritual powers are still active in the world. We need to glimpse the old spiritual world that helped, healed and honored us with its presence and companionship."

Another paradox of present times, in the opinion of many medicine people, is that the medicine men and women of tomorrow are being trained in the prisons of the United States and Canada today. Those who advance this prediction point out that only when today's Indian youth are stripped of materialism and suffer the deprivations of prison do they come to appreciate the teachings of the elders who possess sacred teachings and learning. While a few tribes, such as the Navajo, have structured schools, and while a few individuals are trained from childhood in the sacred ways, a great many medicine people of today came to know and understand their culture and themselves while in prison.

Healing Traditions and Indian Communities

Healing traditions and ceremonies continue to be contentious issues between the dominant controlling culture of the United States (Irwin 1997) and the Indigenous peoples of America, especially in prisons, jails, and detention centers (Bird 2002). However, continuously since the 1970s, organizations such as the American Indian Movement, the Native American Defense Fund, and other organizations (Foster 1998) have generated numerous court suits and volumes of printed literature and Internet sites that center on Indian offender rights in prison. Consequently, these issues are no longer ignored by correctional officials, although religious and racial biases continue to exist. Additionally, subsequent court decisions have resulted in partial changes in correctional policy in some settings. For example, federally recognized Indians in federal custody and those in some states with large Indian populations currently have access to some healing traditions on an individual basis, provided that the individual satisfy certain security conditions. However, other Native people who do not meet the BIA definition of "Indian" continue to be denied access to traditional healing ceremonies in prisons and jails.

Beyond safety and security issues faced by correctional officials who try to address American Indian spiritual issues are others caused by Indians themselves. Medicine people of different tribes, and sometimes within the same tribe, will not agree on the "proper way" of conducting some traditional ceremonies in terms of language, characteristics, and procedural steps. For example, the Sioux and Chippewa practice many of the same traditions, including pipe ceremonies, sweats, and sun dance. However, they differ sharply on specifics of ritual, language, and many other aspects. Additionally, within the same nation, differences between one band and another are as great as that between different tribes. Finally, different medicine leaders within the same band and tribal culture are told in visions to perform ceremonies in particular ways that differ greatly from the rituals followed by others. One of the many consequences of all these different and individualized rituals is that the ceremony performed by one medicine person of one tribe is usually not acceptable to medicine people from other tribes. Similar statements can often be made about individual medicine keepers from the same tribal culture. Personal conflicts among medicine leaders are not uncommon.

All these differences and resulting conflict among medicine keepers also have an effect on tribal politics. Unfortunately, tribal politics on some reservations actually forbids the use of traditional healing ceremonies in tribal jails and correctional facilities. Sometimes political ferment on some reservations over the medicine traditions is fostered by tribal members who have been so indoctrinated with Christian and other religious denominational moral ideology that tribal members actually persecute other more traditional tribal members who engage in traditional ceremonies. Some tribal members consider the practice of their own ancient healing traditions to be *heathen worship*. Opponents of traditional ceremonies use political influence to prevent tribal members under correctional control from having access to traditional ceremonies. Fortunately, there are a great many reservations where tribal politics tends to support traditional medicine ways and extend these to incarcerated offenders as well.

The Utility of Traditional Healing:
Concluding Comments

If traditional healing methods and ceremonies are not acceptable to many American Indian people today, what is their value in dealing with

Native American populations who have become entangled in the web of steel known as the American corrections system? The answer to this question is in seven parts.

First, there is no *silver arrow*, or traditional healing approach that works equally well with all American Indian peoples, in terms of achieving correctional objectives of changing behavior or managing Indian populations.[4] No individual healing ceremony or community restoration ceremony will be equally effective with all tribal offenders. An individual must hold the core tribal beliefs, or at least respect them, and be ready to change before any approach has a chance to work. That an approach works with one individual is no predictor that it will succeed with another person.

Second, little empirical research has focused on the use of healing traditions and ceremonies with offender populations under correctional control, whether housed in custody institutions or carried out on reservations or other community settings. However, anecdotal and informal interview accounts are extensive, both in the United States and Canada. Over the past decade, personal interviews and informal discussions with wardens, former wardens, and former inmates from either the United States or Canada have been fairly consistent. Correctional managers describe the calming effect of inmate participation in traditional ceremonies, involving people who were previously labeled "troublemakers," with histories of violence toward other inmates and correctional staff alike. Former Indian inmates recalled changes in themselves and their behavior when they came to understand and accept their traditional cultures. Discussions with people living on reservations paint a mixed picture of effectiveness for probationers and parolees. Where traditional healing ceremonies are valued and respected by the general reservation community, similar patterns of improvement are noted among community-supervised populations. However, where sacred traditions are not respected on the reservation, participation in these is limited and may not be as effective. In any case, the potential for using traditional methods with offender populations—both in custody institutions and under community supervision—is too promising to be ignored.

Third, any healing ceremony must be based on the traditions of the culture that the offender respects. Ideally, this is the tribal culture of his or her ancestors. However, if the individual has become immersed in the tribal culture and medicine values of another people and accepts these as his or her own, and if the alternative tribal culture is willing for the individual to participate in their ceremonies, then the individual should be allowed to do so. Traditional medicine people sometimes reason that the special knowledge and gifts given to their people are for use only with their people and that such things are not helpful to persons not of the tribe.

Fourth, the offender must make a *voluntary choice* to seek help from a greater power and possess a willingness and readiness to change. No treatment method, whether Indian or dominant-society professional, can succeed unless the person desires help and wants self-change.

Fifth, a *supportive environment* is necessary. Support can come from other members of the tribe, medicine mentors, and/or others who have taken the journey before. While community support and recognition of the efficacy of the traditional ceremony is ideal, it suffices that at least a small group of people support the individual and are respected by him or her.

Sixth, traditional healing ceremonies must be conducted by medicine keepers who are trained by traditional mentors. Not everyone of any given tribe is qualified to conduct ceremonies, nor are ceremonies conducted by New Agers.

Finally, different kinds of healing ceremonies require different supplies, tools, and sacred objects, and the means to use them properly. These will be known by the ceremony leader, who will ask for them or supply them himself or herself. These must be provided if any ceremony is to have a chance of working. Further research into techniques appropriate to Indian populations is needed. Ideas such as the *healing lodge* discussed by Nielsen (2003) need to be given serious consideration. Healing lodges, although developed in institutions, could be used at the community correctional level as well, whether the community is a reservation or a neighborhood of an urban center.

References

Archambeault, William G. 2003a. Soar like an eagle, dive like a loon: Human diversity and social justice in the Native American prison experience. In *Convict Criminology*, ed. Jeffrey I. Ross and Stephen C. Richards, 287–308. Belmont, CA: Thomson/Wadsworth.

———. 2003b. The web of steel and the heart of the eagle: The contextual interface of American corrections and Native Americans. *Prison Journal* 83:3–25.

———. 2006. Imprisonment and American Indian medicine ways: A comparative analysis of conflicting cultural beliefs, values, and practices. In *Native Americans and the Criminal Justice System*, ed. Jeffrey Ross and Larry Gould, 143–60. Boulder, CO: Paradigm Press.

Bird, Michael. 2002. Health and indigenous people: Recommendations for the next generation (editorial). *American Journal of Public Health* 92:1391–93.

Coleman, Victoria, and Phoebe Dufrene. 1994. Art and healing for Native American Indians. *Journal of Multicultural Counseling and Development* 22:145–53.

Deloria, Vine Jr. 2006. *The world we used to live in: Remembering the powers of the medicine men*. Golden, CO: Fulcrum Press.

Deloria, Vine Jr., and Clifford M. Lytle. 1983. *American Indians, American justice*. Golden, CO: Fulcrum Press.

Foster, Len. 1998. Religious intolerance against Indian religion: Native American prisoners' religious freedom. Submitted to the U.S. Special Rapporteur on Religious Intolerance. The National Native American Prisoners Rights Advocacy Coalition.

Gill, Jerry H. 2002. *Native American worldviews: An introduction*. Amherst, NY: Humanity Books.

Guerin, Paul, Robert Hyde, Mitzi Wyatt. 1999. Process evaluation of the Genesis Program at the Southern New Mexico Correctional Facility, Washington, DC: U.S. Dept. of Justice (NCJ 179956).

Ho-Chunk Youth Services Program. 2001. *Ho-Chunk Nation Community Services Program*. Washington, DC: National Institute of Justice.

Hull, Michael. 2000. *Sun dancing: A spiritual journey on the red road*. Rochester, VT: Inner Traditions International.

Irwin, Lee. 1997. Freedom, law, and prophecy: A brief history of Native American religious resistance. *American Indian Quarterly* 21:35–56.

Luna-Firebaugh, Eileen M. 2003. Incarcerating ourselves: Tribal jails and corrections. *Prison Journal* 83:51–77.

Nielsen, Marianne O. 2003. Canadian Aboriginal healing lodges: A model for the United States? *Prison Journal* 83:67–90.

Perry, Steven W. 2004. *American Indians and crime: A BJS statistical profile, 1992–2002*. Washington, DC: National Institute of Justice, U.S. Department of Justice (NCJ 203097).

———. 2005. *Census of tribal justice agencies in Indian country*. Washington, DC: BJS, U.S. Dept. of Justice (NCJ 205332).

Severson, Margaret, and Christine W. Duclos. 2003. *American Indian suicides in jail: Can risk screening be culturally sensitive?* Washington, DC: National Institute of Justice (NCJ 207326).

Tribal Law and Policy Institute. 2003. *Tribal healing to wellness courts: The key components*. Washington, DC: National Institute of Justice (NCJ 188154).

Walters, Karina, Jane Simoni, Teresa Evans-Campbell. 2002. Substance use among American Indians and Alaska Natives: Incorporating culture in an "indigenist" stress-coping paradigm. *Public Health* 117:104–17.

Present and Future Issues for Native American Criminal Justice

Marianne O. Nielsen

SOME YEARS AGO, Robert Silverman and I edited a book called *Native Americans, Crime, and Justice* (Nielsen and Silverman 1996). When I looked at the final "themes" chapter, I was disappointed to realize that many of the issues and needs facing Native American individuals and communities are exactly the same today—but then, when you think about it, how can four hundred years' worth of injustices from colonization and oppression be fixed in just a few short years?[1]

Borrowing words from Native American justice models, there is a need for healing for individuals, communities, and peoples. In what terms, exactly, "healing" is defined will depend on each culture and community. Some of the chapters in this book—for example, those by Archambeault and Meyer—give examples of programs that provide healing. Without such healing, there will continue to be an overrepresentation of Native Americans in the criminal justice system.

This final chapter highlights five main issues that affect the administration of criminal justice to Native American peoples today and likely will continue to do so in the foreseeable future. They are: sovereignty and self-determination, resource needs, cultural revitalization, urbanization, and promoting change.

Sovereignty and Self-Determination

Increased sovereignty has been touted by many Native American and non-Native American scholars, decision makers, and justice personnel as the main solution to the socioeconomic inequalities of Native Americans (as described in chapter 1) and to ending the overrepresentation of Native Americans in criminal justice involvement. *Sovereignty* and *self-determination* are sometimes used interchangeably by scholars but are not exactly the same. *Sovereignty* is a term used loosely in Native American studies, but it can be defined as the "inherent right or power to govern" (Canby 1998, 68), meaning that tribal governments are free to govern their internal affairs except where restricted from doing so by the federal or state governments. Sovereignty influences which level of government (federal, state, or tribal) has the final power over the jurisdictions, mandate, and funding of justice services, and to whose model and standards these services will be held; therefore, sovereignty as it is used in the Native American political arena is aimed at removing federal or state restrictions and regaining a greater degree of legal, political, and economic independence.

The limited sovereignty that Native American nations now have is rooted in paternalistic ideologies that do not see Native Americans as capable of handling their own affairs and being in need of control. Some scholars suggest that governments do not want Native Americans to govern their own affairs because of the economic threat this would produce to the current state of society (Boldt 1993). Historically, the struggle for sovereignty has meant resisting overt and covert assimilationist federal and state government policies that were, and still are, aimed at removing the legal and cultural distinctiveness of Native Americans and turning them into "ordinary citizens" with no special rights or benefits (see Boldt 1993).

Self-determination is related to sovereignty. According to Utter (2001, 277), it is a "catch-all term that covers a variety of concepts including tribal restoration, self-government, cultural renewal, reservation resource development, self-sufficiency, control over education, and equal or controlling input into all policies and programs arising from the American Indian–federal government trust relationship." Self-determination, therefore, could include the control of organizational design as when, for example, a pan-Indian urban service organization offers a prevention program based in cultural practices, or a Native American–operated detox center or family medical center is established in a border town. It could also include a community choosing to use or modify a non–Native American service model or an individual choosing to use non–Native American services, even though Native American alternatives are available. Self-determination choices are hindered, however, by the consequences of marginalization, as discussed in the next section on lack of resources.

Boldt (1993, 72) argues that Native Americans do not have the political or economic power to overcome the interests of more influential segments of society, especially major corporations. Native Americans fall outside the "consciousness and concerns" of politicians. The recent history of Native Americans has been a recounting of attempts to influence the consciousness of politicians and to become an unignorable part of their concerns. Native Americans are trying to remind politicians (and their electorate) of the intent of the treaties that were legal contracts between nations, negotiated in good faith, or at least usually in good faith on the part of the Native American signatories. The intent of the treaties was that Native Americans should retain power over their own affairs and preserve themselves as a people (Boldt 1993, 41; Utter 2001, 83). Legal maneuverings and outright broken promises removed this sovereign power, and today, state gambling compacts and other court decisions continue to nibble away at sovereignty. Government underfunding has forced communities and organizations to make difficult choices about which essential community needs to provide, sometimes having to choose, for example, between repairing police cars or offering a crime prevention program.

Regaining control of criminal justice administration is a vital step in reestablishing sovereignty. The criminal justice system is the enforcement arm of the non–Native American society and as such, it enforces the values of the society and punishes wrongdoers. It is, therefore, a key branch of government for Native Americans to control in their own communities if they wish Native American values to be reinstituted and enforced, and Native American practices to be used. Because so many Native Americans live outside of reservations, it is also important that urban Native American criminal justice services be available, in order to provide culturally appropriate and effective services.

Increased self-determination accompanied by realistic resources would allow communities to negotiate a balance between old and new justice values and practices that work for them. This is an attractive solution, not only because it may decrease poverty (and therefore perhaps crime) and end the jurisdictional labyrinth that currently impedes effective justice services, but also, on a more negative note, because it increases the power of some Native American politicians and provides non–Native American politicians with a scapegoat if a "quick fix" does not occur.

An issue related to sovereignty is indigenization, which, despite its positive aspects, may actually work against sovereignty. *Indigenization* refers to the employment of Native Americans within the dominant government's criminal justice system, either individually or as part of contracted Native American–run organizations (Havemann 1987). Indigenized criminal services operate on the familiar dominant-society model and are under the direct or indirect control of the dominant government. Indigenized jobs are bound by the same job descriptions, standards, and principles as the jobs of any member of the dominant system. There are few efforts made (or even possible) to accommodate the cultural values and needs of the Native American people who are the clients of the service, or of the Native American individuals staffing the jobs. Nevertheless, it is hoped that increasing the numbers of Native American service providers could increase the humane and culturally appropriate operation of the criminal justice system, and could provide Native voices in program design and decision making. Indigenized services may also assist self-determination in that they can increase the legitimacy and skills of Native people working in criminal justice administration and can assist in building the capacity of communities for future development (Nielsen 2003, 2004).

On the other hand, Native Americans' traditional justice values conflict with the values of European-based society (Dumont 1993), which means that indigenization strategies may not be the most effective or satisfactory ones for providing services. Also, indigenized criminal justice organizations may suffer from many constraints, legal ones as described by Cardani in this volume, as well as organizational ones related to following non–Native American models of organizational structure and operation (Redpath and Nielsen 1997). Indigenized services therefore may hinder Native self-determination by hurting the legitimacy of Native American traditional justice-based services, in that the successful operation of indigenized services could be used to argue that autonomous or semi-autonomous Native American–operated criminal justice services are not needed.

Indigenized services may also have another repercussion: because indigenized services can be pointed to as successful initiatives in providing services to Native Americans, they may detract attention from the even more important issue of preventing Native Americans from becoming involved in the criminal justice system in the first place, through improvement of the conditions that encourage Native American overrepresentation.

While indigenization is rooted in the need of dominant governments to acknowledge and at the same time control Native Americans, it is also related to prejudice and, perhaps, to the "melting pot" attitude of the non-Native population. Many non-Native Americans, including political decision makers, feel that Native Americans should give up their traditions and assimilate into the dominant society. This mind-set could be described as a contemporary version of colonial ideology, in that American culture and society, however they may be defined, are assumed to be more desirable and effective than Native American cultures and societies.

Another issue related to sovereignty is that the imposition of European values and criminal justice structures on Native American communities has led to schisms within the communities. Government-imposed political structures invariably conflict with the traditional power structures. This means that divisions in the community develop between those who have political and economic power under the traditional structure, and those who are given power under the imposed structure (see Boldt 1993, 124–27). There are also political schisms rooted in the degree of acculturation of community members. One faction may support a new money-making venture such as a casino or a privatized, for-profit correctional institution, because they will open the community to more economic diversity, while another faction may feel it is against traditional values and refuse to support it (see Zion 1983).

In the development of a new criminal justice initiative, these schisms can have an impact on the degree of community support the project receives and its eventual effectiveness. Some justice service agencies refuse to have any political affiliations, in order to minimize the impact of "Native politics" on the effective operation of their programs. This strategy works well for urban Native justice organizations but is more difficult to accomplish for reservation-based programs when the development of increased political power is a primary concern of their people. Needless to say, the many obstacles to achieving increased sovereignty and self-determination issues will not be resolved quickly.

Resource Needs

"Resource needs" refers to the lack of many different kinds of resources in Native American communities, both rural and urban. This issue is closely related to lack of sovereignty and self-determination. The lack of resources not only hinders the development of new and current criminal justice services (if communities choose to offer them) but makes the provision of services more difficult and stressful than in non–Native American communities (see for example, the chapter by Gould). In general, developmental needs fall into five categories: lack of financial resources, lack of facilities, lack of skilled staff, lack of service support networks, and lack of legitimacy.

Lack of Financial Resources

This is, of course, the primary concern. As mentioned earlier in this book, Native Americans as individuals and communities are among the poorest citizens of this country. Several centuries of economic dependency and social marginalization have meant that most Native American communities not only have an insufficient financial infrastructure to operate effective criminal justice systems but need to learn more about Euro-based economic structures and bureaucratic operations in order to develop their own organizations and to gain legitimacy for their own developmental efforts.

Lack of control of resources is a directly related issue. The common tendency of government bureaucracies to not give up any part of their mandate (in this case the mandates of the Bureau of Indian Affairs or state governments in Public Law 280 states) to control, as opposed to empower, their Native American "wards" may contribute as well. It has also been suggested that "in the national interest," government departments have exploited Native Americans, often in partnership with major corporations (Boldt 1993, 68–72; and Robyn in this volume). The class action lawsuit alleging that since 1887 the Department of the Interior (including the Bureau of Indian Affairs) has misused or lost nearly $100 billion of Native American trust moneys is a prime example (House 2006).

Tribal governments cannot directly access funds without permission. This has led to incidents such as when U.S. Public Law 101–630 authorized

$90 million for the improvement of Native American child protection and family violence prevention, but because the Bureau of Indian Affairs did not request an appropriation, no Indian nations could get access to the money. In his chapter, Zion mentions another such case of inaction with regard to the courts. Funding from other government departments, such as the Department of Justice, must be competed for, sometimes against other Native American groups. Native Americans are caught within what Boldt (1993) calls a "culture of dependence."

Because of these and other factors, the infrastructures of Native American communities are not as developed as those of dominant-society communities; that is, Native American communities do not have the resources necessary to operate some criminal justice services, including juvenile custody facilities or victim protection services. This in turn prevents economic development, because new businesses do not feel the community is secure. Some resource deficiencies are also related to the small size of some Native American communities. They simply do not have enough people or funding to operate the necessary services.

Lack of Facilities

This problem is closely related to a lack of financial resources. Native American communities that would like to develop a youth crime prevention program, for example, may find that they do not have a building to use as a drop-in center and cannot get permission to build one. Similarly, the community may wish to start a detox center or a sexual-victimization prevention program but cannot get funding for space and utilities.

Lack of Skilled Staff

What this means is a lack of community members skilled in areas of expertise that are needed to operate specialized programs such as sexual abuse counseling or alcohol treatment. As problems come to light in Native American communities, a wider range of treatment skills is needed. The skills people need to develop depend on the needs of the community. In addition to lacking community members with specialized training, the community may also lack individuals skilled in traditional Native American practices. Many communities are making strong efforts not only to encourage advanced education for their members, but to teach traditional languages and practices to their young people.

Lack of Service Support Networks

There may not be the community resources needed, for example, to assist a mentally ill offender, to provide substance abuse treatment for a gas-sniffing child, or to provide counseling to a police officer suffering from cultural dissonance. To send the person in need of treatment out of the community is often self-defeating in that the individual may fall into despair at being separated from family and community, which instigates more problem behavior. Access to services is part of this issue. There may be, for example, medicine men and women who hold healing circles or elders who perform sweat lodges, but because these are not seen as legitimate parts of the criminal justice system by non-Native or assimilated Native American justice personnel, offenders and victims may have no knowledge of them and not receive referrals.

It should be noted that there also may be resources available that are operated by the Euro-based system; however, based on past experiences, many Native Americans are reluctant to use services that are culturally insensitive or inappropriate, as Hamby points out with regard to services for sexual victimization.

Lack of Legitimacy

Finally, this lack affects the acquisition of all other resources. Native Americans have been considered inferior peoples for so long in American society that their ability to operate their own services is openly debated. This debate includes not only, justifiably, the resource needs mentioned earlier, but unjustifiably, the stereotypes of Native Americans as incapable of operating organizations or services.

Service programs need legitimacy to get the resources they need to operate—funding, clients, staff, and a mandate to offer services. The legitimacy of one program can be used as a resource to get the funding to develop a different and perhaps more "radical" traditionally based program. Zion (1983) discusses how the "peacemaker courts" were designed to at least outwardly mimic western courts until they were accepted, and were renamed just "peacemaking."

Legitimacy is, however, not only something that is needed in dealing with the non-Native American government decision-makers; it is also needed in dealing with members of the Native American community. In other words, because of the schisms caused by acculturation and conflicting authority structures, not all new programs will be accepted by all members of the community. If the new program is based on Native American cultural practices, it may not be supported by assimilated community members. In order to gain legitimacy from these community members as well as non-Native American decision-makers, new Native American programs need to have the same kind of characteristics that earned them legitimacy with the non-Native American government funders, such as having a bureaucratic organizational structure, following government-set standards of service, having a computerized client information system, and having regular program audits and evaluations. It should be noted that these are not necessarily characteristics that do anything to contribute to the effectiveness of the service and, in fact, may actually detract from it.

On the other hand, in order for the program to gain legitimacy with more traditional community members, the program must incorporate important Native American values regarding justice, such as holistic and respectful treatment of clients, involvement of the family and community in the treatment of the individual, involvement of respected community members in the process, and consensus-building.

Cultural Revitalization

Native American communities are reestablishing and, in some cases, rediscovering their culture and traditions. It must be reemphasized that Native American "culture" is not one culture. There are hundreds of Native American cultures, all different, all based on the unique history, ecology, and values of each group. Nor are Native American cultures static, trapped somewhere in the eighteenth century. Native American cultures, like all cultures, are dynamic and flexible, as discussed in chapter 1. In fact, Native American cultures, more than most cultures perhaps, are adaptive—how else would they have survived so many centuries of active repression and suppression?

Cultural revitalization initiatives have had a tremendous impact on the type of programs that were and still are being developed in the criminal justice field. The majority of traditional justice practices were holistic, stemming from worldviews very different from those that structure the Euro-based justice systems (Dumont 1993). Developing traditionally based programs was very difficult because of legitimacy issues; instead, programs were imposed or developed based on the European model of justice. These services were more familiar and comfortable for non–Native American decision makers and also for some Native American communities. There was, for example, already a history of the Bureau of Indian Affairs using Native people to police their own communities (see the chapter by Luna-Firebaugh).

New Native American–operated programs not only have to overcome the unwillingness of dominant governments to give up control; they also have to overcome the stereotypes of Native American people that are held by Euro-based society. These stereotypes have historically fallen into three categories—the heathen savage Indian, the romantic childlike Indian, and the disadvantaged minority-group member, although the wealthy casino tribe has lately joined the series (Trigger 1985; Mihesuah 1996). These stereotypes grew out of the press representation of Indians during the early years of European exploration and later years of colonization, genocide and ethnocide, and resource exploitation. These images have been perpetuated by today's mass media and work against a realistic view of Native Americans' abilities to handle their own affairs. As mentioned by Archambeault, the mass media is also contributing to the deterioration of traditional Native American values and knowledge among younger generations.

Cultural revitalization is aimed at counteracting these negative stereotypes and reconstructing the reality first created by colonial ideologies. This new reality is a more accurate reflection of Native American cultures, history, concerns, and resources. Media that represent Native American images of reality already exist as films, books, magazines, music, and the Internet, and their proliferation should be encouraged.

Where desired by the community, cultural revitalization efforts are also aimed at replacing Euro-based services such as courts or juvenile treatment programs with more appropriate culturally compatible services, or incorporating aspects of Native American cultures into these services (such as prisons and police). This is another form of self-determination. The wide range of Native American cultures means that a wide range of criminal justice solutions is needed. With growing public awareness and increasing sympathy for multiculturalism, the door is open a crack for more Native American traditionally based programs, which likely will be based on a different model than the adversarial, punishment-oriented, Euro-based system. These models may use respected community members as mediators and counselors, incorporate family members in the process, investigate underlying problems, use consensus building among all participants, and aim at healing for the offender, victim, and community.

On an individual, psychological level, Duran and Duran (1995, 29–30) suggest that many Native Americans suffer from self-hatred, which can lead to family violence, homicide, and suicide. They explain that "once a group of people have been assaulted in a genocidal fashion, there are psychological ramifications. With the victim's complete loss of power comes despair, and the psyche reacts by internalizing what appears to be genuine power—the power of the oppressor. At this point, the self-worth of the individual and/or group has sunk to a level of despair tantamount to self-hatred" (1995, 29). It is recognized in many Native American communities that the development of self-esteem among Native American young people may be an important crime prevention strategy, and the development of an appreciation for heritage and culture a key step. Unfortunately, acculturation may mean that the young people who could benefit the most, because of the impact of Euro-based education and media are the ones least likely to be interested in learning about Native American cultures and have the least knowledge of their Native language. This is particularly an issue for the many Native American young people living in urban areas (Fixico 2000).

The development of feelings of kinship with other Native American groups and indigenous groups worldwide is also part of the process of cultural revitalization. It should be noted that pan-Indian activities such as powwows and arts and crafts exhibitions are not only ways of instilling pride in identity among Native Americans but are also a means of developing increased awareness by the non-Native American population.

Urbanization

The number of Native people living in urban areas has increased dramatically since World War II. Native people migrate to cities because they are "pushed" or "pulled" away from their home communities. Push factors include government relocation policies, lack of employment opportunities, political factionalism, and violence related to drug and alcohol abuse. Pull factors include attending an educational institution, joining the military, finding work, and joining family members (Snipp 1989, 303, 84, 282). Adapting to an urban lifestyle can cause numerous problems: not only does the person face poverty, language barriers, finding employment, a faster pace of living, and a lack of knowledge about places, laws, resources, and social expectations, but they may face social alienation, and active discrimination and exploitation from potential employers, landlords, and the general public. They must also learn to survive without the extensive family and friend support networks that exist in their home communities. This disorientation and isolation contributes to frustration and discouragement, which in turn can lead to alcohol and substance abuse (Fixico 2000) and may well contribute to the increase in the number of Native American inmates who come from urban centers in some American states (Grobsmith 1994, 37).

Native American people in urban areas are a forgotten minority group. Although there are medical clinics and social centers, there are few choices for Native American–specific criminal-justice-related services. If urban Native Americans need assistance with the justice system, they must overcome the additional disadvantages they face in order to find it. They may have to choose between a seemingly insensitive and unknowledgeable Euro-based service, going back to the reservation for services if they are eligible or free to do so, or doing without.

Funding and policy making are focused on reservations, because of the federal government's responsibility for reservations but not for Native American people living outside them. Urban programs often have to rely on an unstable combination of funding from federal, state, county, and local governments, private foundations, and charities. Staff members are usually underpaid, programs are underfunded, and long-term planning is frustrating and seldom successful. The organizations are often unable to expand into other geographic areas in need, or into other service areas.

Promoting Change: The Future of Native American Justice

As Silverman described earlier, Native American crimes rates are going down, as are crime rates worldwide (though research is still needed on why), but the rates remain above those for other groups. This means that the system as it operates now is not working for Native Americans, despite the efforts of both Native and non-Native individuals and organizations. This book has pointed out the most serious issues in each component of the system, and some of the potential solutions. In this section, general trends in promoting change are discussed.

For Native American communities and organizations to continue to provide successful criminal justice services, and for new services to develop, changes are needed to promote more crime prevention and more effective operation of criminal justice system programs. Crime prevention is probably the most difficult to tackle, because it focuses on the hard problems of crime causation. If colonization has led to marginalization, and marginalization to involvement in crime, then prevention will have to tackle marginalization to be effective. Marginalization also affects the ongoing operation of criminal justice system services, as discussed above.

More efforts are needed in a range of interconnected areas, among which increasing sovereignty, economic development, education and skill development, developing healing programs, and developing relationships with other organizations are the most important.

In terms of *sovereignty*, at some point the dominant American society will have to recognize that Native Americans are no longer wards in need of protection (not that they ever were), but peoples with the right to determine their own futures. Native American cultures as they exist now are taking the best of the old ways and the best of the new ways to develop a lifestyle for each group that best fits that group. Keeping this in mind, accusations that programs are not really "traditional" are meaningless. Native Americans do not have to live up to the expectations of outside groups about what they should be like—this is the whole point of self-determination initiatives. They should have the right to choose their own justice paths.

Increased sovereignty doesn't mean, however, that tribes are ready to increase their jurisdictional areas, to run prisons, or to incorporate the death penalty. Few of them have the resources required to operate full-service criminal justice systems; some of them are barely scraping by as it is. With sufficient resources, some communities might choose to handle all aspects of the criminal justice system, up to and including prosecuting and punishing homicide cases; other communities might choose to limit their justice system to handling misdemeanors and minor indictable offences. Sovereignty means that choosing all the parameters of their justice system is up to Native Americans.

Current laws restricting powers of tribal justice services are antiquated and based in colonial ideologies of Native American inferiority. Increasing sovereignty will mean the dominant society making a concerted effort to remove paternalistic policies and laws from federal and state jurisdiction, and educating decision makers about the impacts of colonial ideology. Whether this change is likely is debatable, as pointed out earlier, because of the social and economic changes that would likely result in the dominant society.

To develop new programs and keep ongoing programs operating, *more resources* are needed, either provided by the federal government and states living up to their legal obligations, or by developing other sources of income, such as a tax base. Realistic funding approaches are needed to allow long-term strategic planning where Native American organizations and communities set their own priorities. Based on the federal government's sad historical record, it is not realistic to expect that it will meet its legal and moral fiduciary responsibilities to Native Americans. Understanding this, some nations and organizations are putting great efforts into developing alternate sources of funding, such as tourist facilities, casinos, and urban housing developments.

Education is needed in many areas. Native American administrators need opportunities to develop managerial and leadership skills, because Native Americans have been prevented from governing their own affairs and operating their own services until recently. Native community members need personal skills development to overcome generations of boarding-school socialization, so that they can develop appropriate life skills, parenting skills, interpersonal skills, and work skills. Such programs could do a great deal to prevent child abuse and neglect, substance abuse, suicide, domestic violence, and other forms of interpersonal violence. Communities and organizations could work to change educational curricula at all levels, from kindergarten to university, to accurately and fairly include Native American history, cultures, and issues. On a wider scale, Native American justice programs need to open themselves to learning about the efforts of indigenous groups around the world, through travel and conferences, and membership in national and international organizations if funding allows, but at minimum through the Internet. Colonialism had much the same impacts on indigenous peoples worldwide, and there are innovative programs and problem resolutions operating in many countries that could be modified to serve local clients.

Communities and organizations need to start investing in research. This can range from asking one staff member to cruise the Internet, looking at key terms, to running a full-fledged research department, to partnering with educational institutions. Some Native American communities and organizations are working in cooperation with educational institutions to develop research projects on traditional cultural practices and language, community needs assessments, alternative funding opportunities, and the effectiveness of their programs. Developing more mechanisms for sharing this information, such as publishing through tribal college presses, developing media presentations for community workshops and school curricula, and setting up Web sites for the general public, is essential.

Members of the dominant criminal justice system need to be educated in a meaningful way about Native American culture and issues, and to take their new knowledge into account in their decision making. They need to learn to see Native American communities and organizations as legitimate players within the criminal justice system, with much to offer both Native American clients and non-Native Americans who share those clients. This would mean more than a fifteen-minute segment as part of "diversity training." Law schools and police and correctional-officer training academies should also revamp their curricula. These educational strategies would do much to raise public (and political) awareness of Native Americans and combat stereotypes and prejudice, as well as improve low self-esteem among at-risk Native American youth.

In terms of *healing programs*, more treatment and service programs are needed to handle the conditions that contribute to crime and victimization: substance abuse, intergenerational violence, mental illness, despair, and homelessness. These programs need to be designed and implemented at the local level. Historically, Native American communities and organizations have not done well when experimental programs were thrust on them "from above," that is, by the federal government and other funders out of touch with the reality of Native American issues. More support is needed for traditionally based programs that act as alternatives to incarceration and keep community members within their support network: counseling, peacemaking, restitution, anger management, and community service. Some of these programs are described elsewhere in this book.

Urban Native American service organizations in particular need to develop cordial *interorganizational relations* with Native American political organizations, so that they can work together, though not to the point where the service organization jeopardizes its state funding by appearing "too radical." This strategy has been successfully used in Canada (Nielsen 2003). The role of the political organizations is to raise issues and demand solutions. The role of the service organizations is to offer the possible solutions.

Conclusion

All of these issues—the need for increased sovereignty, the impact of cultural revitalization, resource needs, urbanization, and making changes—will have to be addressed as Native Americans work to develop culturally appropriate and effective criminal justice services. The development of sovereignty for Native American communities and the development of self-determined criminal justice services for Native Americans are intricately linked. They exist in a mutually influential balance—as one progresses, so does the other; as one is damaged, so is the other.

It must not be forgotten, as we discuss crime, victimization, law, police, courts, and corrections, that the goal that Native American individuals, organizations, communities, and nations are working toward is to overcome the results of centuries of oppression and injustice. As mechanisms for addressing poverty, economic dependency, and other forms of marginalization are found, then so will be found the solutions to violence, suicide, substance abuse—and crime. Native American people must not be alone in this struggle. For efforts to succeed, Native Americans and non-Native Americans alike must learn more about this country's history of oppression and the origins of these issues.

Native American crime and incarceration are not "Native American problems"; they are "societal problems." The cost in the waste of human life and potential is shared by us all.

References

Boldt, Menno. 1993. *Surviving as Indians: The challenge of self-government*. Toronto: University of Toronto Press.

Canby, William C. Jr. 1998. *American Indian law*. 3rd ed. St. Paul: West.

Dumont, James. 1993. Justice and Aboriginal people. In *Aboriginal peoples and the justice system*, ed. The Royal Commission on Aboriginal Peoples, 42–85. Ottawa: Canada Communication Group.

Duran, Eduardo, and Bonnie Duran. 1995. *Native American postcolonial psychology*. Albany: SUNY Press.

Fixico, Donald L. 2000. *The urban Indian experience in America*. Albuquerque: University of New Mexico Press.

Grobsmith, Elizabeth S. 1994. *Indians in prison*. Lincoln: University of Nebraska Press.

Hagan, William T. 1966. *Indian police and judges*. New Haven: Yale University Press.

———. 1993. *American Indians*. 3rd ed. Chicago: University of Chicago Press.

Havemann, Paul. 1987. The indigenization of social control in Canada. In *Indigenous law and the state*, ed. Bradford W. Morse and Gordon R. Woodman, 71–100. Dordrecht: Foris.

House, Billy. 2006. Billions in payments to Indians in jeopardy. *Arizona Republic*. October, 6.

Mihesuah, Devon A. 1996. *American Indians: Stereotypes and realities*. Atlanta: Clarity Press.

Nielsen, Marianne O. 2003. Organizational strategies for overcoming the impact of racism on Indigenous justice organizations. *International Journal of Comparative Criminology* 3:191–221.

———. 2004. A Comparison of community roles of Indigenous-operated criminal justice organizations in Canada, the USA and Australia. *American Indian Culture and Research Journal* 28:57–75.

Nielsen, Marianne O., and Robert A. Silverman, eds. 1996. *Native Americans, crime, and justice*. Boulder, CO: Westview.

Redpath, Lindsay, and Marianne O. Nielsen. 1997. A comparison of Native culture, non-Native culture and new management ideology. *Canadian Journal of Administrative Sciences* 14:327–39.

Snipp, C. Matthew. 1989. *American Indians: The first of this land*. New York: Russell Sage Foundation.

Trigger, Bruce G. 1985. *Natives and newcomers*. Kingston: McGill-Queen's University Press.

Utter, Jack. 2001. *American Indians: Answers to today's questions*. 2nd ed., rev. and enl. Norman: University of Oklahoma Press.

Zion, James W. 1983. The Navajo peacemaker court: Deference to the old and accommodation to the new. *American Indian Law Review* 11:89–109.

Notes

Chapter 1. Introduction to the Context of Native American Criminal Justice Involvement

Author's note: The contextualization for the history and present-day world of Native Americans has not changed a great deal in the last ten years; therefore, there is some overlap in ideas and wording with the chapter I wrote for *Native Americans, Crime, and Justice* (Boulder, CO: Westview, 1996).

1. The following short section was written by William Archambeault as part of chapter 13 but seemed better suited for the Introduction. It is included here with Dr. Archambeault's permission.

2. Transitory Indians are those who continuously move from reservation to big cities, often living with relatives, and return to a reservation to live with other relatives, only to return to a city and repeat this cycle again and again.

3. The exact number of tribes changes as the BIA certifies new groups and decertifies others.

4. The Spanish colonists invaded what is now the Southeast and Southwest United States. The Russian colonists invaded what is now Alaska.

This overview of the colonization process is, of necessity, quite superficial. Recommended as excellent overviews of the major change agents on Native American life over the five hundred years from contact to the present day are Trafzer (2000), Hagan (1993), Wright (1992), Deloria and Lytle (1983).

5. One reason it is so difficult to report on all the different aspects of the marginalization of Native Americans is that despite their special historical status, data about them are usually lumped into the "other" category in government statistical reports, and when a differentiation is made, Native Hawaiians are counted together with "Pacific Islanders" and sometimes even "Asians."

Chapter 2. Patterns of Native American Crime, 1984–2005

1. It should be noted that the rates shown in the following tables will generally be lower than some other rates you might see in other publications. The reason is "technical" in the sense that the difference is based on the populations used. If one uses the population indicated by the FBI in the Uniform Crime Reports (UCR),

the number will be lower than population figures provided by the census; hence, higher rates. The UCR population is based on the actual coverage represented by the police forces reporting to them. Unfortunately, they do not also report their estimates of the population for the racial groups that are of interest in this chapter. In the interest of consistency, I have used census data as the denominator for all calculations.

2. The drop in drunkenness rates in 1999 and 2000 is clearly a result of missing data. It should simply be ignored. Assume a smooth line between 1998 and 2001.

3. It has not been possible to determine the specific effect of the population issue mentioned earlier on the rates for Native Americans. It is possible that this effect plays a significant role in these rates.

Chapter 9. More than Just a Red Light in Your Rearview Mirror

1. *Cherokee Nation v. Georgia*, 30 U.S. [5 Pet.] 1 (1831), and *Worcester v. Georgia*, 31 U.S. [6 Pet.] 515 (1832).

2. *Talton v. Mayes*, 163 U.S. 376 (1896).

3. See *Colliflower v. Garland*, 342 F.2d 369 (1965).

4. 435 U.S. 313 (1978).

5. These authors set forth the fundamental premise that tribes have the right to make decisions that assert self-determination for themselves, rather than awaiting a court's determination of their right to undertake certain actions.

6. 25 U.S.C.A. 450a-450n.

7. 25 U.S.C.A. 450–458.

8. See, for example, archives of the Center for American History, University of Texas, Austin, letter to Captain Frank K. Baldwin, Acting Indian Agent, Kiowa Agency from Commissioner of Department of the Interior, Office of Indian Affairs, dated Dec. 26, 1894, denying request to spend $150 to purchase corn for the subsistence of police horses, or the right to hire horses for police use when necessary.

9. See, for example, archives of the Center for American History, University of Texas, Austin, letter to Charles K. Adams, U.S. Indian agent, Kiowa Agency, dated March 28, 1891, from the acting commissioner of the Department of the Interior, Office of Indian Affairs, denying the purchase of leg irons and Winchesters for use in the Indian service, and letter of September 15, 1893, to Capt. H. G. Brown, acting Indian agent for the Kiowa Agency, from the commissioner of the Department of the Interior, Office of Indian Affairs.

10. See, for example, Kim Lonsway, *Equity denied: The status of women in policing 2001* (Washington, DC: National Center for Women and Policing, 2002); S. E. Martin, The Changing Status of Women Officers: Gender and Power in Police Work, in *The changing role of women in the criminal justice system*, ed. I. L. Moyer, 281–305 (Prospect Heights, IL: Waveland, 1992,; and, S. E. Martin, "Outsider within" the station house: The impact of race and gender on Black women police. *Social Problems* 41(1994):383–400.

11. 435 U.S. 191.

12. 18 U.S.C.A., sect. 1153.

Chapter 12. "How Do We Get Rid of Crime? Restore It to Harmony"

1. The author of this chapter has interviewed nearly 100 individuals who have been employed in the Navajo criminal justice system or peacemaking. All interviewees were guaranteed confidentiality, but Mr. Ross wished to have his name linked to his comments, and I am honoring his request. He is the only interviewee identified in any writings based on those interviews. It is important to point out that no other interviewee has contradicted Mr. Ross's recollections of his role in the creation of the modern court-annexed peacemaking program, and some confirmed Mr. Ross's role.

Chapter 13. The Search for the *Silver Arrow*

1. Thus, Indians are lumped together under categories as "Others" or simply ignored on most federally funded government reports that choose to focus on larger minorities, including African Americans and Hispanic people. Regardless of the reason, each year thousands of American Indian peoples become caught in the web of steel known as American corrections.

2. Under this law, states could elect to enforce all state laws on Indian reservations or none at all. This prevented states and local county or parish jurisdictions from arbitrarily or inconsistently enforcing some state laws while ignoring others.

3. Fewer than half (45 percent) of all tribes indicated that they imposed some type of intermediate sanctions. On the other hand, most (75 percent) impose: monetary fines without incarceration, alcohol rehabilitation, counseling or therapy, community services, drug rehabilitation, and restitution without incarceration. More than two out of three impose probation for adults or juveniles. Laws and court orders are of little consequence without enforcement. A little over half the reservations have their own police departments, and nearly all have cross-agency deputizing agreements with another tribal, BIA, or other public agency. However, only about half of the reservations with their own police were recognized by their state as having arrest powers.

4. The *silver arrow* analogy is adapted from the *silver bullet* imagery of the 1970s that described the idealized search for a correctional treatment method that was equally successful with all types of offenders under all circumstances.

Chapter 14. Present and Future Issues for
Native American Criminal Justice

1. There is some overlap in this chapter with the ideas and wording in the "themes" chapter I wrote for *Native Americans, Crime, and Justice* (Boulder, CO: Westview, 1996), because of the ongoing nature of current Native American issues.

About the Editors

Marianne O. Nielsen, PhD, is a professor in the Department of Criminology and Criminal Justice at Northern Arizona University in Flagstaff. She received her doctorate in sociology (criminology specialization) at the University of Alberta in Edmonton, Canada. She is the co-editor, with Robert A. Silverman, of *Native Americans, Crime, and Justice* (Westview 1996) and *Aboriginal Peoples and Canadian Criminal Justice* (Butterworths 1992), and, with James W. Zion, of *Navajo Nation Peacemaking* (University of Arizona Press 2005). Her work has appeared in numerous national and international journals and as chapters in many books. Her current work focuses on the structures, processes, survival, and success of Indigenous-operated justice organizations.

Robert A. Silverman, PhD, is director, Special Projects, Office of the Vice-Principal (Academic) and a professor in the Department of Sociology, Queen's University at Kingston, Ontario, Canada. He received his BA at the University of Toronto in 1965; his MA at the University of Pennsylvania in 1967; and his PhD at the University of Pennsylvania in 1971. He served as chair of the Department of Sociology at the University of Alberta for 10 years and served as dean of the Faculty of Arts and Science at Queen's University between 1996 and 2006. His research interests are in the area of homicide and adolescent delinquent behavior. His homicide interests culminated in the book *Deadly Deeds: Murder in Canada*, with Leslie Kennedy (1993). With Marianne O. Nielsen, he edited *Aboriginal Peoples and Canadian Criminal Justice* (1992) and *Native Americans, Crime, and Justice* (1996).

About the Contributors

William (Bill) G. Archambeault, PhD, is a professor and chair of the Department of Criminal Justice, Minot State University, Minot, North Dakota. In this position, Bill works closely with tribal colleges and teaches courses dealing with American Indian criminal justice issues which have been the focus of his research and publications for over two decades. Before joining MSU's faculty, Bill retired from Louisiana State University in Baton Rouge, Louisiana, after 27.5 years of service. Bill held the rank of Professor and Criminologist in the School of Social Work; Chair, Department of Criminal Justice; Faculty Advisor to the Native American Student Association of LSU; as well as other positions. He earned his PhD in criminology from Florida State University and his criminology master's degree from Indiana State University. Bill is an Ojibwa (Anishinabe, Chippewa) Sun Dancer and a Gourd Dancer who has also been trained in Plains Chippewa pipe and sweat lodge ceremonies. He is of French-Métis, Anishinabe, and Lakota ancestry.

John F. Cardani is the executive director of community and corporate learning at Coconino Community College, where he was formerly department chair for Public Safety, Law, and Allied Health Programs. He retired from law enforcement in 2000, following a twenty-two-year career. He worked on the Hualapai, Havasuapi, Navajo, and Hopi nations, and currently teaches "Criminal Jurisdiction on Federal and Indian Lands." For several years, he traveled to Tuba City, located on the Navajo Nation, and taught Administration of Justice courses to criminal justice personnel working for the Navajo Nation government. John has served on the Arizona Law Enforcement Academy Advisory Board and taught classes for Arizona Law Enforcement Training Academies in Prescott, Tucson, and Phoenix. In 2005, John was asked to present at the Southwestern Indian Gang Summit in Laughlin, Nevada, on jurisdictional issues in Indian country.

Mary Jo Tippeconnic Fox, PhD, an enrolled member of the Comanche Nation, is an associate professor of American Indian Studies (AIS) at the University of Arizona (UA), Tucson, Arizona. She is the former director/chair of AIS and also served in the position of associate director. Prior to joining AIS, she was assistant vice-president for Minority Student Affairs at the UA. Her scholarly activity focuses on American Indian women's issues and roles, historical and contemporary; American Indian education, with a special focus on higher education; and Indian gaming. Her latest publication is *Serving Native American Students*, a New Directions for Student Services monograph, and an article on traditional feminism. Dr. Tippeconnic Fox has extensive experience working with Native communities throughout the United States, and she is active with many organizations, including the National Indian Education Association (NIEA) and the Western Social Science Association (WSSA). She teaches courses on American Indian education, American Indian higher education, American Indian women, and American Indian gaming.

Larry A. Gould, PhD, is currently serving as the associate vice president and campus executive officer of the Yuma Branch Campus of Northern Arizona University. After a career in law enforcement, Dr. Gould graduated from Louisiana State University in 1991, with a PhD in sociology and a minor in criminal justice and experimental statistics. His primary research areas include drug and alcohol issues and law enforcement-related issues. Dr. Gould has been one of the leading researchers on Native American policing. Recent research projects include assaults on National Park Service rangers and studies of Native American law enforcement. His most recent publications include an edited volume entitled, *Native Americans and the Criminal Justice System* (Paradigm Press, 2006) and a research report concerning the *Analysis of Assaults upon National Park Rangers: 1997–2003.*

Sherry Hamby, PhD, is a research associate professor of Psychology at the University of North Carolina at Chapel Hill. She has authored or coauthored more than fifty publications on partner violence, sexual assault, youth victimization, and assessment, including *The Conflict Tactics Scales Handbook.* She is also a licensed clinical psychologist. Her awards include the Wellner Memorial Award from the National Register for Health Service Providers in Psychology and the Outstanding Child Maltreatment Article from the American Professional Society on the Abuse of Children. She has been principal investigator on grants from the Indian Health Service, the National Center for Health Statistics, and other agencies. She lived and worked on the San Carlos Apache Reservation in Arizona, where she and Mary Beth Skupien conducted the first reservation-based study of partner violence. A widely cited scholar, Dr. Hamby has also maintained involvement in grassroots antiviolence programs.

Eileen Luna-Firebaugh, PhD, is an associate professor of American Indian Law and Policy in the American Indian Studies Program at the University of Arizona. She is Choctaw and Cherokee. Professor Luna-Firebaugh is an attorney and a member of the California Bar. She also holds an MPA from the Kennedy School of Government at Harvard University, where she was awarded both the Christian Johnson Endeavor Foundation Native American Fellowship and the John B. Pickett Fellowship in Criminal Justice. She is an appellate judge for the Colorado River Indian Tribes, with jurisdiction in both Arizona and California. She is a faculty member of the National Tribal Judge College, funded by the U.S. Department of Justice. She was principal investigator for the National Institute of Justice evaluation of STOP Violence Against

Indian Women programs, and for a National Institute of Health study of family violence programs in Australian Aboriginal communities. She was also a consultant to the Harvard CIRCLE Project, a joint USDOJ and tribal project on juvenile justice. She is the author of *Policing Indian America: The Juncture of Sovereignty and Justice* (University of Arizona Press), and a number of articles on tribal policing and tribal administration.

Jon'a Meyer, PhD, who is of Mdewakantonwan heritage, is an associate professor of criminology and director of the Criminal Justice program at Rutgers University, Camden. She received her PhD in social ecology at the University of California-Irvine. She has published on many aspects of criminal justice, including Native American legal systems, restorative justice, sentencing, criminal courts, decision making in the criminal justice system, child victims, prison industry and reform, and community-oriented policing. She is the author of *Inaccuracies in Children's Testimony: Memory Suggestibility or Obedience to Authority?, Doing Justice in the People's Court: Sentencing by Municipal Court Judges,* and *The Courts in Our Criminal Justice System.* Her current research focuses on tribal peacemaking, Navajo common law, and denial and concealment of pregnancy by expectant mothers.

Barbara Perry, PhD, is a professor of Criminology, Justice and Policy Studies at the University of Ontario Institute of Technology. She has written extensively in the area of hate crime, including two books on the topic: *In the Name of Hate: Understanding Hate Crime* and *Hate and Bias Crime: A Reader.* Most recently, she has conducted interviews with Native Americans on their experiences of hate crime. The findings of this research will soon appear in print in two books: *Silent Victims: Hate Crimes Against Native Americans* (University of Arizona Press) and *Under- and Over-Policing Native American Communities* (Lexington Press). She is also completing a British Home Office project on antiracism programming in England and Wales. Her work has been published in journals representing diverse disciplines, ranging from criminology, to history, to public policy, and cultural geography. Dr. Perry continues to work in the area of hate crime and has begun to make contributions to the limited scholarship on hate crime in Canada. She is particularly interested in anti-Muslim violence and hate crime against First Nations people.

Linda Robyn, PhD, is from the Anishinabe (Chippewa) nation. She received her doctorate from Western Michigan University in Kalamazoo, Michigan. She is an associate professor in the Department of Criminology and Criminal Justice at Northern Arizona University in Flagstaff. Her current research interests include American Indians and the criminal justice system, wrongful convictions of American Indians, environmental justice including uranium mining and resource acquisition, and the effects of state-corporate crime on American Indian nations. She has published articles in *American Indian Quarterly* and the *Indigenous Nations Studies Journal,* and chapters in books on topics ranging from white-collar crime, to environmental injustice, to Native American justice.

James W. Zion is a lawyer, jurisconsult, and jurist who lives in Albuquerque, New Mexico, and practices law in the Navajo Nation and in international venues. He is a 1966 graduate (BA) of the University of St. Thomas (Minnesota) and a 1969 graduate (JD) of the Columbus School of Law of the Catholic University. He is an adjunct professor in the Department of Criminal Justice of Northern Arizona University and a court commissioner in the Navajo Nation Crownpoint Family Court. He has practiced law in Indian nation courts for approximately thirty years, served as former general counsel of the National American Indian Court Judges Association and as the Solicitor to the Courts of the Navajo Nation. His writing focuses on traditional Indian and customary law and international indigenous human rights. He is a co-editor, with Marianne O. Nielsen, of *Navajo Nation Peacemaking: Living Traditional Justice* (University of Arizona Press, 2005).

Index